DIVIDED POWER

DIVIDED POWER

How Federalism Undermines Reconciliation

EMILY GRAFTON

Fernwood Publishing
Halifax and Winnipeg

Copyright 2025 © Emily Grafton

All rights reserved. No part of this book may be reproduced or transmitted in any form by any means without permission in writing from the publisher, except by a reviewer, who may quote brief passages in a review. The publisher expressly prohibits the use of this work in connection with the development of any software program, including, without limitation, training a machine learning or generative artificial intelligence (AI) system.

Development editor: Tanya Andrusieczko
Copyediting: Erin Seatter
Text design: Lauren Jeanneau
Cover design: John van der Woude
Printed and bound in the UK

Published by Fernwood Publishing
Halifax and Winnipeg
2970 Oxford Street, Halifax, Nova Scotia, B3L 2W4
www.fernwoodpublishing.ca

Fernwood Publishing Company Limited gratefully acknowledges the financial support of the Government of Canada through the Canada Book Fund and the Canada Council for the Arts. We acknowledge the Province of Manitoba for support through the Manitoba Publishers Marketing Assistance Program and the Book Publishing Tax Credit. We acknowledge the Nova Scotia Department of Communities, Culture and Heritage for support through the Publishers Assistance Fund.

Library and Archives Canada Cataloguing in Publication
Title: Divided power : how federalism undermines reconciliation / Emily Grafton.
Names: Grafton, Emily (Emily Katherine), author.
Description: Includes bibliographical references and index.
Identifiers: Canadiana 20250225239 | ISBN 9781773637723 (softcover)
Subjects: LCSH: Indigenous peoples—Canada—Government relations. | LCSH: Federal government—Canada. | LCSH: Canada—Politics and government. | LCSH: Settler colonialism—Canada.
Classification: LCC E92 .G73 2025 | DDC 323.1197/071—dc23

*To my ancestors who walk with me.
To my sweet family: Matt, Sebastian, and Elliotte.
To Bear and Bean, and the people you will become.*

CONTENTS

Acknowledgements viii

Preface: Locating Myself in Settler Colonial Canada 1

1 **Why Federalism Matters for Reconciliation** 6
   A Problem for Reconciliation: Narratives of Canada's Political Structure 9
   What Is Settler Colonialism? 11
   What Is Reconciliation? 17
   Understanding the Terminology: Indigenous Peoples and Political Agency 24
   Making Sense of Indigenous Peoples' Agency in Canada 26
   How These Concepts Come Together 34

2 **Narratives of Settler Colonialism** 37
   Examining Power Relations in Settler Colonial Narratives 38
   Applying Settler Colonial Narratives for Dispossession 43
   Asserting Indigenous Political Agency Through Presence 50
   The Institutional Consequences of Narratives in Settler Canada 54

3 **The Constitution and Settler Colonial Narratives of Federalism** 56
   The Federal Jurisdictional Scope 58
   The Provincial Jurisdictional Scope 66
   Jurisdictional Paths of Exploitation 75

4 **Evolving Federalism and Implications for Indigenous Political Agency** 77
   Federalism in Flux 77
   Opportunities for Indigenous Sovereignty? 95
   A Juncture for Reconciliation 100

| 5 | Beyond Settler Colonial Federalism | 101 |

    Accommodationist Models 103
    Treaty Federalism 107
    Multiplural Sovereignty 113
    Indigenous Resurgences 117
    Exploitation or Liberation? Navigating Reconciliation in Federalism 123

Postscript: Indigenous Sovereignties and the Sustainability of Reconciliation 124

Endnotes 128

Index 151

ACKNOWLEDGEMENTS

These kinds of books come to be as a result of many people's efforts. I'd like to acknowledge the early political awareness afforded to me by parents, Jonine and Wayne. They showed me a world filled with natural beauty and a sense of the ways injustice afflicts it. My father, in particular, shaped my ways of knowing this world through the lens of our Métis family and those broader Indigenous politics situated in the making of Canada.

I would like to acknowledge the many people who have shaped my thinking on the subject matter of this book: at the University of Manitoba (Winnipeg), my PhD advisors, Drs. Peter Kulchyski, Kiera Ladner, and Jean Friesen, as well as my comrades in the trenches, Alena Rosen, Ryan Duplassie, and Max Aulinger; at the Manitoba Legislative Assembly, the Honourable Gerard Jennissen, elected for the Flin Flon constituency, who supported my interest in pursuing a PhD and graciously introduced me to Dr. Kulchyski; at the Assembly of Manitoba Chiefs, Dr. Kathi Avery Kinew, Lisa Clarke, and Leona Starr; at the Canadian Museum for Human Rights, Julia Peristerakis, Dr. Jodi Giesbrecht, Dr. Margaret Kierylo, Dr. Karine Duhamel, Jennefer Nepinak, Elder Peter Anderson, Heather Bidzinski, Dr. Travis Tomchuk, Dr. Jeremy Maron, Alice Lefèvre, Isabelle Masson, Armando Perla, Carly Ciufo, Mireille Lamontagne, and Chandra Erlendson; and at the Newberry Consortium in American Indian Studies, Drs. Jeani O'Brien and Coll Thrush. Developing a scholarly profile is a long journey, and I am indebted to your contributions.

I'd like to thank many people at the University of Regina as well: kēhtē-aya Brenda Dubois, kēhtē-aya Alma Poitras, the late Life Speaker Noel Starblanket, Dr. Jérôme Melançon, Misty Longman, Pheonix

Sparvier, Lori Campbell, Cheyanne Desnomie, Dr. Cassandra Opikokew Wajuntah, Dr. Bettina Schneider, Dr. Merelda Fiddler-Potter, David Garneau, Dr. Sherry Farrell Racette, the late Langan Goforth, Rachel Janzé, Dr. Paul Simard Smith, Heather Carter, John Bird, the late Wendy Whitebear, Dr. Melanie Griffith Brice, Dr. Bob Kayseas, Dr. Chris Yost, Russ Fayant, Dr. Brenda Anderson, Dr. Jim Daschuk, Dr. Mike Capello, Heather Dietz, Dr. Mel Hart, Dr. Vincent Ziffle, Dr. Doug Farenick, Moses Gordon, Dr. Toby Sperlich, Dr. Andrea Sterzuck, Dr. Michelle Coupal, Dr. Shannon Dea, and Karin Rustad. Some incredible students at the University of Regina pushed my thinking, including Zoe Baylis, Jessica Ross-Brown, Winter Ross, and Emily Herzberger. I am additionally grateful to Eric Horbal, who supported some research in Chapter 5 of this book. My gratitude extends further due to the generous funding provided by the University of Regina's President's Publication Fund and the Faculty of Arts' Publication Fund.

In Regina, I am ever grateful to Bev Cardinal, Mark Sylvestre, Dave Slater, Jann Ticknor, and Albert Robillard for the friendship and the conversations on settler relations, which taught me so much. And in broader Saskatchewan, thank you to my colleagues and friends Drs. Allyson Stevenson and Kurt Boyer, who mentored me in countless ways.

I've spent several years on the enormous task of supporting the Reconciliation Committee at the Canadian Political Science Association. I thank past and current members Drs. Joyce Green, Rebecca Major, Mariam Georgis, Christine Sy, Daniel Voth, Daniel Sherwin, and Nisha Nath. Thanks especially to past committee member David MacDonald for the years of generous mentorship through our many projects.

I thank the Expressions of Métis Spirituality and Religion Across the Homelands research team for showing me kinship in the academy: Louise McKay, Michael Thibert, Jacinthe (Jay) Lambert, Alie Johnston, Celina and Darryl Loyer, Josh Morin, Rhonda Ashmore, Joan Pelletier, Calvin Racette, Callie Parisien, Alex Powalinsky, and Lisa Halsall. I am especially grateful for the daring brilliance, compassion, and scholarly integrity of Drs. Chantal Fiola and Paul Gareau.

At Fernwood Publishing, I thank Tanya Andrusieczko for the supportive navigation of making this book and the detailed, deep analysis of my work. I also thank others who supported the project: Fazeela Jiwa, Anumeha Gokhale, Lauren Jeanneau, John van der Woude, Sade Cooke, Erin Seatter, Art Bouman, Beverley Rach, and Brenda Conroy.

I started with my parents, and must return to them. Today, they help daily with my young family, raising a new generation of politically minded and confident Métis citizens. Also, my gratitude goes to my siblings, Brenna, Graham, and Ashleigh, and my dearest friends, Cassandra Hryniw and Talitha Fehr. Thanks to my aunts, uncles, and cousins. No Métis person really knows themselves outside of their relations and I have always known I was rich with (and indebted to) my relations. Relatedly, thanks to the Smith family, which I married into and in many ways was my invitation to Treaty 4 territory, which brought the ever-evolving and expanding gift of family.

Finally, thanks for the patience, Sebastian and Elliotte. I'm not sure that I've ever known anyone who asks more deeply probing and analytical questions of life's many mysteries than you, Sebbie, or anyone with more fearless joy and creative genius than you, Ellie. Thanks the most to Matt.

PREFACE

LOCATING MYSELF IN SETTLER COLONIAL CANADA

I am of Métis heritage and I grew up in Winnipeg, Manitoba. Growing up in the heart of the Red River homeland of the Métis Nation has been a critical element of how I understand Canadian politics. From my family's story, I understand the Métis Peoples as foundational to the establishment of the country through the economic foundations of the fur trade, military conflicts and ongoing Indigenous-centred resistances, and the political development of Manitoba joining the Confederation. Therefore, I understand Canada as an Indigenous place, particularly in relation to Winnipeg, which Anishinaabe scholar Niigaan Sinclair calls an "Indigenous city."[1] In this place, I have been fortunate to have a career that exposed me to Canada's political operations as well as afforded me with intimate exchanges with reconciliation that have made me question the parameters of settler colonial Canada.

An example of how my career has shaped my scholarship begins with the three years I worked in various political positions at the Manitoba Legislative Assembly after completing the Master of Public Administration program at the University of Manitoba. Of particular importance at this time of young adulthood was how much my lens of being Canadian was shaped by the lives of my Métis ancestors and family. Sometimes we come to understand ourselves better when our normative reality clashes with that of the external environment; certainly, this characterizes, in part, my time at the legislature, where I realized how deeply I understood Canada through the conflicts of settler imposition on my ancestors, which were seemingly overlooked by the actors working in the legislative structure.

My ancestors are deeply woven into the story of Canada. Given the persistent issue of inauthentic claims of Indigenous ancestry, I disclose an account of my ancestry that is substantiated in public records, leaving aside those stories of living memory passed down orally over generations. My ancestors include men who arrived from France in the late seventeenth century and the First Nations women they intermarried. They came to engage in the fur trade, and church marriage records for First Nations communities and Métis families show these families moving progressively westward. From these marriages, I share ancestry with many historical Métis families, though I do not list them here as they include families and communities that do not claim me, nor I them. My direct ancestors, the Lafrenières, secured employment as fur traders with the North West Company and Hudson's Bay Company, travelling between the Great Lakes, Cumberland House in the Northwest Territories (later Saskatchewan), and Rat Portage (now Kenora, Ontario). Other records substantiate my family's stories of hunting buffalo and engaging in military resistance. For instance, a great-uncle some generations back participated in the Métis resistance to the Hudson's Bay Company takeover of the North West Company at the Battle of Seven Oaks. (Later, my great-grandfather Alexander Lafrenière fought in World War I, and his contribution is marked at the National Métis Veterans' Memorial Monument in Batoche, Saskatchewan.) As the fur trade came to a close, these ancestors settled in the Northwest Territories, or what became Manitoba, in the mid-nineteenth century. As hunters and traders, they continued to move throughout the Pembina Mountains and Red River. Over several decades, they lived in the historical Métis settlements of Saint François Xavier, where they held Half-Breed land allotment, and then Saint Léon and Saint Boniface. These points of settler-Métis contact, resistance, and perseverance shape the lens through which I understand settler encroachment and how I, through my ancestors, have been personally implicated in the making of Canada.

While working at the Manitoba Legislative Assembly, I saw the making of the many structural barriers that Indigenous Peoples face: The legislature, I came to realize, is a significant part of the decision-making apparatus that creates inequitable conditions for Indigenous people's lives. At that time in my life, I had an underdeveloped understanding of settler colonial political realities. I had earned a Master of Public Administration and developed a particular appreciation for how the government should work in terms of ensuring the collective provision of security for all citizens. However, this education did not align with what I observed working in provincial politics, where I saw the socio-economic marginalization of Indigenous Peoples seemingly dismissed by those involved in the provincial lawmaking structure. Furthermore, what I saw in the legislature did not reflect my understanding of Indigenous Peoples' rights and agency as I understood them based on my lived experiences and the oral histories of my Métis family. The First Peoples as the foundation of Canada were overlooked, and I felt a great deal of disillusion. As fondly as I reflect on my mentors and superiors during this time, I could not find sufficient answers from them about the structural barriers imposed on Indigenous Peoples. Like many who engage in postgraduate studies, these curiosities drove me to pursue a PhD in Native Studies at the University of Manitoba.

Much of the research in this book comes from my PhD dissertation, "Reserved Responsibilities: A Comparative Analysis of Settler Colonial Narratives of Canadian Federalism and Sub-National Jurisdictional Responsibility for Status First Nations Peoples Living On-Reserve in Manitoba, British Columbia, and the Northwest Territories," which I completed in 2017. I developed this book using research directly connected to the political structure of federalism, which I consider vital for understanding barriers to reconciliation in Canada.

During my PhD studies, I worked as a researcher with the Assembly of Manitoba Chiefs and the Manitoba First Nations Education Resource Centre. I also spent a summer as a research fellow at the Newberry Consortium in American Indian Studies in Chicago, Illinois. These positions honed my research experience and capabilities concerning matters related to Indigenous Peoples and our knowledge systems. However, not until later did I begin working in-depth on issues relating to reconciliation, including in my roles as the research-curator for Indigenous content at the Canadian Museum for Human Rights in Winnipeg and the executive lead of Indigenization and the Indigenous research lead at the University of Regina in Saskatchewan. Finally, I became a faculty member in the Department of Politics and International Studies at the University of Regina in 2021, which brought my studies in Canadian politics and reconciliation into synthesis.

These employment experiences are essential to my understanding of reconciliation. Through these opportunities, I had the privilege, for example, to hear folks working directly for the Truth and Reconciliation Commission of Canada (TRC) speak to the importance of their work in transforming the Canadian political landscape. The TRC was situated in Winnipeg, where I lived, and I had the opportunity to visit its offices and speak with staff. As a community-based researcher, I have also had countless opportunities to sit with community members, Elders, Old Ones (called kēhtē-ayak in Cree/nēhiyawēwin), and Knowledge Keepers. These conversations have further shaped how I have come to understand the breadth of what is meant by reconciliation.

Additionally, my family also influences how I understand Canada as a settler colonial society and the opportunities this presents for reconciliation. The oral stories of my ancestors, the Lafrenières, shaped how I understood myself in the sociopolitical fabric of Canada. I grew up understanding our family story as part of the foundation of the country. I also grew up with a mother of Icelandic descent. In my youth, this became a source of contention related to my identity: Any claim to Icelandic ancestry was consistently deemed inauthentic because I do not have the physical characteristics commonly ascribed to Scandinavians, including blond hair and blue eyes. As a result, I found it easier to ignore this ancestry and identify solely as Métis, which was more readily accepted by people unless someone probed my white-passing appearance. Though I became disassociated from an Icelandic identity, I feel it is important to disclose these roots and explain why I lean into my Métis identity. Further, I grew up in an immediate family that I would now describe as active at the fringes of Indigenous politics through different Métis and First Nations organizations. I see now how I always lived at the fringes of cultural spaces and ancestral knowledge systems: They were often present, even if quietly, and informed how I saw the world. However, I am always clear that I am not a traditional Indigenous person. I do not necessarily carry these ancestral knowledge systems, nor do I speak Michif, the language of the Métis. My grandmother was the last in my lineage to speak Michif, a source of cultural loss and assimilation that I am keenly aware of. As such, I am a learner of ancestral knowledges but also an effective bridge builder between colonial structures and Indigenous-related power struggles.

All Indigenous people have likely, at some time, felt shame as a result of experiences of racism, and this shame is in dialectical opposition to the cultural pride that we know in our hearts. I am not the first person of Métis descent to experience this dialectical tug. Importantly, all of these academic pursuits and employment opportunities taught me how to process it and attempt to decolonize my being. I think of the late Métis writer Howard Adams, who conceptualized this dialectic, or the opposing forces of shame and pride, as the "prison of grass."[2] As Adams explained, a decolonizing of our cognition — here I borrow from Marie Battiste's (Mi'kmaq Nation) concept of "cognitive imperialism"[3] — is necessary for many Indigenous people living in settler societies. Importantly, I am active in my cognitive decolonizing. In this way I observe and comment on — but do not dictate — a path forward for reconciliation in settler Canada.

I hope that this book offers its readers some sense of the complexities of settler colonialism in Canada. Mainly, I hope to illuminate some aspects of how settler colonialism operates through Canada's governance systems. For me, these lessons demonstrate how settler colonialism is an invisible force, difficult — in some instances — to point directly to, and even more difficult to reconcile with Indigenous Peoples' liberation movements. This book responds to a central question: How do settler colonial narratives of Canadian federalism circumvent Indigenous Peoples' agency? In this book I provide Canadians with a straightforward account of the challenges that the political system of Canadian federalism presents for reconciliation. With structural limitations on reconciliation, the possibilities of overcoming colonial inequities in Canada are also limited. Such restrictions on reconciliation might exist in social, political, or economic realms of Canada. This book, however, focuses on the political structure of Canadian federalism, as I argue that alternative approaches to this political system exist, as does the potential to better foster reconciliation in Canada.

Finally, this book is an invitation to think more critically about the many barriers to reconciliation, as well as a practical guide to equip Canadians with tools to change the country's political structures.

CHAPTER ONE

WHY FEDERALISM MATTERS FOR RECONCILIATION

Canada is a settler colonial state that has tried to assimilate and erase Indigenous Peoples' lands, agency, and difference in its attempts to provide benefits to non-Indigenous settlers. One way to make Canada confront its ongoing practices of settler colonialism is through reconciliation. For many, reconciliation means alleviation of the injustices and socioeconomic inequities brought on by colonialism. The TRC as well as Survivors and Intergenerational Survivors of the Indian residential school (IRS) system have advocated for reconciliation. Reconciliation builds on the long legacy of Indigenous-centred resistance to Canadian settler power, centring Indigenous difference in defiance of the settler tactics of elimination and erasure.

Reconciliation efforts are ongoing through education, court cases and settlements, and celebratory or commemorative events. Markers of social

Indigenous Difference

Indigenous difference includes those Indigenous ways of thinking and being that are exclusive to Indigenous Peoples, shaped by their worldviews, and specific to distinct nations and communities. Indigenous worldviews encompass the knowledge systems and ways of being that Indigenous Peoples cultivate in their relationships with the land. Elder Norman Sunchild (Thunderchild First Nation) explains Indigenous worldviews as the "connectedness" that Indigenous Peoples gain through knowledge and understanding of the Creator.[1] These connections are embedded in Indigenous Peoples' languages; frame approaches to social organization, political practice, and economic systems; and are held in specific Indigenous lands. Such Indigenous lands, which can also be understood as Indigenous title,[2] are understood as those with which Indigenous Peoples hold a stewardship role, or a sacred relationship built through responsibility with the land but also with other-than-human beings.

and political change related to reconciliation vary, often due to the context of a situation (e.g., What is the history of structural oppression at hand?), the actor(s) undertaking the work (e.g., Are they individuals or organizations, settlers or Indigenous?), or the metrics being used (e.g., the TRC report). We might point to tangible change through the growth of days of recognition (such as National Indigenous Peoples Day, National Day for Truth and Reconciliation, National Day of Awareness for Missing and Murdered Indigenous Women and Girls and 2SLGBTQIA+ People [Two-Spirit, Lesbian, Gay, Bisexual, Transgender, Queer, Intersex, Asexual, and others], also known as Red Dress Day, and National Ribbon Skirt Day), the increased practice of land acknowledgements, or the Canadian Parliament's declaration on October 27, 2022, that the IRS system was genocidal.

Alongside these developments, however, colonial inequities remain embedded in Indigenous Peoples' realities. Water quality in reserve communities, for example, remains a pervasive problem despite Justin Trudeau's 2015 campaign promise to address the issue and nearly ten years in office as prime minister.[3] Indigenous women, girls, and Two-Spirit folks experience disproportionate rates of violence.[4] Objectively clear markers of racism limit Indigenous people's access to equitable healthcare.[5] These cross-Canada inequities all entrench Indigenous dispossession while securing settler benefits.

While I can drive from my home in Regina in Treaty 4 territory to Saskatoon in Treaty 6 territory and pass provincial signage honouring these Treaties, these signs do not translate into land back for Indigenous Peoples. These signs represent a kind of moment of reconciliatory change — an opportunity for education — but not the decolonial change that one might hope the settler state would make to address the ongoing colonial legacies of inequity.

Scholars Eve Tuck (Unangax̂) and K. Wayne Yang have argued that decolonization cannot be understood as a metaphor; it must entail the return and restitution of Indigenous lands stolen through colonization.[6] Decolonization includes the activities and processes that respond to, resist, and undo colonial oppressions. Decolonization ought to encompass the reclamation of everything connected to these lands. This includes Indigenous rights; cultural, linguistic, and political practices; and Indigenous difference. Indigenous rights in Canada can be unclear, as they are often referred to as Aboriginal rights, which may be influenced by colonial perspectives. When I mention Indigenous rights, I am referring to the rights defined and upheld by Indigenous Peoples themselves, in line with their worldviews and concepts of political autonomy. Thus, the targets of decolonization include all of the processes, structures, and institutions that have supported the theft of Indigenous Peoples' lands, sources of rights and political autonomy, and ways of being. While reconciliation is distinct from decolonization, it should also seek to address and rectify colonial inequities such as the disproportionate rates of poverty, racism, and violence experienced by Indigenous people.

Tony Ballantyne has explained colonialism as a structure built upon a set of webs that interconnect imperial colonial nations, or empires, with colonies through economic trade, diplomatic presence, and the movement of people or subjects of the colonial enterprise.[7] Canadian federalism is caught up in a similar web of colonial operations supporting the settler structure. As a political system, federalism shapes the operation and structure of Canadian settler governance and is integral to untangling the web of settler colonial inequities through contemporary reconciliation.

Notably, Canada's application of federalism has evolved according to the hallmark of settler colonial intent: Indigenous Peoples' dispossession for settler benefit. In Canada, matters pertaining to the lives of Indigenous Peoples fall under the jurisdiction (or responsibility and decision-making authority) of both the federal and provincial governments. This federalist structure inherently denies powers to Indigenous orders of government. The denial of Indigenous Peoples' right to self-determination and agency is a central feature of settler colonial oppression and thus a central concern for reconciliation.

While the operation of settler colonialism has deprived Indigenous Peoples of lands and rights, Indigenous Peoples do continue to practise traditional or ancestral laws according to ancestral worldviews. However,

Indigenous Rights

Aboriginal rights are recognized in Canada's Constitution Act, 1982, and have evolved through case law. In contrast, Indigenous rights are defined and upheld by Indigenous Peoples themselves, rooted in their own worldviews and concepts of political autonomy. These rights can be viewed as inherent, stemming from their status as the First Peoples to inhabit what would become Canada, prior to European colonialism and settler occupation.

the impact of Canadian sovereignty on Indigenous Peoples and their rights in relation to land ought not to be overlooked. The exercise of Canadian sovereignty through the federalist political arrangement is shaped by the settler colonial intent to wrest agency from Indigenous Peoples and transfer it to the state, a common standard in settlerism.

That settler colonial dispossession for settler benefit is embedded within the political system of federalism limits the transformative potential of reconciliation if left unexamined in the work of reconciliation. In Canada, changes to federalist power sharing occur alongside shifts in the social and political landscape, creating an opportunity to adjust jurisdictional power-sharing models. Alternatives to federalism exist, too, varying in scope and application from marginal reconciliatory change to revolutionary decolonial agendas. Without adequate consideration of the political system of federalism — including how jurisdiction related to Indigenous Peoples is made and operates — the sociopolitical change of reconciliation will face obstacles across Canada.

A Problem for Reconciliation: Narratives of Canada's Political Structure

Canadian federalism is rooted in settler colonialism, and this political arrangement has been used to generate orders of government that explicitly deny Indigenous Peoples' agency. This denial is evidenced in the Constitution and case law that inform the division of powers and provide the federal government with jurisdictional power related to Indigenous Peoples. This federal jurisdiction was established in the British North America Act, 1867 (BNA Act), which served as Canadian's first constitutional document. Throughout the twentieth century, however, changes to the federalist power-sharing model enhanced the role of the provinces over Indigenous Peoples through decentralization,

Federalism

Federalism is a system of governance in which decision-making power is distributed among various political units. In Canada, this power sharing takes place across multiple orders of government, including federal, provincial, territorial, and municipal authorities. Both the federal and provincial governments are considered sovereign in this arrangement, meaning they operate as autonomous powers that hold independent and intermingled powers, which are set out in the Constitution Act, 1982.

power sharing, and devolution. Both jurisdictional arrangements — the national and provincial — present settler colonial restrictions for the agency and self-determination of Indigenous Peoples.

Central to this federalist situation are narratives of settler colonialism. These narratives are comprised of foundational stories or myths, giving form to the nation, or what Benedict Anderson calls "imagined communities."[8] Settler colonial narratives are commonly developed in settler society to justify settler land theft and intrusive settler laws. To give shape to the nation, an imagined community, narratives serve to distort the principal equation of settlerism, where Indigenous dispossession produces settler benefit. For example, settler colonial narratives can include the myth of Canada as a peacekeeping nation[9] or the notion of a pioneering or frontier past,[10] which aims to obscure and nullify settler colonial violence that has shaped nation building. Other narratives, such as the myth of the "savage,"[11] are used to denigrate Indigenous Peoples in the process of rationalizing the theft of Indigenous lands or the erosion of Indigenous cultures and languages through assimilation tactics. Settler colonial narratives that frame federalism as a neutral political system of governance mask the assimilative purview of the colonial state.

Typically, Indigenous Peoples, government decision-makers, and citizens alike understand that in Canada, the federal government has jurisdictional decision-making power for Indigenous Peoples, though as this book will show, provinces also have a role. But Indigenous agency within the structure of Canadian federalism is consistently denied. The question that gets asked within the settler colonial framework is "Which order of government is responsible for Indigenous Peoples?" and not "How do we restore nation-to-nation relations that recognize Indigenous sovereignty?"

The concept of sovereignty has a complex history that is closely tied to the mechanisms of dispossession in settler colonialism. Sovereignty is typically understood as a mechanism of legitimacy for the state as an actor in the international system.[12] However, this idea is not fixed; it has evolved over time, moving from its origins in religious and monarchical rule to a secular political concept that is deeply rooted in broader imperial colonialism.[13] Today, settler colonial states are significantly affected by this history because, as Lorenzo Veracini writes, settlers assume an "inherent sovereign claim that travels with them"[14] to new lands and territories. Settler mobility brings an assertion of sovereignty, derived from an imperial land base, that is used to undermine the agency of Indigenous Peoples on their lands.

Although federalism is typically not a focus of reconciliation conversations, it offers opportunities for related change. Indigenous Nations have effective political and constitutional standing in Canadian government, yet federalism remains a structure of divided powers that by design withholds fundamental access to sovereignty from Indigenous Peoples. To foster reconciliation, this book explores alternative approaches to federalist governance, including different political arrangements to better recognize Indigenous Peoples' agency so that reconciliation can contribute to restoring Indigenous and Crown nation-to-nation relations within the federalist model.

What Is Settler Colonialism?

Many Canadians likely understand that their country evolved from the ongoing presence of British and French powers throughout the seventeenth to nineteenth centuries. This Euro-colonial presence across North America was part of the global imperial colonial order that saw many European powers carry out similar travel, contact, and supposed "discovery" of new lands, leading to violent conflicts as foreign powers laid claim to these lands. The initial elements of this process began in the fifteenth century when European powers were engaged in global competition to enhance power and influence vis-à-vis neighbouring empires.[15] A key aspect of these operations was the identification and extraction of natural resources from regions across Africa, Asia, Oceania, and the Americas, and the process of religious expansion.

This growing imperial action was operationalized and justified through international laws that treated European-style politics, economics, and culture as superior to those practised elsewhere. European explorers and merchants relied on two significant legal concepts to justify these operations: *terra nullius* — a Latin term for vacant or unused lands — and the doctrine of discovery. While the primary motives for imperial operations were power and wealth, religion played a role in justifying European expansion; the legal concepts of *terra nullius* and the doctrine of discovery originated from papal bulls, formal documents created by the Catholic Church that endorsed imperial expansion by justifying the acquisition of Indigenous Peoples' lands.[16]

Framed by philosophical motives based on European superiority and greed, the concepts of *terra nullius* and the doctrine of discovery had significant impacts, serving European political domination and becoming entrenched in settler lawmaking.[17]

Settler colonialism is an evolutionary outcome of this imperial colonialism. Over time, imperial presence and occupation can give way to differing patterns of settlement that produce a settler colony. For example, Veracini has demonstrated that imperial colonies relate to an empire as a home country to which they will return.[18] As time progresses, the possibility — or inevitability — of return diminishes, and the colony starts to function as a home base. This transition of the home base from empire to the colony signifies the shift toward settler colonialism. Veracini referred to this as *animus manendi,* which captures the settler intent to remain or take up residency on new lands.[19] This change is accompanied by what settler scholars Emma Battell Lowman and Adam J. Barker describe as "Settler sovereignties" that are "carried with" settlers until they establish them elsewhere,[20] a practice based on the foundations of land theft set by *terra nullius* and the doctrine of discovery. The desire to stay, along with the anchoring of sovereignty, is frequently supported and justified through settler colonial narratives. These narratives, discussed in relation to Canada's settler state in Chapter 2, erase Indigenous Peoples' sacred connections and relationships with the lands now settler-colonized.[21]

Another critical factor of settler colonialism is its economic foundation. Imperial colonialism is considered the basis for contemporary capitalism, where the wealth generated by settler colonialism is rooted in the theft of Indigenous lands and the extraction of resources.[22] For instance, imperial corporations such as the Hudson's Bay Company helped establish settler presence in Canada and drew Indigenous Peoples into a corporate system through trade. The company used existing Indigenous trade routes and increased the purchasing power of Indigenous communities to promote the sale of imperial goods. These economic operations laid the groundwork for the expansion of the Dominion of Canada, including the purchase of Rupert's Land from the Hudson's Bay Company and the subsequent Numbered Treaties.[23] The economic exploitation of lands and resources raises significant concerns for Indigenous relations with federal and provincial governments, as disagreements over jurisdiction continue to shape contemporary economic projects.

Indigenous Peoples face several outcomes from the lasting colonial contact, engagement, and settlement by European people as the agents of the Crowns they represented. Principally, Indigenous nationhood impedes the development and entrenchment of settler political economies.[24] Thus, settler colonies attempt to overcome Indigenous nationhood by destabilizing the relationships that the First Peoples, as the legitimate caretakers of their territory, hold with their neighbours and with more-than-human beings (or relatives) such as plants and animals. This destabilization is done to concretize settler claims to the lands and allow settlers to continue to build wealth and prosperity through natural resource access and use.

The progression of settler colonialism was violent and it aimed to undermine Indigenous sovereignty to establish the legitimacy of the settler state. While settler colonies are inherently violent,[25] such practices are often obscured, dismissed, or ignored by settler states and societies, and settler narratives play a role in this, too.[26] In Canada, settler colonial violence and dispossession are evident in the reserve system, which physically removed First Nations people from their lands and severely restricted their access to healthcare, economic activities, and family relations. Another example is the IRS system, through which the Canadian state apprehended, or stole, Indigenous children from their communities and sent them to schools to assimilate them according to settler-based norms and thus eradicate Indigenous difference — a measure of genocide.[27] Additionally, the Canadian state has created various mechanisms to construct and manipulate Indigenous identity in an effort to eliminate it, such as through the Indian Act or Inuit disc numbers.

Drawing from British and French practices, the Canadian government established its governance system, which has been key to enabling various processes of dispossession. However, as Indigenous legal scholar John Borrows (Anishinaabe Nation) has illustrated, these processes of dispossession through political displacement are not absolute: Canadian legal and political structures are informed by Indigenous Peoples' laws and political practices. In fact, the origin of the federalist power-sharing model is typically attributed to the Haudenosaunee (Hodinohso:ni) Nation, or the Iroquois Confederacy, which has a long-standing tradition of federalist governance that contributed to the development not only of Canada but also the US federation.[28] In addition, Borrows explains that the Treaties in North America involve Indigenous laws, evidencing

Indigenous legal traditions that are tied up in Canadian governance.[29] There are also other examples of Indigenous legal traditions tied up in Canadian governance. For instance, Borrows writes, "It could be said that Canada is a legally pluralistic state: civil law, common law, and Indigenous legal traditions organize dispute resolution in our country in different ways."[30] In this way, the foundations of the Canadian state are entrenched with Indigenous-derived laws and political arrangements.

Settler colonial societies often draw on Indigenous legal structures in these ways. American Indian scholar Jodi Byrd (Chickasaw Nation), discussing the settler colonial context of the United States, argues that British-origin settler states maintain a complex dialectical relationship with Indigenous nationhood, characterized by both recognition and erasure. She builds on the concept of "cacophony," or the existence of discordant realities coexisting simultaneously. In this context, settler states recognize Indigenous nationhood while also undermining it.[31] Byrd explains that this "cacophonous discourse" is applied in settler projects to transform Indigenous ancestral political constructs for settler purposes while suppressing these Indigenous traditions. This dynamic minimizes the visibility of Indigeneity within the framework of colonial domination, thereby justifying ongoing settler domination. Byrd describes these mechanics as a dialectic tension (referring to the coexistence of two seemingly opposite characteristics) that both recognizes and renders absent or erases Indigenous difference.

Building on Borrows' work, we can understand that Indigenous political approaches of federalism, Indigenous legal traditions, and Treaties have been incorporated into Canadian political structures. This incorporation — while empowering in some circumstances — serves to, as Byrd states, suppress or absent Indigenous Peoples within the settler state. The Indigenous foundations of Canada's political framework are largely unrecognizable to most Canadians and have been co-opted by settler systems to support those very systems. As a result, these foundations are used to obscure domination tactics that justify the ongoing continuation of colonial domination.

This dialectic of recognition and suppression is further effected in Canada's justice system. Legal scholar Brenna Bhandar explains the paradox of iterability, which is the court's practice of iteration that both produces and reproduces Canadian sovereignty.[32] Though the courts contribute to recognition of Aboriginal rights in Canadian law, they also use these rulings as opportunity to restate (and thereby produce and reproduce) Crown sovereignty. In this way, the "law attempts to hold on to and retrench its own foundations."[33] This practice works to ensure that the Crown is not displaced but rather maintains its dominance through the subordination of Indigenous Peoples' political autonomy.

In Canada, these processes of settler colonial expansion built on Indigenous legal and governance foundations unfolded in a series of stages: bilateral diplomacy, protectionism, and assimilation.[34] This evolutionary unfolding of Canadian settler intent and dispossession has been demonstrated by countless Canadian historians. In the Prairies, I understand this evolution through the work of Allyson Stevenson (Métis), Sarah Carter, and James Daschuk.[35] Canada's economic origin in the fur trade and diplomatic bilateralism are typically pointed to in the making of the Royal Proclamation of 1763 and early Treaties. Settler encroachment through land theft and European-derived disease then led to Crown protectionism. Throughout the nineteenth and twentieth centuries, assimilation tactics were increasingly regimented by the state and bolstered by discrimination and racism in society, pushing Indigenous dispossession and, in some cases, genocidal assimilation. The IRS and Sixties Scoop are often recognized by contemporary Canadian society as examples of significant policies that have impacted Indigenous Peoples. Other harmful practices include relocation projects, disease spreading, tactics of starvation, and underresourced social services.

As Canada developed as a country, social change was influenced by immigration. In the 1970s, the government established its multicultural policy. This practice of multiculturalism in Canada, intended to foster inclusion, can be understood as an assimilative force: It presents a façade of diversity that exerts pressure to conform or assimilate. Feminist sociologist Sunera Thobani explains that Canadian society is, first and foremost, bilingual and bicultural (English and French),[36] so newcomers may feel compelled to assimilate in order to navigate the social landscape. Thobani writes, "It is the nation's proper responsibility to oversee the practices of immigrants and govern cultural difference: 'we' may let 'you' in, but you must become who we say should be."[37]

These complexities of settler inclusion and exclusion have increasingly led to an understanding of contemporary settler societies through a triad or triangular organization. This framework consists of settler populations, Indigenous Others, and Exogenous Others. The latter group includes those from diasporic communities who might be immigrants, refugees, or newcomers[38] — or arrivants.[39] Exogenous Others often encounter challenges trying to fit into the settler colonial social order, which determines who has access to benefits. The triad is underpinned by settler-oriented power relations: Settlers arrive with a form of sovereignty that supplants Indigenous political authority, whereas Exogenous Others or arrivants must adapt to the dominant culture.[40] One social mechanism that sustains the dominant settler structure is the "complicity" of these populations in reinforcing it. American feminist philosophers Corwin Aragon and Alison M. Jaggar write, "People are structurally complicit when they exercise their agency in ways that reinforce the unjust social structures in which they participate, regardless of their conscious intentions."[41] Complicity effectively operationalizes social structures, normalizing the conditions that dictate the provision, access, and denial of political agency within settler society.

Many settlers are grappling with the complicated history of their country's domination — attempted, actual, and ongoing — of Indigenous Peoples. When the benefits that settlers derive from this history are challenged or disrupted, a number of social responses can arise. One such response is settler guilt. When the ongoing legacies of the IRS system became widely known, they undermined the national narrative of Canada as a peacemaker and led to feelings of guilt among some Canadians.[42] Another response is fear of losing the benefits that settlers enjoy as derived from the dispossession of Indigenous Peoples' lands.[43] Faced with these uncomfortable feelings, some settler folks may resort to "moves to innocence," a series of actions that deflect accountability and divert decolonial efforts, often with an intention to assuage settler guilt.[44] Additionally, many settlers may display a lack of empathy for the suffering experienced by Indigenous Peoples as a result of socioeconomic disparities and outright violence. This attitude can lead to what scholars Mary Jane McCallum (Munsee-Delaware Nation) and Adele Perry have coined a "structure of indifference" in settler Canada. In this structure, the mistreatment of Indigenous Peoples becomes normalized and overlooked, further reinforcing colonial practices.[45]

This description of settler society, while brief, should be further understood through Indigenous-led resistance against settler colonial dominance. There are concrete examples of and results from resistance to state-driven and socially constructed settlerism. These resistances have been expressed in various manners, from silent uprisings to violent clashes. In the Prairies, for instance, the Treaty and reserve-making processes in the nineteenth century saw uprisings against the Crown. As historian Michel Hogue has explained, the First Nations and Métis Nation in the Prairies co-constructed resistances, including the Battle of Batoche in 1885, on the basis of long-standing kinship relations.[46] The TRC has also brought to light stories of children running away from residential schools, such as Chanie Wenjack's story from 1966, which was later shared by musician Gord Downie in an album and graphic novel, *The Secret Path*. Other examples include episodes of resistance against large-scale, mega-projects such as the James Bay hydroelectric project and Mackenzie Valley pipeline in the 1970s. These practices of resistance continued through to the Kanesatake resistance at Kahnawá:ke in 1990 and the present-day standoff against the Trans Mountain pipeline and the Wet'suwet'en land defence against Coastal GasLink, to name only a few examples. These are not isolated incidents; they are part of a continuous struggle by Indigenous Peoples to resist colonial domination. The outcomes of these resistances are significant and include the historical Treaties, Aboriginal rights recognition in the Constitution Act of 1982, Aboriginal self-government agreements and modern-day Treaties, commissions and inquiries concerned with rights assertion or protection, defence of the land against encroachment by resource corporations, and the continued expression of Indigenous cultures, languages, and enduring Indigenous difference.

What Is Reconciliation?

Reconciliation is a practice of healing and repairing harmed relationships. It is not specific to Canada. Sometimes it follows periods of conflict, war, atrocity, genocide, and apartheid. In Canada, it is shaped by Indigenous-centred perspectives, principally those that led to the TRC (2009–15). Truth and reconciliation in Canada originated in the advocacy and resistance work of Survivors as well as Intergenerational Survivors of the IRS system. The descendants of IRS Survivors have come to be referred to as Intergenerational Survivors to indicate the deep, lasting impact of residential schools. Importantly, through political advocacy and court litigation, Survivors and Intergenerational Survivors brought to light the various abuses, assimilation tactics, and genocidal intent and outcomes of the IRS system. Many court cases related to the IRS were litigated — *Blackwater v. Plint* (2005) and *Baxter v. Canada* (2006) are two examples.[47] This Survivor-led action ultimately led to the Indian Residential Schools Settlement Agreement (IRSSA), the second-largest class action settlement in Canadian history. The IRSSA included five core components: Common Experience Payment and Independent Assessment Process, which were two distinct financial processes for resolving IRS-related claims, and the TRC, commemoration initiatives, and health and healing services.[48]

The TRC is critical to understanding reconciliation in Canada. Like the IRSSA, the TRC resulted from significant Survivor advocacy and resistance work. The TRC had its roots in the global transitional justice and reconciliation approach — various justice, truth, and reconciliation organizations have been implemented in countries around the world, including, to name only a few, Argentina (1983–84), South Africa (1995–98), Rwanda (1999–2002), and East Timor (2001–2005) — but was shaped by the specific experiences and interests of Survivors across Canada.[49] Scholar Rosemary Nagy has written extensively on the significant care and effort that Survivors took to ensure the TRC "embrace[d] a community-based process that was self-consciously identified as home-grown and indigenous, rather than an internationalized, legalistic approach."[50]

Canada's TRC had unique components in its design and operation thanks to the input of Survivors, which differentiated it from other such commissions.[51] For example, many survivors preferred the IRSSA over pursuing litigation as it was understood to be less adversarial.[52] Another measure of Survivor influence on the TRC was the process of public *truth-telling*. Foundational to the commission's activities were the public and private hearings in which Survivors and Intergenerational Survivors gave testimony and spoke of their or their family members' personal experiences prior to, during, and after attending residential schools.[53] To this end, the TRC held hundreds of hearings along with seven national events in Winnipeg, Manitoba (2010); Inuvik, Northwest Territories (2011); Halifax, Nova Scotia (2011); Saskatoon, Saskatchewan (2012); Montreal, Quebec (2013); Vancouver, British Columbia (2013); and Edmonton, Alberta (2014).[54]

These public hearings and national events collected nearly seven thousand statements, which make up much of the *truth* aspect of the

TRC. These histories did not occur in a vacuum and their impacts did not stay at the schools: They were carried by the Survivors and shared with Intergenerational Survivors in a Canadian society deeply shaped by anti-Indigenous racism. Another contribution to the truth aspect of the TRC comes from research and archival records, which inform how Canadians understand the parameters, extent, and impact of the IRS system on individuals, families, and communities.[55] Additionally, bearing witness, or deep and concerted listening by the public audience, contributes to the truth aspect of the TRC.[56] How Canadians listen to, honour, and effect change as a result of Survivors' and Intergenerational Survivors' truth-telling profoundly shapes the truth aspect of reconciliation. Truth-telling and bearing witness are practices centred on the histories of abuse, familial and community breakdown, and cultural and linguistic disconnect experienced by Indigenous Peoples.

From this truth, we can start to understand better what might be entailed, broadly speaking, by the *reconciliation* component of the TRC. The TRC ultimately issued a six-volume final report and 94 Calls to Action.[57] The first volume considers the history of colonization in Canada. The next volume looks at the ongoing legacies of the residential schools. Two volumes look at the specific experiences of Inuit and Métis students. The fifth volume is dedicated to the burial grounds at residential schools, marking the many children who did not survive the IRS system and return home to their families and communities. The sixth volume focuses on reconciliation and relationships between Indigenous Peoples and settler society.

Two central components of reconciliation emerge from the reports. First, reconciliation involves responses to the history and breadth of colonial injustices that have shaped the Canadian state's and society's structural development. Although the impetus for reconciliation can be located in the advocacy and resistance of Survivors and Intergenerational Survivors of residential schools, the entirety of the structure of settler colonial inequity is critical to reconciliation. Second, reconciliation is the responsibility of all Canadians, as made clear by the Calls to Action, which offer suggested starting points to effect change in the Indigenous-settler relationship. In Volume 6 of the final report, the TRC writes, "Together, Canadians must do more than just talk about reconciliation; we must learn how to practice reconciliation in our everyday lives — within ourselves and our families, and in our communities, governments, places of worship, schools, and work places."[58] As illustrated, reconciliation is conceptually broad for the TRC, yet it is understood as key to how Canadians live together. To reconcile the atrocities of the IRS system is to hold to account all structures involved and those who benefited. That is to say, the Canadian state, which founded and legislated these schools, and the churches that operated the schools are beholden to these truths.

The TRC released its Calls to Action in June 2015 and its Final Report in December 2015. That same year, Prime Minister Justin Trudeau won a majority government, after pledging to implement the Calls to Action.[59] However, progress has been limited and uneven. In 2023, the federal government claimed that 85 percent of the Calls to Action were in process or completed, whereas the nonprofit organization Indigenous Watchdog suggested that only 66 percent were underway or completed.[60] The Yellowhead Institute monitored and reported on government progress annually from 2019 to 2023, finding a paucity of implemented Calls to Action. In the institute's 2023 report, authors Eva Jewell and Ian Mosby explained that over the five years of analysis and reporting, reconciliation was stalled by government inaction.[61]

Due to the government's slow progress, reconciliation practices have garnered criticism. Some criticisms relate to an actor's intent, when reconciliation efforts seem inauthentic. Years ago, as an example, the claim that "reconciliation is dead" was often heard.[62] Critics have argued that reconciliatory intents need to be more genuine than is typically demonstrated in order to generate tangible or revolutionary change in Canadian society.[63] In this sense, many reconciliation efforts are arguably performative[64] — they use language that indicates commitment but do not lead to meaningful change — or "reconciliation lite" — they use language that minimizes colonial harms or provide insufficient solutions related to culture that do not address political power imbalances.[65] Such approaches lack sincere interest in reconciliation and are nontransformative, which only fosters or delays colonial plans for the elimination of Indigenous difference.[66] These critiques map various deficiencies in understandings of what reconciliation asks of Canadians.

Other criticisms result because the work of reconciliation across Canada is not politically neutral. Yellowknives Dene scholar Glen Coulthard's concept of the "politics of recognition" demonstrates how the Canadian state has for decades responded to Indigenous Peoples' claims of colonial dispossession with superficial actions that reinforce the legitimacy of the state. Coulthard argues that these politics have merged with reconciliation.[67] From this perspective, we can understand that reconciliation can be used to serve the interests of the settler state and society. Human rights scholar Damien Short, writing from the Australian perspective, also argues that state legitimacy is the primary concern for the state in reconciliation procedures.[68] These scholars and others point to harms that arise from reconciliation measures that are transactional or offer little transformative change of settler colonial dispossession.[69]

Political scientists Corey Snelgrove and Matthew Wildcat (Ermineskin Cree Nation) also argue that reconciliation as underway in Canada demonstrates the state's ability to "reconfigure" itself to enable new or adjusted measures of colonial domination.[70] They say that reconciliation is often used by state actors in a way that "downplays and depoliticizes non-state actors,"[71] which hold serious implications for Indigenous Nations, which are not states. Yet these authors also offer a differing perspective, that reconciliation exposes a weakness in colonial orders:

> The reproduction of colonial power is never guaranteed and must constantly respond to the efforts of Indigenous peoples to seek justice. Colonial power is constantly in need of new strategies to reproduce itself, and the reconciliation project represents a vulnerability that signals new openings within colonial power structures.[72]

Colonial orders, founded on the theft of Indigenous Peoples' lands, continuously need to "produce and reproduce" their legitimacy. Reconciliation does not inherently provide the conditions for political change that can support Indigenous-centred liberation in settler Canada, but it does offer an opening for actors to generate struggle against settler domination.

I agree with much of the breadth of critical and engaged dialogue on reconciliation. This dialogue is essential to maintaining accountability in the movement: It requires individuals, nongovernmental organizations, and the state to ensure their actions are not vacuous of transformative change. The critiques of reconciliation are not directed at the work of the Survivors and Intergenerational Survivors of the IRS system and instead focus on the take-up of the TRC's Calls to Action by state or political and civic actors,[73] prolonged "government inaction,"[74] inauthentic or performative behaviours, and the failure to achieve "more than just talk about reconciliation."[75] This book sits adjacent to these criticisms in that while I know deficiencies in reconciliation approaches exist, I still believe that reconciliation presents an opportunity for change, though the implementation of change faces various restrictions partly due to the political system of federalism.

Furthermore, I also have observed the ways that both Indigenous and settler organizations and governments are investing in reconciliation. These investments are facilitated by funding grants, programs, and newly structured committees dedicated to reconciliation work. While it remains unclear whether these efforts contribute to reconciliation, I do see some financial and resource commitment to reconciliation that I do not see for other initiatives, such as decolonization. In part due to this commitment, I argue that reconciliation is a process that can effect change and occur in tandem with decolonial pursuits. As I have written elsewhere with my colleague Dr. Jérôme Melançon at the University of Regina, reconciliation and decolonization can work in supportive collaboration or be opposing forces.[76] Certainly, reconciliation — or efforts made in the name of reconciliation — in no way guarantees the outcomes of transformative change needed to address Indigenous Peoples' dispossession of lands, rights, and difference. Nevertheless, the current political willingness to support reconciliation opens some possibilities for positive and beneficial changes, which can support decolonial change. Yet there remains a gap in terms of the multitude of political processes that impede reconciliation, including federalism.

In this sense, I start with the premise that reconciliation is a cornerstone of the decolonization of settler colonial Canada. Many would disagree with this assumption. Reconciliation and decolonization are separate political processes, and this book is primarily concerned with reconciliation and not decolonization. As Tuck and Yang explain in arguing against decolonization as metaphor,[77] decolonization is always about the land and its restitution. This form of decolonial reparation differs from what is usually offered through reconciliation. Central to reconciliation in Canada is reparation of the social contract that has enabled settler benefit through Indigenous dispossession; reconciliation is not consistently concerned with a restitution of lands, though it can be. An example of a model that effectively bridges reconciliatory actions with tangible decolonial efforts is the Treaty Land Sharing Network in Saskatchewan, through which settler farmers give access to these agricultural lands to Indigenous Peoples, who can then exercise their Treaty rights or inherent Indigenous rights to hunt and gather foods or medicines.[78]

It is noteworthy that Call to Action 45 speaks directly to the core of my argument concerning Canadian federalism as an overlooked aspect of the settler colonial project of Canada. While the TRC does not directly discuss the structure of federalism, it does take up many components of settler colonialism that shaped the Canadian state and jurisdictional powers. In the coming pages, I take an in-depth look at these components, including the Royal Proclamation of 1763, Treaty of Niagara of 1764, doctrine of discovery, *terra nullius*, and the constitutional and legal orders of the Confederation. These aspects of the state are integral to settler colonial structures of invasion and ongoing dispossession.[79] I demonstrate how these structures connect with federalism and how settler colonialism is present in contemporary jurisdiction making in Canada.

Federalism's power-sharing model is only one part of the overall change required to redistribute power in Canada. That said, federalism is a structure that insists on constraining Indigenous Peoples' political autonomy, which stalls reconciliatory progress. Thus, we ought to focus reconciliation efforts here.

Call To Action 45

We call upon the Government of Canada, on behalf of all Canadians, to jointly develop with Aboriginal peoples a Royal Proclamation of Reconciliation to be issued by the Crown. The proclamation would build on the Royal Proclamation of 1763 and the Treaty of Niagara of 1764, and reaffirm the nation-to-nation relationship between Aboriginal peoples and the Crown. The proclamation would include, but not be limited to, the following commitments:

i. Repudiate concepts used to justify European sovereignty over Indigenous lands and peoples such as the Doctrine of Discovery and *terra nullius*.
ii. Adopt and implement the *United Nations Declaration on the Rights of Indigenous Peoples* as the framework for reconciliation.
iii. Renew or establish Treaty relationships based on principles of mutual recognition, mutual respect, and shared responsibility for maintaining those relationships into the future.
iv. Reconcile Aboriginal and Crown Constitutional and legal orders to ensure that Aboriginal peoples are full partners in Confederation, including the recognition and integration of Indigenous laws and legal traditions in negotiation and implementation processes involving Treaties, land claims, and other constructive agreements.[80]

Understanding the Terminology: Indigenous Peoples and Political Agency

There are state-generated determinations of Indigenous identity, and then there are determinations that Indigenous communities make about who belongs. Authentic Indigeneity goes beyond ancestry; it is determined by cultural facets such as collective social kinship agreements, which are understood and practised differently by different Indigenous Nations.

In Canada, Indigenous Peoples maintain nation-to-nation relationships with the Crown. As political scientist Martin Papillon notes, "The insistence on nation-to-nation relations stems from the principle that Indigenous peoples were organized as political societies well before the arrival of Europeans, who themselves recognized this fact through the negotiation of military and economic alliances and treaties."[81] While the concept of nation-to-nation relationships affirms Indigenous political agency and has been foundational to Indigenous Peoples' political legitimacy in the face of colonial delegitimation, the settler state has sought to control Indigenous identity through colonial tools of elimination and assimilation.[82] For example, the state has historically used rules about Indian status to keep Indigenous people in or out of Indigenous communities.[83] Early Indian Act legislation included the marrying-out rule (a First Nations woman who married a man without Indian status would lose her own status) and other conditions that would lead to loss of Indian status, such as attending a postsecondary education institution, serving in the state military, or holding employment outside of a reserve. These are only some of the government practices aimed at eliminating Indian status.[84]

In Canada, the term "Indian," misapplied by early imperial explorers to the First Peoples throughout North America, is legally complex. Under the Indian Act, 1867, the term includes those registered with an Indian Band. In a constitutional sense, section 91(24) of the BNA Act creates a "special relationship" between the state and Indians.[85] Lawyer Alan Pratt writes about section 91(24), noting that "Aboriginal people often argue that it is the source, or at least the embodiment, of a 'special relationship' between them and the Crown in right of Canada, which gives rise to legal and political obligations of protection and trust."[86] This special relationship can also be traced through the Treaties, which detail state fiduciary obligations to Indigenous Peoples and are meant to be upheld by the Crown. Notable Supreme Court cases, including *Reference Re: Eskimos* (1939) and *Daniels v. Canada* (2016), have established that these fiduciary obligations extend to Inuit and Métis communities.[87]

Because of the long history of racism in Canada and the derogatory nature of the term "Indian" in mainstream Canadian vernacular,[88] I use this term only when it appears in quotations or refers to legal status through the Treaties or the Indian Act. But there are Indigenous people who use this term in the spirit of reclamation, such as Patricia Monture-Angus (Mohawk Nation), who wrote, "I want to reclaim that word, Indian, once forced upon us and make it feel mine."[89] In my experience, many Indigenous people grow up using this term in their homes and communities, and they identify as Indian with much cultural pride and knowledge.

The Constitution Act of 1982 provided Canadian law with a new term, "Aboriginal." This term includes Indian (Status First Nations), Inuit, and Métis people. It does not include nonregistered Indians, colloquially referred to as non-Status First Nations. Through this denial of Indigeneity, the term is an exclusionary state mechanism that enfranchises (gives Canadian citizenship to) some Indigenous people, stripping them of Indigenous difference to forcibly assimilate them into the Canadian body politic. The term "Aboriginal" is also criticized for glossing over differences. As Harold Cardinal (Cree Nation) argues, this term can dilute the distinctiveness of Indigenous Nations, which confuses debates about the specific rights and identities of these various peoples.[90] The term certainly discourages acknowledgement of the diversity of Indigenous Peoples, and overlooks, dilutes, or misconstrues specific Indigenous rights and differences. However, the term's constitutional entrenchment has an empowering aspect: While it can facilitate assimilation, it also safeguards Indigenous difference.[91] Given the outdatedness of the term "Aboriginal," I use it only when it appears in quotations or when discussing a Canadian legal concept such as Aboriginal rights or title.

Today, "Indigenous" is commonly used in the Canadian context to encompass First Nations (Status and non-Status Indians), Métis, and Inuit. As with the term "Aboriginal," the term "Indigenous" is critiqued for muting distinctions between Indigenous Nations, which have their own terms to describe themselves. There are over six hundred First Nations reserve communities, numerous Inuit and Métis communities, and many urban Indigenous people in Canada. However, this diversity gives rise to a practical need for a general term to be used in discussions of collective experiences of colonialism.

The legal scope of section 91(24) is often understood as restricted to Status First Nations people living on-reserve. This is not a closed group of people; many First Nations people, for example, live or have family members both on- and off-reserve. In many ways — legally, politically, socially — the mechanics of Canadian federalism extend to all Indigenous Peoples. In this book, I sometimes speak directly to the situation of Status First Nations people living on-reserve within the scope of law, but this book is more generally about Indigenous Peoples, who are all affected by the colonial project in Canada. This book follows Greg Youngings *Elements of Indigenous Style* to inform the representation of Indigenous Peoples.

Making Sense of Indigenous Peoples' Agency in Canada

The settler colonial state is one external force that hinders Indigenous Peoples' agency and autonomy. Agency is a political concept that refers to decision-making capacity. The concept of autonomy articulates the capacity for individuals or a collective to exercise agency unencumbered by external interference. Politically speaking, the agency and autonomy of Indigenous Peoples in settler colonial Canada can be understood through three generalized concepts: self-determination, self-government, and sovereignty. Navigating Indigenous Peoples' rights through the lens of these three concepts demonstrates the many challenges that the settler colonial federation presents to Indigenous agency and autonomy in Canada.

At the core of each of these three concepts are Inherent rights, which are the rights of Indigenous Peoples that predate the colonial context and exist independently of colonial legal orders.[92] Canadian courts have recognized these rights as *sui generis*, a Latin legal term meaning unique and distinct, as in not derived from the Crown. Inherent rights should not be understood as having a singular source or application. They are grounded in Indigenous ontologies or the intergenerational and ancestral knowledges that are specific to a place, community, or Nation. Thus, they have particular characteristics depending on where they originate from. Inherent rights are tied up in practice and expressed as kinship responsibilities to a collective, the land, and more-than-human beings. Today, Indigenous knowledge systems form the basis for Indigenous resurgence and resistance movements.

In the context of settler colonialism, Cherokee scholar Jeff Corntassel argues that state-centric rights discourses will promote state-centric frameworks, thus promoting state interests.[93] These state-centric rights discourses fundamentally oppose Indigenous Peoples' conceptualization of Inherent rights as responsibilities and limit how they are exercised.[94] For Corntassel, Indigenous pathways to decolonization rely on Indigenous resurgence practices, especially how Indigenous Peoples conceptualize rights as responsibilities: This is foundational to self-determination.

Self-determination for Indigenous Nations is a concept most readily understood through the *United Nations Declaration on the Rights of Indigenous Peoples* (UNDRIP).[95] Article 3 of UNDRIP states, "Indigenous Peoples have the right of self-determination. By virtue of that right, they freely determine their political status and freely pursue their economic, social, and cultural development."[96] UNDRIP is the result of over thirty years of advocacy by Indigenous Peoples to achieve a rights recognition framework that is not liberally construed.[97] Liberal definitions of rights, which rest upon individualism and not collectivity, often support assimilation and negatively impact Indigenous Peoples' pursuit of collective rights recognition. To generate an Indigenous-centred rights framework, the United Nations established the Working Group on Indigenous Populations in 1982. UNDRIP took effect in 2007. Canada was not originally a signatory to UNDRIP and actively resisted recognizing it in order to continue settler colonial dispossession practices. However, under a new government, Canada signed on in 2016 and formally brought the declaration into Canadian law in 2021 through Bill C-15: An Act Respecting the United Nations Declaration on the Rights of Indigenous Peoples. While UNDRIP remains largely unenforced in Canada (British Columbia is the only province or territory that has established legislative standing for the declaration), it serves as a significant validation of the rights of all Indigenous Peoples, emphasizing self-determination as a means to shape the collective rights of agency and autonomy.

Anishinaabe scholar Sheryl R. Lightfoot, using the work of legal scholars such as James Anaya (United Nations special rapporteur on the rights of Indigenous Peoples from 2008 to 2014) and Alexandra Xanthaki (United Nations special rapporteur in the field of cultural rights since 2021), demonstrates that the definition of self-determination in UNDRIP need not be limiting and can offer a "broadening" of the conceptual frameworks of sovereignty for Indigenous Peoples outside of state mechanisms. To articulate this point, Lightfoot argues that the Haudenosaunee Confederacy's passport is a tool of self-determination: The nation's repatriation of citizenship is "decolonizing the concept of self-determination."[98] Indigenous political writers and leaders Arthur Manuel (Secwepemc Nation) and Grand Chief Ronald Derrickson (Westbank First Nation) also agree with the merits of UNDRIP, describing it as a "virtual declaration of independence for Indigenous Peoples."[99]

However, UNDRIP's conceptualization of self-determination is also routinely criticized. Lightfoot explains that, for some scholars, Article 3 can be understood as indicating that Indigenous Peoples hold diminished political rights under domestic laws.[100] Ktunaxa and Métis scholar Joyce Green sees self-determination as a clear challenge to the settler state's monopoly over decision-making in Indigenous communities. However, she also argues that "self-determination does not require transformation to statehood."[101] These positions articulate tensions regarding the extent of change that self-determination can achieve as a legal mechanism.

In addition to UNDRIP, a long-standing source of rights recognition is section 35 of the Canadian Constitution Act, 1982. This section provides constitutional recognition of the pre–Canadian Confederation existence of Aboriginal and Treaty rights, including the right to self-government. The codification of Aboriginal and Treaty rights in section 35 was the result of years of tremendous effort by Indigenous Peoples, as illustrated most notably by the Constitution Express. Organized by the Union of British Columbia Indian Chiefs in 1980–81, this initiative saw Indigenous leaders from across the country travel by train to Ottawa to advocate for the constitutional recognition of their peoples' rights, and later to the United Nations in New York and Europe.[102] Ultimately, this mobilization achieved a decision-making role for several Indigenous leaders in Canada's constitutional negotiations, and this seat at the negotiating table led to section 35. In my view, section 35 recognizes that Indigenous Peoples in Canada are rights holders, not interest groups or minority groups. In addition to their Inherent rights, Indigenous Peoples hold constitutionally recognized Aboriginal rights in domestic law, as well as those international Indigenous rights articulated in UNDRIP. Aboriginal self-government, in terms of this constitutional recognition and protection, is important to Indigenous liberation.

One issue with the constitutional recognition of rights is how it has been implemented in Canadian law. Instead of defining the recognition of Aboriginal rights and the contours of self-government in the Constitution Act, 1982, the constitutional authors deferred the matter to later First Ministers' meetings.[103] The parameters of Aboriginal self-government, however, proved too difficult to define, and the job was ultimately left to the courts. That we do not know precisely how UNDRIP and section 35 of the Constitution Act enable Indigenous Peoples' political autonomy is a challenge for determining broader responses to questions on reconciliation as they relate to Canadian politics and Indigenous Peoples' rights.

Another key criticism of Aboriginal rights as contained in the Constitution Act relates to the previous points made by Corntassel and Green. Remember, Indigenous Peoples' rights are *sui generis*, or unique, and are recognized by but not generated by the state. For many, section 35 exemplifies Corntassel's view of state-centric rights, which differ from Indigenous notions of rights as sacred responsibilities and relationships, and Green's assertion these do not necessarily transform the state. Similarly, Coulthard's assessment of rights recognition demonstrates that these state-centric rights fold Indigenous Peoples into the colonial state model. Some may contend that these rights challenge Canadian state sovereignty, while others argue that they further entangle Indigenous Peoples' political autonomy within the Canadian federation.

The concept of Indigenous Peoples' sovereignty is also a source of much debate. Sovereignty is a global political structure in which the state is the authoritative or legitimate political unit.[104] With roots in Eurocentrism,[105] this understanding of sovereignty developed primarily in the sixteenth and seventeenth centuries across much of Europe,[106] in part arising after the Peace of Westphalia in 1648 to become the basis of the international system. The transnational context of sovereignty, as I demonstrate, has implication for discussions on Indigenous sovereignty in the Canadian settler colonial context.

Writing from an international perspective, legal scholar Rashwet Shrinkhal asks, "Does sovereignty matter to Indigenous Peoples?"[107] As the following paragraphs show, the responses across Canada are inconsistent at best: Some say that sovereignty is a colonial concept that will only reinscribe the oppression of Indigenous Peoples. Others see sovereignty as a political tool to recognize and respect those precolonial

Inherent rights of Indigenous Peoples and to advance liberation from colonial oppression. Both points of view make clear that sovereignty has implications for Indigenous Peoples: It does, indeed, matter.

To understand why Indigenous sovereignty is a contested conceptual framework, we can start with a broader discussion of sovereignty itself. The term signifies political organization and activity, but whose activity — the state's or Indigenous Peoples'? More commonly, sovereignty is assumed to be the political organization and activity of the state. In Canada, sovereignty is understood to be held by the Crown. Through federalism's division of powers, the Crown's representatives — the governor general and lieutenant governor — ensure that the federal and provincial governments are sovereign or, in other words, can act with legitimate authority as independent political actors. This understanding of the state demonstrates the colonial intention of state sovereignty, as the process of imperial colonialism has shaped the contemporary global order through the conception of sovereignty.[108] Imperial powers assumed that they possessed sovereign authority. Initially, they exercised this authority through imperial contact, trading practices, the spread of religion, and the extraction of resources. However, over time, it came to guarantee that settler states held ultimate authority. In this sense, "sovereignty is an exclusionary concept rooted in an adversarial and coercive nation of power."[109]

As Anishinaabe scholar Dale Turner argues, state sovereignty as understood in this way is a Western concept.[110] Critics understand state sovereignty as political organization and activity that is Eurocentric,[111] or framed by a value system that understands knowledge — and its associated power — as derived from European sources. Eurocentrism is central to establishing colonial intent, procedures, and outcomes.[112] Those working from a Eurocentric framework or perspective understand Euro-derived sources of knowledge and practice as superior to other sources of knowledge, including the specific knowledge sources of Indigenous Peoples throughout what has become Canada.

EUROCENTRISM

Eurocentrism refers to a worldview that perceives European culture as superior and holding intellectual authority, thereby diminishing other cultures as inferior. This perspective became prominent in the eighteenth century through colonization, conquest, and trade. This superior/inferior binary was often used to justify the exploitation of colonized regions.[113]

From this, we can understand the concept of sovereignty as a construct that reinforces colonial intent. Much like other colonial constructs, state sovereignty can be assimilative.[114] As international relations scholar Ajay Parasram has demonstrated, by adhering to this understanding of state sovereignty, "We [continue to be] actively engaged in the process of colonization ... complicit in the violence perpetuated by the modern colonial state."[115] Mohawk scholar Audra Simpson argues that any Indigenous claims to sovereignty cannot be separated from the Eurocentric nature of sovereignty; as such, these claims are assimilative into Canadian political frameworks. In this way, Indigenous sovereignty does not challenge state sovereignty; instead, it unintentionally legitimizes the state's authority, drawing Indigenous autonomy further under its control.[116] For these reasons, some thinkers have argued that the search for Indigenous liberation through the concept of sovereignty should be abandoned.[117]

Not all scholars and thought leaders interested in Indigenous Peoples' anticolonialism agree. Let's turn to strategies that use a conceptualization of Indigenous sovereignty for liberation. Understanding the basic premise of sovereignty is central to these arguments: Again, sovereignty is a Euro-colonial conception of political organization centred on the state that cannot support Indigenous Peoples' differing worldviews and ontological orientations because of the Eurocentric disregard of other knowledge systems. This description of state sovereignty, however, also offers opportunity for the political power that comes with Indigenous Peoples' claims to sovereignty. In fact, Indigenous claims to sovereignty make these state-based sovereignty claims vulnerable. Competing claims to sovereignty or plural sovereignties are considered a threat to state sovereignty,[118] as they render settler colonies fragile.[119] Effectively, Indigenous Peoples' claims to sovereignty disturb the very grounding or framework of the exclusive power of the state.[120] Here, we see real liberatory potential for Indigenous Peoples in asserting sovereignty.

One way that theorists contemplate including the sovereignties of Indigenous Peoples in settler colonial states is alongside or differentiated from state sovereignty. This can be called pluriversal sovereignties or, as Parasram puts it, multiple sovereignties that overlap.[121] Some theorists argue this conceptualization provides an effective way to approach Indigenous sovereignty. In a sense, this approach can make room for what American scholar Stuart Christie describes as those Indigenous sovereignties that "never departed."[122]

What does this kind of Indigenous sovereignty look like in settler colonial Canada? Heidi Kiiwetinepinesiik Stark (Turtle Mountain Ojibwe) writes, "Sovereignty in contemporary understandings has often been applied to mean that nations are autonomous and independent, self-governing, and generally free of external interference."[123] Similarly, political scientists Ludvig Beckman, Kirsty Gover, and Ulf Mörkenstam add, "The theoretical traditions of Indigenous Peoples have authority independently of settler recognition or endorsement."[124] Accordingly, Indigenous Peoples have a political or legal autonomy that is not located in or traced back to the Canadian state — it is *sui generis*. Typically, this autonomy is associated with Indigenous Peoples' sacred responsibilities and relationship with place, or those responsibilities that are "derive[d] from within the collective will of the community."[125] I understand this autonomy through the concept of Inherent rights: those collective rights that are sourced from relationships with place[126] and that are inalienable (i.e., the state cannot compromise these rights because they do not originate in the state).

In his work, international relations scholar Justin de Leon quotes Kelsey Wrightson, a non-Indigenous scholar and the executive director of the Dechinta Centre for Research and Learning (Yellowknife, Northwest Territories): "I spend time working to create and protect the spaces and practices that I have come to know as sovereign — space for young ones to learn, space for Elders to teach. Space to learn the boat trails, set the nets, and speak the language."[127] Here, Indigenous Peoples' sovereignty is not defined, but we see how it is located in practice, passed through intergenerational knowledge transmission, and sustained in language. Moreover, as scholar Sarah Hunt (Kwakwaka'wakw Nation) has explained of Indigenous knowledge, "Its relational, alive, emergent nature means that as we come to know something, as we attempt to fix its meaning, we are always at risk of just missing something."[128] In considering the practice of Indigenous sovereignty, we can borrow from Hunt's description of Indigenous knowledge as indefinable because it is relational, alive, and emergent.

The notion of Indigenous sovereignty as distinct expressions of collective agency entails autonomous decision-making power specific to Indigenous Nations. Legal scholars Wallace Coffey (Comanche Nation) and Rebecca Tsosie (Yaqui descent) build on this political understanding to introduce the idea of cultural sovereignty:

> By understanding the philosophical structure of Native cultures, we can appreciate "sovereignty" as a cultural as well as a political phenomenon. In many ways, political sovereignty for Native peoples has become an external phenomenon that posits the overriding sovereignty of the federal government and the centrality of American citizenship for Native people. Cultural sovereignty is an internal phenomenon: the "heart and soul" of the Indian nation is located within Indian people, as communities and as individuals.[129]

Here, we see Indigenous sovereignty elevated from a state-centric definition to one that also includes cultural specificities. In a sense, we see a similarity to Corntassel's critique of self-determination through notions of Indigenous rights as responsibilities instead of state-centred rights. Moreover, as Parasram argues, pluriversal sovereignty can adequately recognize all of these ontological differences between Indigenous Nations ignored and overruled by Eurocentric framings.[130] Toward this, Shrinkhal writes, "Indigenous sovereignty may not have fixed contour, but it essentially confronts the idea of 'empire of uniformity.'"[131]

Today, the idea and application of Indigenous Peoples' sovereignty is still being developed and defined in light of these debates. Multiple conceptualizations of Indigenous sovereignty exist, because of the distinctiveness of different Indigenous Nations. But Indigenous sovereignty is not interchangeable or synonymous with state sovereignty. It is something of a different nature. Some thinkers, such as Federico Lenzerini, understand Indigenous sovereignty as running parallel to state-centred sovereignty.[132] Battell Lowman and Barker write, "Indigenous sovereignties are bound by sacred responsibilities," whereas settler sovereignties are derived from imperial orders.[133] Similarly, Stark explains that state sovereignty is imposed on the populace, but Indigenous sovereignty emerges from the collective. Ultimately, Indigenous and state sovereignties are derived from differing sources that hold differing expressions of autonomy and agency. Importantly, Indigenous sovereignties are processes that confront colonial power or state sovereignty.

In many ways, this brief overview of Indigenous Peoples' agency and sovereignty is the beginning. I would not be alone in arguing that a fuller understanding of sovereignty can be found by listening to the Knowledge Keepers in any particular Indigenous Nation address the concept. I have spent a lot of time sitting with Knowledge Keepers and community members, hearing about what sovereignty and political autonomy look like and used to look like, and how they can benefit people in a specific community context. In many ways, these various voices reflect a struggle over the core concept of sovereignty: Is it an abstract construct at the state level that crushes Indigenous independence? Is it the community-level realization that agency and autonomy exist and can correct the many colonial outcomes of dispossession? While I do not have the answers to these questions, Indigenous sovereignty does shape how I navigate my explanation of settler colonial narratives of federalism and possible paths for reconciliation. The conceptual framework of sovereignty — particularly through Indigenous resurgences — is given more attention in Chapter 5, as I expand on moving past the restrictions imposed on reconciliation through Canadian federalism.

How These Concepts Come Together

Each of the core concepts in this book — settler colonialism, reconciliation, and federalism — is complex. This book carefully maps these concepts to evidence the settler colonial inequity fostered by Canadian federalism that acts as a barrier to reconciliation. Central to each chapter are Indigenous Peoples' Inherent rights, which are fundamental to dismantling the settler colonial project.

Chapter 2, "Narratives of Settler Colonialism," delves into the historical context of narrative making and its application in settler colonial contexts. It is crucial to understand that scholars have meticulously explored settler nations' development of narratives that circumvent Indigenous Peoples' political autonomy in Canada. These narratives, often associated with cultivated stereotypes of Indigenous Peoples' inadequacies or disappearance, are tools of Indigenous erasure. This overview of settler colonial narratives explains why such narratives have developed in the assistance and advancement of settler colonial states. In Canada, particular narratives exist that ensure social, political, and economic structures marginalize Indigenous Peoples and dispossess them of their lands. These narratives unquestionably benefit non-Indigenous settlers. Canadian federalism, too, can be understood and practised through settler colonialism narratives: It is used to circumvent Indigenous agency and advance settler betterment.

Chapter 3, "The Constitution and Settler Colonial Narratives of Federalism," maps the evolution of Canada's Constitution and how Indigenous Peoples' self-determination is marginalized by the BNA Act's section 91(24), which states, "Indians, and Lands reserved for the Indians" are a jurisdiction of the federal government.[134] This section effectively gives authority over Indigenous Peoples to the federal government, though that jurisdiction of colonial domination is not clear-cut. Chapter 3 maps what it has meant in terms of lands (which lands?) and peoplehood (who is included and what does it mean to be included?).

As is true of federalist systems — because they are structured on power sharing — the provision of authority to one order of government denotes a relationship of power over another. In Canada, provincial jurisdiction over Indigenous Peoples exists alongside federal jurisdiction. However, discussions of Canadian federalism often overlook this reality, which reflects settler colonial narratives that obscure the power relations stemming from settler colonial dispossession. Over time, provincial governments have gradually expanded their jurisdiction over Indigenous Peoples through legislation and public policy, actions that ultimately serve settler colonial interests, which are often hidden by prevailing narratives that prioritize settler perspectives.

Chapter 4, "Evolving Canadian Federalism and Implications for Indigenous Political Agency," illustrates the flexibility of Canadian federalism. It is not a static political system of governance, and changes since Confederation in 1867 have had significant consequences for Indigenous Peoples. For example, more recent arrangements of Canadian federalism place growing responsibility for many governance matters with the provincial governments, impacting Indigenous Peoples and self-determination movements. For many, when the provincial order replaces the Crown at the negotiating table, it complicates and strains the nation-to-nation structure. Additionally, as powers shift from federal to provincial orders, jurisdictional football occurs, which means governments each refuse their responsibility and toss it to a different order of government. These kinds of tactics related to jurisdiction or federalism can have harmful impacts on Indigenous Nations, but can also present opportunities for decolonial advancements.

Chapter 5, "Beyond Settler Colonial Federalism," presents a range of scholarship about changes to federalism that may reduce the structural oppression of Indigenous Peoples. These alternatives envision liberation on a spectrum of change, offering hope for a more equitable future. One example is Treaty federalism, which advocates say can advance Indigenous Peoples' self-determination within the federalist system.[135] Treaty federalism would require a significant shift in the federalist power-sharing model, but it would leave the broader political system of Canadian federalism intact. Still, others suggest we burn it all to the ground. Coulthard's work on political recognition remains essential here: Developments in Canadian politics that take up Indigenous-related matters do not amount to advancements in Indigenous-centred agency or liberation and instead are an extension of colonial manifestation and dispossession.[136] Indigenous resurgence movements are central to liberation. Leanne Betasamosake Simpson (Michi Saagiig Nishnaabeg Nation) describes Indigenous resurgences that call for Indigenous Peoples to rekindle ancestors' political actions and structures in order to rid themselves of settler colonial domination.[137]

In some ways, I wonder how much we can truly ask of reconciliation when we want real change, not the metaphor.[138] Reconciliation is a practice that only sometimes fits well. It is a complicated application of international justice that is then applied through Survivor guidance in the Canadian context, and the scholarship and public perception related to reconciliation is split on its merits and deficits. Although these complexities have been discussed generally in this chapter, I hope that the coming pages demonstrate why federalism must be brought into this conversation: Members of Canadian society relate — even without our realization — through the country's political systems. When a system such as federalism shapes decision-making in ways that dictate settler colonial dispossession, it must be part of our national conversation on reconciliation. To dismiss the influence of federalism as a mechanism of the settler colonial project limits any real progress through reconciliation.

CHAPTER TWO

NARRATIVES OF SETTLER COLONIALISM

Settler colonial narratives are foundational to settler colonial states and societies. These narratives are sociopolitical conceptions that include stories, myths, or tropes that shape a collective identity. These kinds of stories are evident in historical and contemporary conversation, literary and media sources, and government decision-making. These stories have a utility in settler-based efforts to dispossess Indigenous Peoples of lands and difference. They can also foster settler complicitness by masking settler colonial oppression that deprives Indigenous Peoples of agency and the power differentials that provide the settler state and society with benefits. These tandem settler colonial mechanisms — Indigenous Peoples' dispossession and settler benefit — become entrenched or a status quo that is reproduced by settler colonial narratives as unquestioned myths about the origin or function of society.

These settler colonial narratives exist in the ordering of Canadian federalism. As the state's division of powers gives the federal government decision-making authority over Indigenous Peoples, we can see a current of settler colonial narrative develop. This narrative is multifaceted. It deprives Indigenous Peoples of agency and manufactures a dependence by placing them under the jurisdiction of the federal government. This jurisdictional role is accounted for in the Constitution, which is discussed in Chapter 3, and becomes an unquestioned determinant. Due to the nature of federalist structures, the federal government does share decision-making powers with the provinces. However, the role of the provinces, also mapped in Chapter 3, is rarely acknowledged in country-wide conversations of jurisdictional arrangements affecting

Indigenous Peoples. This omission is crucial to settler colonial narratives that seek to obscure and erase evidence of power relations that oppress Indigenous Peoples, further concealing colonial power and compromising nation-to-nation relations, which hinders opportunities for reconciliation.

At the heart of reconciliation is building better relations between settler colonial society and Indigenous Peoples. This multifaceted work requires attention to Canada's social, economic, and political aspects. As Arthur Manuel and Ronald Derrickson write, "The fight was against a colonial government using colonial laws against Indigenous Peoples and it would require a battle on many fronts."[1] Within current discussions on reconciliation, I see a lack of attention given to how federalism divides powers across jurisdictions: These are colonial fronts that must be included in reconciliation. As this chapter makes clear, the division of powers is steeped in settler colonial narratives that fuel Indigenous Peoples' dispossession and settler benefit.

Examining Power Relations in Settler Colonial Narratives

The practice of narrative making and application that shapes settler colonial state and society is premised on power relations generated by acts of Indigenous dispossession. These settler colonial narratives are often pervasive in settler colonial societies, disguised as national myths or origin stories that tell a mythologized version of a country's founding, building social cohesion through the imagined nation.[2] As an exhibit at the Museum of Civilization in Quebec City states, "Myths are said to be the collective dreams of a society."[3] In this way, national myths infiltrate the social consciousness and are consensually practised and upheld by society.[4] Settler colonial narratives can reinforce social power relations through these mythologized collective dreams.

The purpose of settler colonial narratives is to dispossess Indigenous Peoples of their long-standing histories of presence on the land, use of the land, and relationships with lands, waters, and animals. The Inherent rights of Indigenous Peoples stand as a barrier to settler social presence, extraction of resources, and political occupation. Indigenous Peoples' histories and ongoing presence are, thus, supplanted by settler-oriented narratives to legitimate the presence and occupation of the settler state.

There are many examples of settler colonial narratives. The process of place-story, developed by American historian Coll Thrush, describes settler-generated stories of geographic regions that replace Indigenous Peoples' ties to place — histories of presence, use, and relationships — with settler-based occupation.[5] Considering this practice in Canada, we might point to the provincial, territorial, or municipal boundaries on maps. When we understand what has become Canada through these political maps, we are erasing aspects of Indigenous Peoples' political and historical presence, along with Indigenous Peoples' inherent sovereignty connected to place. Mapping, or cartography, is a vital tool of writing over or reinscribing land with the occupation of settler colonialism through political borders or renamed territorial locations.[6] In this way, we might understand land or territorial acknowledgements as disrupting how a place is understood as an assumed settler location and returning Indigenous Peoples' histories of presence, use, and relationships. These acknowledgements can, in part, disrupt settler-manufactured place-story.

Related to these settler colonial narratives that dispossess Indigenous Peoples through place making are narratives based on cultivated stereotypes of Indigenous Peoples' inadequacies or disappearance. These narratives are tools of Indigenous erasure. In Canada, specific narratives of Indigenous inadequacy and settler benevolence ensure that social, political, and economic structures support the marginalization of Indigenous Peoples and the dispossession of their lands. This work to justify Indigenous Peoples' displacement can leave the marginalization unquestioned or even deemed necessary to "save" Indigenous Peoples from themselves.[7] These narratives of inadequacy and benevolence, in turn, contribute to national myths that frame collective identities, and ultimately justify settler benefits that might be derived from Indigenous Peoples' dispossession.

Métis scholar Emma LaRocque captures the twofold process of Indigenous dispossession for settler benefits through the binary of civilization/savage.[8] She argues that Canadian society is structured along two categories, settler society as civilized and Indigenous Peoples as "savage." The stark contrast of the binary demonstrates how the supposed superiority of settler society is propagated through juxtaposition to the supposed inferiority of Indigenous Peoples. This binary is built through a betterment discourse that implies that the colonial presence inherently and unquestionably improves the lives of Indigenous Peoples. This kind of discourse is used for assimilation practices.[9] The manufactured inferiority of Indigenous Peoples is integral to the mechanics of settler colonial narratives. This positioning deepens the sense of Indigenous Peoples' disappearance and erasure as an inevitability in settler societies.[10] As scholar and past director of research for the TRC Paulette Regan explains, this superiority/inferiority binary and betterment discourse enable settler society to legitimize its presence, in part, as a benevolent saviour of Indigenous Peoples.[11]

Narratives of Indigenous inadequacy or settler benevolence can also serve as national myth-making stories in Canada. Regan describes the peacekeeping myth that frames the making of Canada, premised on the idea that the colonial presence established law and order through benevolence.[12] Another example is the foundational myth of the pioneer. As Canadian historian Paul Litt writes, "Local histories, school textbooks, and historical plaques honored the pioneer with the parable of how he (and it was always he) was cast into the wilderness with meager resources, yet, through hard work survived, and, in time, was rewarded with bountiful harvests and an enduring dynasty."[13] These kinds of narratives often understand the social outcome of colonial dispossession through assimilative tendencies: Indigenous Peoples will prosper if they are more like settlers. This assumption ignores the prosperity that existed prior to European contact and devalues the very structures and practices of being Indigenous.

These narratives effectively work to maintain relational power imbalances. Contemporary societies are generally understood to be structured on power relations. According to Italian philosopher Antonio Gramsci, hegemonic power operates in societies such that those in power do not need to use force to secure consent to their power from those who lack it. Instead, this consent is relinquished through a process of coercion exerted by political and capitalist-framed cultural institutions. These institutions develop an ideological framework that society adheres to, leading people to accept the existing power structure and its associated norms with minimal intervention from those in power. In a sense, hegemonic power structures establish a status quo, or an unquestioned hierarchy of power within society.

These power relations are essential to a discussion of settler colonial narratives of federalism and reconciliation. Federalism delineates who does and does not have power or decision-making authority on all sorts of matters related to governance and, well, life. Thus, power relations and structures of power — how decisions are made, who makes these decisions, and who benefits from these decisions — are central to the conversation at hand. Specifically, the federal and provincial governments have decision-making authority in relation to Indigenous Peoples as legitimized in the Constitution, case law, and policymaking practices. In a sense, it is a hegemonic authority; the power-sharing model coerces consent and power enacted is through settler colonial constructions of governance that are not accessible to Indigenous Peoples, because they are constrained by federalism. In other words, they hold no space as sovereign decision-makers in the federation.[14]

Power relations in any society are complicated. Applying reconciliation to address colonial inequities in Canada, which are partly manufactured by federalist power sharing, is also complicated. The TRC explains that reconciliation primarily concerns power relations between Indigenous and non-Indigenous or settler populations. These societal relations are steeped in power imbalances. To better understand the dynamic, we can draw from the analysis of French philosopher Michel Foucault, whose poststructuralist work examines how power relations operate and are influenced by social institutions. Foucault contended that different social contexts lead to varying experiences of power.[15] His arguments shape, in part, how the philosophy of poststructuralism understands power relations as deeply intertwined with discourse, which encompasses how knowledge is expressed, relayed, and determined.[16] Discourse can be seen as the representation of knowledge in identities, societal relations, languages, and expressions. As a result, power relations are ingrained within social structures and enacted through discourse or knowledge representations. People embody and enact power relations in all matters of everyday life: Societal relations, then, are reproduced through these power differentials.

Understanding how power influences societal relations and is reproduced is crucial to identifying barriers to reconciliation. For instance, a society that remains unaware of or does not face the "hard truths"[17] of colonial inequities will struggle to engage effectively in reconciliation. Additionally, a society that reflects and reproduces colonial inequities will perpetuate these injustices, hindering the progress of reconciliatory justice.

These entrenched power relations are central to settler narratives of dispossession. As Regan explains, many Canadians understood the founding of Canada as an altruistic benefit to Indigenous Peoples,[18] as settler colonial narratives obscure the effects of the dispossession of Indigenous Peoples. In Canada, power dynamics are structured in such a way that minimal coercion of settler colonial society is needed to perpetuate the dispossession of Indigenous Peoples; this has become a normative arrangement. Thus, the issue of dispossession is not merely historical, but remains relevant today, driven by a fundamental intention: the unchallenged benefit of settlers.

Central to securing settler benefit is the enactment of violence against Indigenous Peoples and structures of indifference that create the conditions for normalizing this violence.[19] Métis scholar Chelsea Vowel articulates this point by stating, "The violence that national myths commit is to delegitimize the very real pain that is the legacy of abuse and oppression."[20] The hegemonic social reproductions of relational power imbalances are embedded in Canadian society through settler colonial narratives, which mask and legitimate the violence of settler colonial social and political formations in efforts to ensure settler benefit continues. The perpetuation of this violence becomes normalized over time, as settler colonial violence against Indigenous Peoples is deeply ingrained in society.[21] We need to look no further than the genocidal crisis of Missing and Murdered Indigenous Women, Girls, and Two-Spirit People to evidence the normalization of this violence in settler Canada.[22]

These dynamics of power relations, including violence and indifference, are closely linked to reconciliation and settler colonial narratives. Reconciliation, as described by the TRC, centres on how Canadians live together: "Together, Canadians must do more than just talk about reconciliation; we must learn how to practice reconciliation in our everyday lives — within ourselves and our families, and in our communities, governments, places of worship, schools, and work places."[23] Societal relations of power are deeply embedded in settler colonial narratives intended to dispossess Indigenous Peoples for settler benefit. Wrapped up in these narratives are discourses that ascribe power through representations of knowledge, building a status quo of power differentials, which Manuel and Derrickson describe "as the interplay of dispossession, dependency and oppression."[24] The Canadian state uses the political system of federalism to circumvent and undermine Indigenous agency, a process partially sustained through settler colonial narratives.

Applying Settler Colonial Narratives for Dispossession

Historian Jean O'Brien (White Earth Ojibwe Nation) argues that settler colonial society constructs "replacement narratives" to erase Indigenous Peoples' histories.[25] Replacement narratives are local narratives built on a national discourse of the "vanishing Indian," or the idea that Indigenous Peoples were dying after European contact, due in part to European-derived diseases, and would not have survived without colonial intervention. Looking at written sources, public speeches and performances, and public commemorative plaques and statues to evidence the pervasiveness of replacement narratives in New England, O'Brien writes, "The collective story these texts told insisted that non-Indians held exclusive sway over modernity, denied modernity to Indians, and in the process created a narrative of Indian extinction that has stubbornly remained in the consciousness and unconsciousness of Americans."[26] O'Brien argues that this collective story of vanishing continues to shape settler colonial America.

Replacement narratives are similar to Thrush's place-story, which describes a process in which settler colonial stories of place fail to recognize Indigenous Peoples' historical ties to an area or ancestral lands, which support the relationships that form the basis of Inherent rights.[27] Both approaches understand that settler narratives are created to write Indigenous Peoples out of existence in service of the interests of settler society. Further to this point, as evidenced by historian James Joseph Buss, American place-story emerged from historical settler narratives, which continue to frame contemporary narratives.[28] The concepts of replacement narrative and place-story show us that the historical narratives of settler colonial societies inform contemporary settler society, and these narratives have been developed in ways that continue to omit or silence Indigenous Peoples.

These practices of narrative reframing are used to support settler political structures. Australian historian Patrick Wolfe describes settler colonial projects as constructed on the "logic of elimination." He argues that settler colonialism is a pervasive, ongoing structure, not a historical event, that is built on the destruction of Indigenous Peoples and also requires the continual functioning of this destruction.[29] This elimination, explains Wolfe, enables structural domination through the "obtaining and maintaining" of Indigenous Peoples' territory.[30] Wolfe writes, "Settler colonialism destroys to replace."[31] What is destroyed is replaced with the "legitimate" settler society. Although not all settler colonies resort to acts of genocide, every settler colony engages in some form of assimilation. The intent and outcome of genocide and assimilation are elimination of Indigenous populations. To underscore the harm caused by these processes of elimination, Wolfe asks, "But just what kind of death is it that is involved in assimilation?"[32] I argue that the consequence of this death, as described by scholar Peter Kulchyski, is a colonial social fabric "where being itself is the question in question."[33] The logic of elimination — whether based on practices of assimilation or genocide — makes Indigenous presence, or simply being, a matter of contention for the settler state.

Although Wolfe situates his work in the Australian context, we can apply his insights to the development of settler Canada. Through claims of title to North America's territory, Europeans attempted to eliminate Indigenous Peoples' title. This logic persists through place-story or replacement narratives, supporting practices of erasure and dispossession.[34] Canadian settler society is also built upon and requires the continued destruction of Indigenous Peoples, specifically Indigenous difference. Settler colonial narratives were created to disavow Indigenous Peoples' presence, use, and history in relation to the land while instilling settler fixity and legimating settler use of land and resources.[35]

One settler colonial judicial narrative of erasure and dispossession concerns the Canadian state's sovereignty. Constitutional scholar Michael McCrossan and Cree political scientist Kiera Ladner argue that the courts cannot comprehend Indigenous ancestral legal orders, which predate Canada. They write that "the court continues to perpetuate the myth that without settler colonial governments, no one would be regulating vast areas of the country."[36] The courts assume that Crown sovereignty is both legitimate and permanent, and they reproduce this assumption every time they perceive Indigenous rights to territory as a threat to that sovereign existence or as a lack of regulatory presence.[37] Consequently, the courts deny Indigenous claims of sovereignty through the narrative of Crown sovereignty.[38] This raises the question: How do narratives of federalism similarly deny Indigenous Peoples' rights to sovereignty by reinforcing settler colonial narratives of federal jurisdiction over Indigenous Peoples?

To answer this, we can examine the processes of settler colonialism and claims of settler state sovereignty that arise from imperial expansion and result in complex political, economic, and social effects.[39] In imperial colonialism, a distant foreign power uses ideology and settlement to dominate a colonized people.[40] In contrast, settler colonialism requires a population from the foreign power to establish itself locally and work to render Indigenous history, place, and presence obsolete for the benefit of the colonial settlers. Over time, the source of political legitimacy or regulatory influence shifts from the distant colonial power (metropole) to the local colonial power (colony). As the settlers' intention to stay and assert sovereignty supplants Indigenous Peoples' nationhood, the settler population and their structures of economy, politics, and society become more firmly regimented as the "legitimate" structures in the region.[41]

Although imperial and settler forms of colonialism differ, they also share some characteristics. Both exert a set of foreign economic, political, and cultural values and procedures onto another people, resulting in structural domination. The work of postcolonial theorists Edward Said, Albert Memmi, and Frantz Fanon reveals these parallels through examination of the factors that led to structural domination and attempts to overcome it.[42] They demonstrate that the primary concern for all colonial projects is unencumbered land access through structural domination, and these dynamics continue in postcolonial environments.

Although access to the land is central for both forms of colonial power, imperial and settler colonialism are distinguished by the role of the Indigenous population. According to Wolfe, imperial colonialism requires Indigenous Peoples' labour for the perpetuation of the colonial regime.[43] Imperial colonialism, therefore, entails the expansion of the colonial power through a military and trade, and it uses (and even requires) the Indigenous populations to maintain the momentum of these activities on the territory of the colony.[44] Settler colonialism, on the other hand, is based on the displacement of Indigenous Peoples by the settler community in order to access the land and its resources. The settler population does not use the Indigenous population to maintain the colonial project — it pushes the Indigenous population to the margins of the colonial project.[45] To survive, settler colonies import a labour force so large that settlers and their descendants become the majority of the population.[46]

This transition from imperial to settler colonialism can be evidenced in Canada. In early periods of the colonial project, Europeans relied on Indigenous populations for basic survival, learning about the geographies and climates and adjusting practices of travel, food cultivation, and shelter building.[47] Political relations were often built on alliances and economic systems of exchange (a significant reason for the imperial power's presence was to access resources and have a new market for imperial-made goods). Over time, however, settler colonial societies — through power shifts and European-derived population growth — no longer relied on Indigenous populations. As settler society expanded control over lands through a military and political diplomacy and economics, it developed a corresponding attitude that the Indigenous populations were impediments to settlement and needed to be cleared away through assimilation, physical removal (e.g., through the reserve system), or marginalization, meaning they were displaced to the periphery of society, their power fundamentally limited.[48] Hence, Indigenous Nations were displaced under the regime of settler colonialism in Canada.

The colonization of Indigenous lands required replacement narratives and place-stories that overlook the lived histories of Indigenous Peoples on their lands and their ongoing connections to those areas. These narratives continue to facilitate the settlement of the land by settlers.[49] One consequence of colonial land acquisition is its impact on Indigenous Peoples' relationships with land and rights. This impact is particularly acute for urban Indigenous people who lack access to outdoor space beyond the confines of the urban environment. Some individuals may lack relationships with Indigenous Knowledge Keepers, which are needed to engage in kin-based teachings, learn language, or participate in ceremony. Additionally, those living in rural and reserve communities may experience cultural disconnection stemming from the colonial assertion of legitimacy through land ownership and state regulation, which impacts Indigenous Peoples' access to land. Thus, reasserting ancestral and ongoing rights to land to overcome these narratives of place is a fundamental aspect of contemporary Indigenous liberation movements.

Settler historian James Daschuk has described the serious impact of settler land acquisition on Indigenous Peoples.[50] Writing from the Canadian Prairies, he explains how alongside Canadian Confederation and Treaty making, the state dispossessed Indigenous Peoples of lands, resulting in devastating social, economic, and health outcomes. For example, restricting Indigenous Peoples to reserves limited their access to economic livelihoods, thus also limiting access to foods and medical care. Daschuk asserts that starvation was a policy practice to ensure the plains were cleared of Indigenous Peoples, the rights holders in this territory.

Indigenous scholars Gina Starblanket (Star Blanket Cree Nation) and Dallas Hunt (Wapsewsipi, Swan River First Nation), also writing on the Canadian Prairies, illustrate how settler colonial narratives from this same period of settlement continue to influence contemporary society.[51] In *Storying Violence,* they address the trial of Gerald Stanley, a settler farmer who shot and killed Colten Boushie, an Indigenous youth, in 2016. The authors analyze how settler state propaganda — based, in part, on omitting Indigenous Peoples from official narratives of lands — was used during the historical settlement of the Prairies to promote settler farming. This propaganda contributed to the formation of a prairie settler society that prioritizes its own interests and benefits at the expense of Indigenous people's lives. During the Stanley trial, this settler priority was further reinforced by the media, some public opinion in Saskatchewan, and the court verdict acquitting Stanley.

A critical practice in the theft of Indigenous lands is the colonial power's assertion of its authority over a people. To justify this practice, international legal concepts such as *terra nullius* and the doctrine of discovery have been invoked.[52] These concepts, which have been widely criticized, had significant implications for Indigenous Peoples. *Terra nullius,* a Latin term meaning "vacant lands," asserted that when a foreign power travelled to a land that was not being cultivated to the degree that the foreign power thought reasonable, the lands could be considered vacant. This practice of determining a territory to be *terra nullius* is steeped in Eurocentrism. The concept of *terra nullius* was also used to justify and enable the foreign power to exert its authority or sovereignty over these lands.

Aboriginal Title

Aboriginal title refers to the collective rights of Indigenous Peoples to their lands. Defining these rights has been a crucial aspect of Canadian law. From an Indigenous perspective, these rights can be viewed as a guardianship of the land and, as explained by Elder Norman Sunchild, entrusted to Indigenous Peoples by the Creator. The colonial state often suppresses these rights through colonial laws. Canadian law concerning Aboriginal title, or what was once understood as Indian title, has evolved through policy and the courts. It now acknowledges that the prior occupancy of Indigenous Peoples provides them with interests that deserve legal protection.[53]

As Indigenous scholar Sharon Venne (Muskeg Lake Cree First Nation) explains, *terra nullius* was designed to divest Indigenous Peoples of legal rights to lands so they could be used by European powers.[54] Both imperial and settler colonial contexts saw the invocation of *terra nullius* in this way. By doing so, the European power also exerted its sovereignty over Indigenous Peoples, effectively diminishing Indigenous sovereignty. For many, *terra nullius* provides a tenuous justification for land seizure, an issue at the heart of many Aboriginal title and Aboriginal rights court cases in Canada.

In a similar vein, the doctrine of discovery asserts that if land is occupied by a people who are not socially and politically organized to a degree that satisfies a foreign power, that foreign power can be said to have discovered the land and can seize it. John Borrows (Anishinaabe Nation) explains that the doctrine of discovery was enabled by the perceived notion that Indigenous Peoples were inferior to others due to their insufficient social and political organization.[55] Philosopher Paul Patton writes, "According to this doctrine, a 'civilised' power could claim territory occupied by native peoples considered so primitive as to be without laws and without a sovereign."[56] One example of the exercise of the doctrine of discovery concerns the acquisition of lands by colonial powers who then ascribed new meanings and histories to the lands that helped generate new settler place-stories. This process could involve renaming places, recording explorer and settler histories and not those of Indigenous Peoples, or recasting the value of land based on extractive use and capitalist profits.[57] The concepts of *terra nullius* and doctrine of discovery are intertwined, connected by a Eurocentric framing. European powers used these concepts to create a legal and moral justification for conquering Indigenous lands (and Inherent rights to these lands) based on the dubious premise that the lands were "empty" and "unused" and that Indigenous Peoples lacked proper social and political organization according to criteria constructed by the European powers. Indigenous Peoples have never accepted these justifications. It is no coincidence that when Indigenous Peoples did not meet the criteria developed by European powers, it was the European powers that benefited from the Indigenous Peoples' "shortfall."

Terra nullius and the doctrine of discovery continue to superimpose European worldviews and undermine Indigenous Peoples' worldviews, including social organization, governance and legal systems, and political practices. European laws and economic practices were introduced to disconnect Indigenous Peoples from the land so the land could be used to serve colonial interests such as settlement or, as happened in Canada, settler economies such as the fur trade. Put simply, the justification is embedded in the doctrine of discovery and *terra nullius,* allowing land to be taken from Indigenous Peoples to serve colonial settlement requirements. In the process, Indigenous Peoples' worldviews are invalidated and displaced.

In Canada, *terra nullius* and the doctrine of discovery undergird settler colonial narratives, which are then reflected in the Canadian legal system and by extension inform the structures of the Canadian government and society as a whole. Brenna Bhandar argues that "legal-historical narratives" about the founding of Canada have contributed to the myth of the legitimacy of colonial-state sovereignty. The application of *terra nullius* and the doctrine of discovery creates a weak foundation for the settler colonial state, which, consequently, settler colonial narratives must strengthen. Bhandar writes, "Narratives about settlement and the assertion of sovereignty are central to the legitimacy and foundation of the law itself."[58] She explains that these legal-historical narratives are created to legitimize settler colonial laws, which are then continuously relegitimated through the same narratives. In a manner similar to Wolfe's "logic of elimination," Bhandar argues that society is constructed upon and relies on the destruction of Indigenous Peoples, a relationship that is ingrained in Canada's colonial legal framework.

Delgamuukw

Delgamuukw v. British Columbia (1997) is a ruling by the Supreme Court of Canada that helped clarify Aboriginal title in Canadian laws. In this case, the Gitxsan and Wet'suwet'en Nations sued the British Columbia government to assert their title and jurisdiction over that of the province.[59] The central questions of this case were as follows: How is Aboriginal title protected by section 35(1) of the Constitution Act? What is needed to prove Aboriginal title? Could the province extinguish Aboriginal rights after 1871 using section 88 of the Indian Act?[60] The Gitxsan and Wet'suwet'en Nations successfully asserted their ancestral guardianship, known in Canadian law as Aboriginal title, of over 58,000 hectares of land in northern British Columbia. The judgment stated that Aboriginal title is *sui generis,* or unique, in that "its characteristics cannot be completely explained by reference either to the common law rules of real property or to the rules found in aboriginal legal systems."[61] This broadened the understanding of Aboriginal rights to land, beyond harvesting rights, to a standalone entitlement.[62]

McCrossan similarly argues that the erasure of Indigenous sovereignty through the Canadian legal system extends to the courts: "The guiding narrative presented by judicial actors is one in which Indigenous laws, sovereignty, and jurisdiction over land must always yield to the territorial interests and perpetual presence of the larger setter society."[63] This narrative is derived from past colonial constructs and contributes to the territorial displacement and dispossession of Indigenous Peoples. For example, Justice Allan McEachern's judgment in the *Delgamuukw* case (1997) included an analysis that no Hudson's Bay Company fort was present in the region, suggesting the region was desolate and remains so. McCrossan emphasizes that this analysis "temporally collapses the 'Canadian' present into the 'British' past to arrive at a single vision of territorial uniformity."[64] This merging of the historical past and the judicial present, a function of settler colonial narratives, allows the courts to produce and reproduce notions of Canadian sovereignty over Indigenous Peoples and their territories.[65]

In this way, the courts create a narrative that portrays Indigenous Peoples' presence on their ancestral lands as a historical event rather than a current reality or future matter. They utilize this narrative foundation to support the overarching myth of settler sovereignty. Bhandar explains this as the paradox of iterability, where the myth must be repeated by the courts to establish it as the foundational story of the Canadian nation. The paradox of iterability "requires the original to repeat itself originarily, to alter itself so as to have the value of origin."[66]

Asserting Indigenous Political Agency Through Presence

Clearly, the doctrine of discovery and *terra nullius* are influential kinds of replacement narratives in settler operations. As historian Kate Brown explains, colonial portrayals depicted Indigenous lands as empty and barren, suggesting they needed to be filled.[67] Colonial projects established this assumption through the doctrine of discovery and *terra nullius*, a tenuous foundation that requires reproduction in power relations to be sustained. The TRC writes that these concepts "cannot serve as the basis for a legitimate claim to the lands that were colonized."[68] But colonial powers used them to empty territory — to erase the presence of Indigenous Peoples — and the practices of relocation, settlement, and disease functioned to make this seem the reality.[69]

In the context of legal frameworks rooted in colonial narratives of erasure and dispossession that influence state regulation, Indigenous Peoples have asserted political agency. Many have shown that the doctrine of discovery is unfounded,[70] and the Vatican also drew this conclusion in 2023.[71] Contemporary understandings — supported by scholarship and Indigenous communities — recognize that the lands now known as Canada were fundamentally under the guardianship of Indigenous Peoples, who continue to hold and maintain long-standing relational practices in governance, commerce, and social organization.[72]

Indigenous Peoples have always known their lands were not "empty" or "unused." Anishinaabe scholar Aaron Mills explains that Inherent rights tied to relationships with the lands have not diminished for Indigenous Peoples.[73] Indigenous oral traditions provide evidence of an ongoing presence on these lands, highlighting the continuation of Indigenous legal traditions and governance structures rooted in relationship with the lands.[74] Additional sources of Indigenous presence and land use include anthropological and archaeological records and travel accounts of early settlers.[75]

However, the courts continue to rely on proof of continuous social organization, or precontact and continued occupancy, to establish title.[76] Canada's judiciary has developed this requirement of occupation and continued use in several court cases regarding Aboriginal title. For instance, since the 1997 *Delgamuukw* ruling, Indigenous Nations are required to prove exclusive occupation of land prior to European contact and to show continuity of that occupation from precontact times to the present day.[77] Meeting these criteria can be a challenge due to the implications of settler colonial disruption, encroachment, and forced resettlement and relocation processes.

The doctrine of discovery and *terra nullius* were not based on facts or moral principles. As Eurocentric tools designed to take lands from Indigenous Peoples, they have had a damaging impact on Indigenous Peoples' connection to their lands and their rights to it. As the Royal Commission on Aboriginal Peoples (RCAP) outlined, the doctrine of discovery "gave the discovering European nation the exclusive right 'of acquiring the soil from the natives.'" Thus, it "resulted in an impairment of the rights of Indigenous Peoples."[78]

Borrows argues that "Canadian law still has *terra nullius* written all over it."[79] He explains that although the judgment in *Tsilhqot'in* (2014) asserts that the lands in what became Canada were not *terra nullius* — and thus, the concept did not justify the sovereignty of the state over Indigenous Peoples' lands — it simultaneously reinforces the idea of *terra nullius* by citing *Guerin* (1984). The verdict in the *Guerin* case, which involved the Musqueam Nation in British Columbia, states, "At the time of assertion of European sovereignty, the Crown acquired radical or underlying title to all the land in the province."[80] The use of the *Guerin* verdict in *Tsilhqot'in* affirms or reinscribes (produces and reproduces) sovereignty. Thus, Borrows argues that while *Tsilhqot'in* asserts lands were not *terra nullius*, it also undermines this assertion by relying on a prior ruling that employed the concept of *terra nullius* to endorse Crown sovereignty.

The rationale behind this legal perspective that asserts European sovereignty on a basis of *terra nullius* may stem from the constraints that settler colonial states face in reconciling both historical and ongoing processes of colonialism, which serve settler interests at the expense of Indigenous rights. Bhandar explains that efforts to reconcile the effects of settler colonialism and the narratives supporting it can only go so far in Canada. This limitation arises because the legitimacy of settler colonial frameworks relies on the false narrative of legitimate acquisition of land. When courts acknowledge the political agency of Indigenous Peoples, they do so because they are compelled to recognize Indigenous dispossession. However, the inherent flaw in the Crown's sovereign power — the myth of legitimacy — means that these courts ultimately reaffirm the Crown's legitimacy, which undermines the recognition of Indigenous dispossession.[81] Furthermore, the practices within broader

---

Tsilhqot'in

Tsilhqot'in Nation v. British Columbia (2014) is a landmark Supreme Court ruling concerning Aboriginal title that was brought by the Tsilhqot'in Nation after the British Columbia government issued a commercial logging licence on their traditional territory. The Tsilhqot'in Nation, residing in a southern region of the province with no Treaty relationship with the Crown, claimed Aboriginal title to their ancestral lands beyond reserve holdings. The Supreme Court of Canada ruled in their favour, for the first time extending Aboriginal title beyond reserve holdings in an area not held in Treaty.[82] This decision holds broader implications for how government and the private sector approach Indigenous Nations, extending the duty to consult beyond reserve lands to ancestral Indigenous lands.[83] Duty to consult arises from section 35 of the Constitution Act, 1982, to ensure that Indigenous Peoples, as rights holders, are consulted by governments and businesses regarding matters that affect their rights.

settler colonial political structures continue to reinforce this false legitimacy through these narratives.[84] For example, on the Aboriginal and Treaty rights written into section 35 of the Constitution Act, 1982, Bhandar writes:

> I argue that the production of historical narratives about the founding and settling of Canada serves a dual purpose: the production of historical narratives that recognize the injustice of colonial settlement is central to the recently recognized objective of reconciliation; and, at the same time, it is a means through which the law re-establishes the unquestioned and unproblematized legitimacy of the colonial assertion of sovereignty.[85]

The authority of the settler state is embedded in a narrative of legitimacy that is re-established through the structures of the settler colonial state. Therefore, court cases and judicial rulings, such as the *Tsilhqot'in* (2014) decision, continue to operate under the assumption that Aboriginal title exists only with the establishment and recognition of the Crown, rather than Indigenous-derived tenets of sovereignty.[86] Courts reinforce this assumption by relying on narratives of colonial legitimacy that underpin their decisions.

The construction and implementation of the doctrine of discovery and *terra nullius* enabled settler governments and society to effectively limit and control Indigenous Peoples' access and rights to their lands and sovereignty. However, Indigenous Peoples have persistently fought back, maintaining varying degrees of autonomy or agency, or the ability to exercise decision-making, even when colonial forces have abrogated

Guerin

R v. Guerin (1984) established Aboriginal rights as *sui generis* (unique) and determined that the relationship between First Nations and the Crown is both fiduciary-like and trust-like. The case centred on the Musqueam First Nation in the area of Vancouver, British Columbia, and surrounding territory. Chief Delbert Guerin led the suit against the Crown on the grounds that the federal government had inappropriately leased or misappropriated reserve lands to a golf club. This stems from a long-standing lease on Musqueam territory, initially negotiated by the Department of Indian Affairs. At the time the lease with the golf club was negotiated, the federal government denied legal representation to the Musqueam Nation and did not share the final lease, which was later found to include terms they had not agreed to.[87]

their sovereignty.[88] While this resistance has often been obscured by replacement narratives that overlook Indigenous Peoples' presence in settler colonial society, it does exist. For example, First Nations were marginalized through the reserve system, and yet one result of reserves is that these community structures have enabled continuance of cultural knowledge systems rather than advancing the colonial project through the state's assimilation agenda. Despite the Indian Act, the IRS system, and countless other Indigenous-related policies, Indigenous-centred knowledge systems — including cultures, social structures, ancestral laws, and languages — often persist alongside or outside of settler colonial knowledge systems.[89] Thus, ancestral Indigenous-centred knowledge systems often remain intact in settler colonialism and are neither assimilated into nor overridden by the mainstream settler colonial knowledge systems.

However, as James Anaya has shown, the doctrine of discovery and *terra nullius* have posed significant challenges to Indigenous rights, particularly for those who have been separated from their lands or prohibited from practising their laws on those lands. Further, he writes, "This doctrine [of discovery] shamefully persists in the jurisprudence of national judicial systems and in many of the domestic laws and regulatory regimes that affect Indigenous Peoples."[90] Indigenous Peoples who have been unable to maintain legal traditions and customs tied to ancestral lands often face legal, geographical, and other restrictions rooted in colonialism. This marginalization reflects a historical pattern of exclusion, where the perspectives and rights of Indigenous communities are often overlooked in favour of dominant governmental interests.

The Institutional Consequences of Narratives in Settler Canada

The institutional structures of Canadian governance are significantly shaped by the transition from imperial to settler colonialism. Canadian federalism, too, is shaped by this shift. One clear example is the question of whether Indigenous-related matters of governance fall under federal or provincial jurisdiction. This question, driven by a settler colonial framework, ignores Indigenous agency and sovereignty. In other instances, provincial jurisdiction is overlooked, aligning with settler colonial narratives that ignore power imbalances, present lands as empty, and erase or replace Indigenous Peoples.

That the narratives of federalism contribute to the ongoing omission of this provincial jurisdiction and Indigenous Peoples in Canadian federalism is a feature of settler colonial narratives. Specifically, the governance relationship between provincial governments and Status Indians who live on-reserve is often overlooked in favour of the more straightforward relations with the federal government. Why the focus on federal responsibility? Who benefits from this narrative of sole federal jurisdiction for Indigenous-related matters of governance? Or put another way, who gains from the neglect of the provincial jurisdiction?

Ignoring provincial jurisdiction serves the marginalization of Indigenous Peoples within the narrative of Canadian federalism. The structure of government and the division of powers often perpetuate settler colonial practices that deprive Indigenous Peoples of agency. Reconciliation cannot function or thrive when the legitimacy of jurisdiction relating to Indigenous Peoples is understood in terms of an authority belonging to the Canadian orders of the state.

CHAPTER THREE

THE CONSTITUTION AND SETTLER COLONIAL NARRATIVES OF FEDERALISM

Federalism is a way of organizing a state's political system that divides the powers of governance (or decision-making) between a centralized government order and noncentralized orders.[1] In Canada, this means the central government (i.e., the federal government) shares powers with the provincial governments. In this way, each order of government is sovereign and can exercise autonomous decision-making, known as jurisdiction. This jurisdictional delineation is carved out in the Constitution, including the BNA Act, 1867, and later the Constitution Act, 1982.

Political scientist Jennifer Smith writes that as matters arise related to constitutional delineation of responsibility, these are tested through case law and governance practices of devolution, and a shift in decision-making authority from central to provincial powers may result.[2] If a new governance issue arises that lies outside of the Constitution, it is standard practice that the matter be deferred to the central government. Practices of devolution and deferral (or federal paramountcy, a principle under which the federal government's jurisdiction has traditionally

---

Sections 91, 92, and 95

The Constitution Act, 1982, defines the distribution of powers between the federal and provincial governments. Section 91 outlines the powers of the federal government; some examples of its jurisdiction include postal services, the military, and currency management. Section 92 details the powers of the provincial governments, including regulating businesses within the province, overseeing healthcare, and managing municipal bodies. Section 95 addresses shared powers in areas such as pensions, agriculture, and immigration.[3]

extended to matters not explicitly named as provincial responsibilities) make federalism a flexible system of power sharing. Significant changes have been made in modern governance practices as the federal government decentralizes and devolves powers to the provinces and sometimes to the territorial governments. Here, a note about the territories: In Canada, the federal and provincial governments are sovereign or have autonomous decision-making capabilities within their jurisdictional scopes. The territories are not considered sovereign, though their governance authority has increased over time due to devolution practices and other political changes.

This chapter examines how federalism has evolved as governance that excludes Indigenous Peoples' agency in Canada. We begin with the settler colonial narrative about the specific governance relationship between the Canadian state and Indigenous Peoples. In the BNA Act's section 91(24), "Indians, and Lands reserved for Indians" fall under federal jurisdiction. This section authorizes Parliament to enact laws in relation to Indians and their lands while erasing Indigenous sovereignty.[4]

This jurisdiction is not, however, clear-cut. As political scientist Radha Jhappan writes, "In fact, the provinces exercise a wide range of roles with respect to Aboriginal peoples."[5] This relationship between the provincial governments and status First Nations people living on-reserve can be evidenced in the Constitution, legislation, case law, and political and public administration practices. Accordingly, the provinces have both political and legal responsibilities for Status First Nations people, and these responsibilities have consistently increased since the end of World War II through devolution and provincial encroachment.[6]

In Canada, however, the role of the provinces in relation to First Nations communities (reserves) has been overlooked or omitted from the narrative of Canadian federalism. Settler colonialism has shaped the narrative to its advantage by narrowing the discourse of jurisdictional responsibility for First Nations people who reside on-reserve, placing — more broadly speaking — all Indigenous Peoples on the periphery of the narrative of Canadian federalism. Neglecting to acknowledge provincial jurisdiction minimizes or obscures power imbalances, thus downplaying the oppression and dispossession experienced by Indigenous Peoples within settler colonial projects. Indigenous Peoples' agency and sovereignty are restricted for settler benefit, demonstrating the opportunity for and necessity of reconciliatory attention.

The Federal Jurisdictional Scope

The power relations entrenched in federal jurisdiction arise from the Royal Proclamation of 1763, a precursor of section 91(24) of the BNA Act. As scholar Anthony J. Hall writes, the Royal Proclamation left many questions unanswered regarding land ownership and management, presenting broader questions of government jurisdiction to Canadian federalism.[7] What defines "Indian" and "Indian lands"? Or, as articulated in modern political debates, what is the nature of Indigenous rights and title? These questions continue to challenge modern-day Canadian politics and Indigenous sovereignty.

Many interpret the wording of the Royal Proclamation of 1763 as evidence that at the time, Indigenous Peoples and the Crown dealt with each other as equal and independent, or autonomous, nations. The TRC's Call to Action 45 — that the Canadian government jointly develop with Indigenous Peoples a Royal Proclamation of Reconciliation that reaffirms the nation-to-nation relationship[8] — seeks a return to this diplomacy. The Royal Proclamation of 1763 offers an approach in stark contrast to contemporary settler colonial relations, which are hierarchical and paternalistic. Today, many Indigenous Nations struggle for settler society and state recognition of their sovereignty, as demonstrated through the various modern land claims, self-government, and Aboriginal rights court cases.

Borrows has argued that the Royal Proclamation of 1763 was based on the principles of diplomacy between equal, sovereign nations, reflecting the diplomatic practices that existed between the European settlers and Indigenous Peoples at the time.[9] From the perspective of many Indigenous Peoples, the Royal Proclamation affirms their right to

---

Ambiguous Wording

The Royal Proclamation of 1763 raises questions in modern Canadian politics regarding Indigenous sovereignty due to its ambiguous wording: "And We do further declare it to be Our Royal Will and Pleasure, for the present as aforesaid, to reserve under our Sovereignty, Protection, and Dominion, for the use of the said Indians, all the Lands and Territories not included within the Limits of Our said Three new Governments, or within the Limits of the Territory granted to the Hudson's Bay Company, as also all the Lands and Territories lying to the Westward of the Sources of the Rivers which fall into the Sea from the West and North West as aforesaid."

Indigenous-centred sovereignty. Thus, the document is often referred to as the "Indian Magna Carta." (A foundational document of legal rights, Magna Carta received the king's seal in Runnymede, England, in 1215, with subsequent versions developed over the next century.[10] Though its impact is contested, many argue it was an essential symbolic or actual embodiment of rights.) By informing Treaty-making practices and cementing Indigenous-based land title into Canadian law, the Royal Proclamation of 1763 was arguably not *making* rights but instead *recognizing* the existing land rights of Indigenous Peoples. In this regard, the Royal Proclamation remains significant to Indigenous sovereignty today.

The Treaty of Niagara, signed in 1764 between twenty-four First Nations and the Crown in the Niagara region, ratified the provision that the Crown can create Treaty with Indigenous Nations as set out in the Royal Proclamation of 1763.[11] Essentially, the Treaty of Niagara represented Indigenous Peoples' acceptance of the terms of the Royal Proclamation, underscoring Indigenous agency.[12] However, although the Royal Proclamation was created in part to mitigate settler theft and conflict over lands, it also provided a tool to expand "British sovereignty and dominion over Indian lands."[13] The Treaty of Niagara stands in contrast to this; it was a gathering of the Crown and Indigenous Peoples in a nation-to-nation spirit and also an expression of Indigenous diplomacy, as captured by a Wampum Belt recording the Covenant Chain of Friendship, an alliance affirming Indigenous sovereignty.[14] Wampum is an aspect of ancestral Indigenous-centred governance that European powers often participated in when negotiating and forming alliances with Indigenous Nations in this region. Wampum Belts continue to be used by Indigenous Nations to mark Treaty or political milestones,[15] and the use of Wampum at the Treaty of Niagara demonstrates that "First Nations were not passive objects, but active participants in the formulation and ratification of the Royal Proclamation."[16] The Treaty of Niagara, as a diplomatic event that highlights both Indigenous agency

Wampum Belt

The Two-Row Wampum Belt of the 1764 Treaty of Niagara is made of two purple lines of wampum (shell beads), set against a backdrop of white wampum. The two rows depict Indigenous Peoples and European settlers travelling in two separate boats along the same river, symbolizing the equal coexistence of the two political entities.

and sovereignty as well as nation-to-nation diplomacy, is recognized in the TRC's Call to Action 45, emphasizing the need to better entrench nation-to-nation relations in contemporary governance.

Another essential feature of modern-day Canadian federalism derived from the Royal Proclamation of 1763 is the property relations between the federal government and First Nation communities. One of the purposes of the Royal Proclamation was to deter conflict over land acquisitions and holdings between the settler colonies and Indigenous Peoples by ensuring the protection of lands belonging to the Indigenous Peoples.[17] Thus, the Royal Proclamation enabled a relationship of "special" status between Indigenous Peoples and what became the federal government by determining that Indigenous lands are inalienable — they cannot be surrendered to any party but the Crown.[18] Thus, the Royal Proclamation established a legal process of title, which consequently is one of the reasons that issues of Indigenous policy have consistently been placed with the federal government: Ownership of land can pass from Indigenous Peoples only to the federal Crown.

This stipulation for land transfer between the Indigenous Peoples and the Crown was originally a measure intended to protect Indigenous Peoples from land theft by settlers. However, over time, it was utilized by the Crown to advance its own settlement agenda. As colonial projects sought possession and control over land, property laws became a crucial mechanism to achieve this goal. Bhandar states this connection explicitly: "If the possession of land was (and remains) the ultimate objective of colonial power, then property law is the primary means of realizing this desire."[19] Transforming collective land holdings into private property has been essential for the success of colonial endeavours. As Indigenous scholars Clifford Atleo (Tsimshian and Nuu-chah-nulth Nations) and Jonathon Boron (Haudenosaunee; Cayuga Nation) explain, the lands of Indigenous Peoples were transformed into property that could be bought, sold, and owned by individuals, disrupting collective Indigenous relationships with these lands.[20] Property holdings are steeped in the dynamics of settler power relations, but Indigenous dispossession and settler complicity are often unrecognizable.

Over time, the Royal Proclamation of 1763 enabled the state to find ways, in its pursuit of land as per the colonial project, to "manage the displacement of the Indians."[21] The impact of these property relations, or the housing of Indigenous lands under federal authority, led to the federal government using section 91(24) of the BNA Act to narrow the nature and scope of Indigenous rights and title by aligning Indigenous policy with the federal government's agenda of settler colonial exploitation. For example, the ministerial portfolio of Indian Affairs (now called Crown-Indigenous Relations and Northern Affairs Canada) has consistently existed under a larger bureaucratic profile charged with land appropriation and regulation,[22] representing a serious conflict of interest as the government controls Indigenous lands, which it also seeks to appropriate.

The Royal Proclamation of 1763 was later used as the framework for the BNA Act, 1867, section 91(24), which states, "Indians, and Lands reserved for the Indians" are the jurisdiction of the federal state. The fundamental responsibilities of protection that the Royal Proclamation placed on the Crown were thus extended. Since 1867, section 91(24) has been used to frame how the federal government understands its relationship to sovereign Indigenous Nations or, perhaps more accurately, how it has interpreted its authority over Indigenous Peoples. This relationship is not imagined on a scale of nation-to-nation equity — the federal government's interpretation of section 91(24) as a provision of wide-sweeping authority over Indigenous Peoples is a departure from the Royal Proclamation's recognition of nation-to-nation diplomacy.

The evolution of Indigenous-related policy in Canada reflects this changed interpretation of authority. Increasingly, policy became a tool of assimilation.[23] This understanding of authority over Indigenous Peoples and assimilationist intent have been expressed through two significant avenues — how government defines Indians, and how it defines Indian lands — that are discussed shortly. The state's approach to authority later fuelled Canada's long history of Indian reserves, residential schools, and Indigenous policy. This context illuminates why the state's governance system is central to reconciliation efforts.

Today, the Royal Proclamation of 1763 and the notion of original occupancy are the two foundational sources of Aboriginal rights used in modern legal practice. Original occupancy is a Western understanding of rights and title that the state and courts use to determine ownership and legitimate use of lands and resources.[24] Although it is accepted that the First Peoples occupied the territory now known as Canada prior to European contact, the significance of this prior occupation — the cultures, political diplomacy, and economic systems — has been consistently downplayed and often completely ignored by colonial powers through settler colonial narratives. As well, the assertion of the Canadian state's sovereignty is rarely questioned, even though, as the legal narratives demonstrate, it rests on a tenuous platform of settler-manufactured sovereignty.[25] However, as a source of Aboriginal rights, the Royal Proclamation presents a significant problem concerning whether these rights are acknowledged by the Crown or created by the Crown. If these rights are created by the Crown, then the Crown can extinguish them. If these rights are acknowledged by the Crown, then the nation-to-nation sovereign relationship must be maintained or upheld by the Crown. In either case, however, these rights have been violated by the Crown.[26]

Indigenous Peoples have never ceased asserting that their rights existed prior to European colonial contact and occupation. Yet the settler state commonly frames this relationship not as nation-to-nation but as a relationship between sovereign and subject, or state and citizen. This tension over the Royal Proclamation of 1763 and whether Aboriginal rights are acknowledged or created presents a question as to the power the federal government has regarding Aboriginal rights and the nature of federal authority over Indigenous Peoples.

Up to this point, the discussion has outlined how the settler colonial state defines jurisdiction. The state positions Indigenous Nations in terms set by, managed, and controlled by the state. Indigenous Nations, however, have different definitions. As former Grand Chief of the Assembly of Manitoba Chiefs Derek Nepinak says, "Our jurisdiction is one that has never been surrendered. The corner stones have been built on the foundation of Treaty. A relationship of jurisdiction and sovereignty is recognized; this created affirmations that have not happened, but we maintain our jurisdiction. These rights are the Treaty lands, ancestral lands, and rights that are not recognized by settler experience."[27] Jurisdiction, to Indigenous Peoples, is not defined by the narrative of settler colonial federalism. Put another way, the Canadian state does not have jurisdiction over Indigenous Nations. Indigenous Nations are sovereign, with rights that predate imperial colonialism and settler colonialism, and these have, as Nepinak maintains, been recognized by the Treaties, relationships with lands, and rights discourses. These rights include those continued and contemporary rights and responsibilities tied to ancestral use and occupancy of lands that have been recognized and affirmed by section 35 of the Constitution Act, 1982, which says, in section 35(1), "The existing aboriginal and treaty rights of the aboriginal peoples of Canada are hereby recognized and affirmed."

The settler colonial interpretation of section 91(24) that holds that the federal government has jurisdictional authority over Indians has allowed the federal government the authority to create and regulate those who are defined as Indian through state-generated rules about who belongs. As mentioned, many argue that this legal authority is tenuous: Indigenous Nations continue to hold ancestral or inherent authority to determine membership and identity, and many continue to exercise this right.[28] In 1857, the Gradual Civilization Act (a precursor to the Indian Act), containing the first provision of "special" Indian status, was enacted by the early colonial governments of Upper and Lower Canada with the intention of erasing distinctions through enfranchised assimilation. Enfranchised assimilation is the process of stripping Indigeneity through the provision of Canadian citizenship (enfranchisement). However, this process of assimilation was not limited to simply gaining Canadian citizenship: Indian status was lost at the same time as enfranchisement, which could occur through marriage, education, military service, and often just living off of the reserve, for example. Though these provisions came long after 1857, most remained until revisions were made to the Indian Act in 1951 and 1985 and some continue. Although the intention was to erase Indigenous distinctions through enfranchisement, the creation of Indian status established a legal distinction between Indians and non-Indigenous Canadians based on citizenship differentiation, and developed parameters for land ownership and management exclusive to that of First Nations.[29] Initially, the definition of Indian included all people with Indian ancestry; however, this definition was narrowed through Treaties and legislation, specifically the Indian Act,[30] and then broadened through case law. For example, the Federal Court in *Daniels v. Canada* (2013) and Supreme Court in *Daniels v. Canada* (2016) made

Section 35

The Constitution Act, 1982, section 35(1) states, "The existing aboriginal and treaty rights of the aboriginal peoples of Canada are hereby recognized and affirmed." Today it is generally understood that the Constitution does not create these rights; rather, it recognizes in Canadian law that Indigenous Peoples have pre-existing or *sui generis* rights that are distinct from this legal source and not derived from the Crown.

the historic decision that the Métis are Indians as per section 91(24) of the Constitution Act, as was previously determined for Inuit through the Supreme Court case of *Reference Re: Eskimos* (1939).[31]

One of the consequences of the state determining who is included in the definition of "Indian" in section 91(24) is the use of that section as a tool for assimilation. Indigenous perspectives of membership are often more fluid and inclusive than those of the Indian Act or section 91(24) and are not limited to who has status or resides on- or off-reserve, focusing instead on community affiliation, family ties, or ancestral relations such as kinship or clan systems, as some examples.[32] The Canadian government has used its power under section 91(24) to control who is an Indian in an attempt to reduce this demographic, and it has been argued that shifts in the definition of Indian are attempts to eliminate this special status through assimilation.[33] As historian John L. Tobias writes on section 91(24), "The legislation by which the governments of Canada sought to fulfill their responsibility always had as its ultimate purpose the elimination of the Indian's special status."[34] Thus, while section 91(24) creates jurisdiction for the federal government over Indigenous Peoples and matters of Indigenous policy, it also provides a tool for the state to control who is an Indian in attempts to assimilate Indigenous Peoples. Clearly, the federal definition serves the interests of the state at the expense of the interests of Indigenous Peoples.

Though section 91(24) states that the federal government has authority and responsibility for Indian lands, it is not clear what constitutes these lands. For example, are Indian lands those lands used traditionally, or are Indian lands only reserve lands, or all lands with Indian title such as Treaty lands? Answers to this question reveal a complex mix of settler colonial intentions of land acquisitions. For example, both the 1927 and 1951 Indian Acts define a reserve as the following: " 'Reserve' means a tract of land, the legal title to which is vested in His Majesty, that has been set apart by His Majesty for the use and benefit of a band."[35] Reserve lands, which often exist next to provincial Crown lands, are typically small tracts of land that were, at the time of reserve establishment, the least desirable land in terms of access to wood, water, and later agriculture. In fact, the Cree/nēhiyawēwin names for reserves, *askihkan* and *iskonikan*, mean fake land and leftovers.[36] Other Indigenous-centred perspectives on reserves, of which there are many, see them as land holdings or property, places for cultural resistance and continuance, or, simply, home.

In contemporary Canadian law, there are ongoing tensions regarding the interpretation of section 91(24). The settler state defines Aboriginal title on the basis of three tenets: (1) Aboriginal title is held collectively rather than by individuals, as detailed in *Delgamuukw* (1997); (2) Aboriginal title is inalienable — it cannot be extinguished or surrendered, except to the Crown, which has a fiduciary responsibility to protect the interests of those who surrender title; and (3) Aboriginal title is legally protected because of Indigenous Peoples' occupancy of the land prior to the establishment of Canada.[37] However, these tenets do not go far enough to enshrine Indigenous worldviews. As Hereditary Chief E. Richard Atleo (Nuu-chah-nulth Nation) writes, "Constitutional, federal, state, provincial, and municipal laws are oriented around human issues and concerns, while Gitksan and Wet'suwet'en laws are oriented around humans, animals, and spirits in an equitable, or balanced relationship."[38] When the state attempts to define Aboriginal title, it does so in a manner that links title to Western concepts of property. But Aboriginal title is not just the use and ownership of land; it is tied to the right of self-government.[39] Land entails a relationship of reciprocal care and as ancestral rights; this stewardship of land is upheld through Indigenous sovereignties.

Constitutional legal scholar Peter Hogg writes that Indigenous lands do not include just reserve lands, but all lands set aside by the Royal Proclamation of 1763 as not ceded to the Crown.[40] In fact, the Royal Proclamation designated all lands west of the Mississippi River as lands "reserved to the ... Indians."[41] This interpretation of Indigenous lands extends well beyond the limitations of reserves to include all lands under Aboriginal title, including, in many cases, lands that are now settled or urban areas.

Deciphering how these lands ought to be used to enable a proper interpretation of the jurisdiction as per section 91(24) is a difficult task in modern Canadian politics, because of contemporary state conceptualizations of Aboriginal title based on the tenets of collective holding, inalienability (excepting land transfer to the Crown), and prior occupancy.[42] This tenet of prior occupancy means that to prove title to land, Indigenous Peoples must demonstrate use of land in a traditional way with little to no interruption by colonial settlement. However, this is difficult for a variety of reasons, most of which have to do with settler colonial contact and occupation and the resultant disruption of Indigenous

Peoples' access to their land and practice of their cultures, languages, political systems, and economic structures. Further, as mentioned, historical state definitions of Aboriginal title have excluded Indigenous-based determinants of title.[43] Thus, tests of Aboriginal title are developed by the state and look at factors such as Treaties, reserves, and culture.

These types of state-generated tests are colonial measures that seek to test "authentic" Indigeneity in an era shaped by centuries of attempted colonial assimilation. The *Delgamuukw* test, for example, contends that a First Nation must have had exclusive occupation of the land prior to European contact and a continuity of occupation to the present in order to prove Aboriginal title.[44] The criteria for these tests change over time, but consistently exclude Indigenous-centred definitions, relying instead on state-centric definitions that assume Indian lands must be held in trust by the government. In contemporary management of lands and land claims, therefore, conflicting understandings of what constitutes Indian lands exist.

These interpretations of the scope and nature of section 91(24) regarding Indigenous Peoples and their lands have shaped how the federal government has perceived and acted upon its responsibility — or jurisdiction — to Indigenous Peoples. The federal government has been able to use section 91(24) to empower itself by expanding its authority, often to the disadvantage of Indigenous Peoples.[45] Legal scholar Brian Slattery, however, interestingly demonstrates a different interpretation and argues that section 91(24) "opens the door" for Indigenous self-government as reaffirmed by the right to self-government entrenched in the Constitution Act, 1982.[46] While this notion is explored further in Chapter 5, I argue here that the settler colonial state has used section 91(24) to marginalize Indigenous Nations and control Indigenous Peoples. Settler government-based interpretations of section 91(24) have empowered colonial authority through federal jurisdiction. The settler colonial narrative of federalism and jurisdiction foster Indigenous dispossession for settler benefit and is, therefore, critical to reconciliation efforts.

The Provincial Jurisdictional Scope

While section 91(24) facilitates a settler colonial narrative regarding federal jurisdiction and entrenched settler dominance, the provincial governments also hold a significant role within Canada's federal system.

The Constitution, case law, and public policy affirm the existence of provincial jurisdictional responsibilities concerning Indigenous Peoples. This provincial authority can hinder the agency of Indigenous Peoples, much like federal jurisdiction does. That the settler colonial narrative of federalism ignores or omits this provincial jurisdictional responsibility highlights broader issues stemming from settler colonial narratives. When settler colonial mechanics operate in ways that are ignored or go unnoticed, a pervasive power dynamic remains obscure. At this time of reconciliation, it is crucial to include provincial roles in the national dialogue on reconciliatory change.

Provincial jurisdictional activity on-reserve is determined by section 88 of the Indian Act, which states that, subject to federal law and Treaties, "all laws of general application from time to time in force in any province are applicable to and in respect of Indians in the province." Laws of general application include laws that are not specific to one group of citizens.[47] Examples of provincial laws that fall within this scope relate to traffic,[48] minimum wage, automobile insurance, and hunting.[49] Additionally, provincial programs may operate in reserve communities through "the occasional special program or small funding agency," which is service delivery beyond laws of generality.[50]

Provincial laws of generality face certain legal restrictions: They cannot single out Indians, dampen Indianness (or dilute Indigenous cultural identities), supersede federal jurisdiction (a principle called federal paramountcy), or infringe upon the tenets of Aboriginal rights as protected by section 35 of the Constitution Act, 1982.[51] The restriction related to Indianness warrants some attention. It means that provincial laws of general application must not be intended to impact Indianness, nor can they have any such resulting effect. Therefore, even if there is no

Indianness

"Indianness" is not an everyday term in Canada, but it has a conceptual place in the country's legal system. In this regard, it refers to what I describe as Indigenous difference: the unique ancestral worldviews of Indigenous Peoples that are fundamentally distinct from European-derived colonial worldviews. This Indigenous difference is encompassed in and expressed through languages, cultures, and political practices. As provinces have assumed more colonial-centred authority related to Indigenous Peoples, the scope of their powers has been evaluated through the lens of impacting Indigenous difference, or Indianness, to minimize the infringement on this Indigeneity.

intent to infringe, if the operational impact of a law affects Indianness, it is not considered a law of general application under section 88.[52]

Section 88 was not included in the Indian Act until 1951 (at which time it was actually section 87). Initially, because it reflected state practices that had been laid out in a pamphlet issued by the Department of Indian Affairs nearly forty years earlier,[53] it did not significantly change policy. Over time, it began to have a greater impact. Tobias has argued that this enhanced provincial engagement was a strategy to lessen federal responsibility for Indigenous Peoples.[54] Scholar Hugh Shewell elaborates that section 88, which enabled the federal government to transfer responsibility and cost-sharing to the provinces, was designed to increase assimilation by reducing the federal constitutional responsibility to Indigenous Peoples.[55] In effect, Indigenous Peoples' political agency — or exercise of their sovereignty — was to be overwritten by the provinces.

The provincial power to legislate for Indigenous Peoples has been tested in the courts. Historically, any provincial laws that affect Indigenous Peoples must apply generally and cannot negatively impact Indianness.[56] *Delgamuukw* (1997) examined whether provinces could extinguish Aboriginal title. Chief Justice Antonio Lamer argued against such a power due to section 88 of the Indian Act disallowing legislation that infringes on "Indianness."[57] The situation shifted slightly with the *Tsilhqot'in* decision in 2014, which established that provincial laws of general application can infringe on Aboriginal rights if justified, effectively removing some protection for Indigenous Peoples against provincial interference.[58] However, section 88 clarifies that Treaties take precedence over provincial laws,[59] and in cases such as *Simon v. R* (1985) and *R. v. Sioui* (1990) the court has found that Treaty rights and hunting rights are exempt from the jurisdictional regime of section 88.[60]

While section 88 of the Indian Act provides a limited role for provincial activity on-reserve through general application, there is also a restricted involvement for provinces derived from section 91(24) of the BNA Act, which is related to section 88. The provinces argue that this section restricts their involvement due to the "special" relationship between the federal government and First Nations.[61] Again, we see that section 91(24) grants the federal state powers over "Indians, and Lands reserved for the Indians," which is interpreted as giving the federal government authority and responsibility for Indigenous Peoples. Therefore, "by contrast, a provincial legislature is not entitled to pass legislation directly in relation to Indians or lands reserved for Indians; legislation to the effect would be in essence, legislation in relation to a federal head of power and therefore ultra vires [beyond the powers of] a provincial legislature."[62] As a result, provinces are limited in their ability to develop policy in this area, and they have been reluctant to do so.[63]

The limitations on provincial authority carved out through section 91(24) of the BNA Act and the courts have led the provinces to argue that they are not obligated or responsible for providing for First Nations people that live in reserve communities. Thus, the provinces maintain that governance related to Indians and lands reserved for Indians are solely under federal authority. Again, this special relationship is constitutionally entrenched, and the federal government does mostly accept that it is obligated to "pay for most or all programs" for on-reserve Indians.[64] Historically, this meant that the federal government delivered all on-reserve services, including infrastructure, healthcare, education, roadways, housing, water, energy, and more, through the Department of Indian Affairs. Many of these services, such as federally covered health benefits, are also provided for those with Indian status living off-reserve, non-Status First Nations, and Inuit.

However, a major drawback of this centralized approach to service delivery is that the services provided to Indigenous populations by the federal government are often below the standards of those offered by provincial departments. Provincial ministries, which are responsible for specific areas, become experts in their fields. According to scholars James Frideres and Rene Gadacz, historical colonial projects result in inadequate or low-quality social service provision to Indigenous populations.[65] Federal, as well as provincial, service delivery seems to follow this trend. Practical challenges, such as servicing small, isolated rural and reserve communities and cultural differences, can also complicate the effectiveness of standardized programs.

As a consequence, contemporary service delivery on reserves has evolved in a complicated and patchwork manner that has split delivery

Ultra Vires

Ultra vires in Latin means "outside of powers," and it refers to being beyond the scope of authority or legality. It is used to assess whether a government or entity oversteps its jurisdictional boundaries by acting beyond constitutional powers.

into various arrangements between the federal and province governments. In some cases, the Department of Indian Affairs provides services, while in other instances, provinces offer services and are reimbursed for their expenses by the federal government. Additionally, some provinces have established agreements with the federal government that devolve authority to the provinces, and more recently both orders might devolve authority to Indigenous governments, to provide services through transfer-of-payment schedules on an ongoing basis. This situation has created duplication, overlap, and vacuums in service delivery.

One example of a policy vacuum is Jordan's Principle. This principle is named after Jordan Anderson, a young First Nations child whose complex medical needs could not be met in his home community of Norway House Cree Nation in Manitoba due to a lack of services and a dispute over healthcare provision and cost coverage between the Manitoba and Canadian governments. Jordan's Principle addresses jurisdictional disputes in which both levels of government minimize their responsibility, resulting in inadequate healthcare coverage for First Nations people living in reserve communities. The Canadian Human Rights Tribunal concluded that the gap in healthcare service spending for First Nations people living on-reserve "amounted to a form of systemic discrimination."[66] Jordan's Principle demands that, as a mitigating solution, the government of first contact immediately provide the necessary medical services to First Nations children on-reserve — services that are available to non–First Nations children living off-reserve — with responsibility for payment determined afterward, in an attempt to reduce wait times and denial of services to children with complex medical and healthcare needs.[67]

One result of the division of authority and responsibility arising from section 91(24) is how the provinces interpret their role regarding Indigenous Peoples as nonfiduciary. Lawyer Timothy McCabe argues that provinces have interpreted their jurisdictional responsibility regarding fiduciary duties as limited; though the fiduciary responsibility is primarily federal, provincial duty does exist.[68] Likewise, professor of law Bradford Morse asserts that the federal government cannot transfer the *sui generis* or unique fiduciary relationship it has with Indigenous Peoples to the provinces; however, it can share fiduciary obligations with them.[69] This point raises an important question: If provinces can fill legislative vacuums and have fiduciary authority, what are the limits to their exercise of laws of generality? As Hogg writes, "[Court] decisions establish that the provincial Legislatures have the power to make their laws applicable to Indians and on Indian reserves, so long as the law is in relation to a matter coming within a provincial head of power."[70] Therefore, as discussed, provincial legislation can impact Indigenous Peoples through laws of general application if the issue falls under provincial authority. A provincial law that is not of general application or that does (negatively) impact Indianness is *ultra vires,* meaning it is outside the scope of provincial constitutional authority.[71] The *Tsilhqot'in* (2014) decision held that provincial laws of general application can apply to Aboriginal title lands.[72]

Another question arises: If the provinces cannot legislate in a way that deters Indianness, can they legislate to promote it? According to McCabe, they can: "Provincial legislation enacted with the intent, purpose or policy of singling out Indians for special treatment is permissible where the intent is benefit to the Indians."[73] Indigenous-centred legislation does not fall outside the jurisdiction of the province unless it has to do with Indian lands.[74] And yet, historically, the provinces have argued otherwise, claiming that they cannot legislate in ways that promote Indianness. As Martin Papillon writes, "In Canada too, Indigenous Peoples have historically faced hostile provincial governments with little interest in maintaining their unique status and protected land regimes."[75]

Thus far, this overview of provincial jurisdictional roles has highlighted how provinces can address legislative gaps, exercise fiduciary authority, and enact laws that promote or enhance Indigenous identity. A follow-up question related to the jurisdiction of natural resources management arises: What provincial jurisdiction exists for Indigenous Peoples' lands? The courts have maintained that the provinces cannot legislate on Indian lands, which includes reserves, in accordance with section 88 of the Indian Act. *Delgamuukw* (1997) clarified that this restriction also pertains to lands where Aboriginal title remains intact.[76] If provincial Crown lands are adjacent to or overlap with reserve lands, these lands remain regulated by the federal domain. However, when provincial Crown lands are in conjunction with Treaty lands or Aboriginal title lands, the legal implications of provincial laws must be considered to ensure they do not infringe upon Indianness.[77]

Provincial governments have jurisdictional responsibility over Crown lands outside of reserves, except for areas designated as federal, such as national parks. In fact, as Jhappan writes, section 91(24) of the

BNA Act "is misleading as it provides the federal government with very little authority over lands (just reserve lands) and instead it is the provinces that have authority over [Indigenous] ancestral lands that are outside of the reserves."[78] Provincial jurisdiction over lands and natural resources outside of reserves was established for Ontario, Quebec, Nova Scotia, and New Brunswick through the BNA Act, section 109, which also applied to Prince Edward Island and British Columbia when they joined the Confederation. The same jurisdiction was established for Alberta, Saskatchewan, and Manitoba in a series of natural resource transfer agreements made with the federal government in 1930.[79] In recent years, devolution agreements have granted regulatory authority over lands to the territorial governments in Yukon (2003), the Northwest Territories (2013), and Nunavut (2024).[80] The provinces are significantly involved in Indigenous politics regarding the regulation of natural resources on lands that are outside of reserves but within the ancestral territories of Indigenous Nations. The question of regulatory authority over provincial Crown lands is a key aspect of modern land claims.

McCabe argues that in a situation where provincial Crown lands and lands reserved for Indians or under Aboriginal title are in conjunction, the province must account for and fulfill the fiduciary obligations to Indigenous Peoples for which the federal government would otherwise be accountable. Essentially, the province can promote Indianness in such a situation. The *Keewatin* (2014) decision clarified that provincial laws of general application do not apply to lands under Aboriginal title unless proper consultation has been undertaken (in line with the duty to consult) and, if appropriate, Indigenous interests have been accommodated.[81]

All of these lands in question are, however, the ancestral lands of Indigenous Peoples. Indigenous Peoples have Inherent rights to these lands, but the state considers these rights surrendered through Treaty

---

Keewatin

Grassy Narrows First Nation v. Ontario (Natural Resources) (2014), also known as *Keewatin* (2014), was a case initiated by the Grassy Narrows First Nation in Northwest Ontario to determine whether the Ontario government had the authority to restrict harvesting rights in Treaty 3 territory. The Supreme Court of Canada ruled that because Treaties are made with the Crown, which includes federal and provincial orders of government, the provinces have the power to override a Treaty but must still respect the duty to consult. This case, in part, tested the extent of provincial powers outlined under section 91(24) and section 109 of the BNA Act.[82]

where applicable. This discrepancy creates a tension for land management and access within the framework of Canadian federalism. Both Indigenous Peoples and the provincial Crown assert claims to the same lands, and both governance systems — Indigenous and Canadian — support these claims. There is clear overlap between Indigenous Peoples and provincial governments in terms of policy, regulation, use, and rights to these lands. However, when provincial authority conflicts with Indigenous rights, it undermines the nation-to-nation relationship established in the Royal Proclamation of 1763, Treaties, and broader diplomatic agreements, diminishing the political agency of Indigenous Peoples.

Historically, the provinces have acted "without much regard for Indigenous rights and interests,"[83] and conflicts over oil and gas, mining, and forestry continue to occur. For instance, in 2016, the Saskatchewan government initiated a series of public auctions to sell Crown lands.[84] Critics argue that these lands should first undergo a Treaty Land Entitlement (TLE) process before any privatization or sale to private entities. Failure to do so hinders Indigenous Nations from acquiring these lands through the TLE framework, in violation of the *Saskatchewan Treaty Land Entitlement Framework Agreement*.[85] As the provincial government moves forward with the sale of Crown lands to private investors, TLE issues remain unsettled. This situation has serious negative ramifications for Indigenous rights concerning these lands. As Betty Nippi-Albright, Saulteaux and Cree from Kinistin Saulteaux Nation and a member of the Legislative Assembly of Saskatchewan, stated, "What good are the rights to hunt, fish and gather if there's no Crown land left to do it on?"[86]

One final consideration of provincial jurisdiction within Canada's constitutional framework is how different interpretations of it align with the intended distribution of governmental powers. The founders

---

Treaty Land Entitlement

The *Saskatchewan Treaty Land Entitlement Framework Agreement* was established in 1992 to fulfill Treaty obligations to First Nations that did not receive the land they were promised by the federal Crown and to ensure that First Nations communities have the right of first refusal on any Crown land available for sale.[87] The agreement lists reserve communities in the province that "have not received Reserves of sufficient area to fulfil the requirements of that Treaty" pertaining to them.[88]

of the Constitution put Indigenous policy under federal jurisdiction to ensure uniformity in policy and regulation in the interests of Indigenous Peoples. However, was this constitutional responsibility always meant to remain at the federal level, or was it anticipated to shift to provincial or Indigenous governments when the time was right? Discussions prior to the Confederation debates hinted at the possibility of transferring jurisdictional responsibility to provincial governments. A letter from Archibald Acheson, Earl of Gosford and the governor-in-chief to British North America, to Lord Glenelg (Charles Grant), the secretary of state for war and the colonies, written July 13, 1837, states that Indigenous Peoples must remain under federal jurisdiction "until Circumstances make it expedient that they should be turned over by the Crown to the Provincial legislature and receive Legislative Provision and Care."[89] Lord Glenelg expressed the same sentiment the next year, on August 22, 1838, in a letter to John George Lambton, Earl of Durham and governor general and high commissioner of British North America.[90] It seems unlikely that transferring responsibility to provincial governments was seen as practical before or immediately following Confederation, as legislators were likely focused on immediate nation-building efforts. However, the correspondence outlined in this paragraph suggests an expectation that provincial governments would eventually assume responsibility for Indigenous policy. Current practices of federal offloading indicate that this moment may have finally arrived. This jurisdictional transfer aligns with the settler state's desire for assimilation, suggesting that entrusting the provinces with the responsibility for Indigenous Peoples will facilitate their assimilation.

To summarize, the federal government's responsibility for First Nations peoples on-reserve does not negate provincial involvement, except where the restrictions found in section 88 of the Indian Act are concerned. When a vacuum of state authority arises, along with a gap in services, the provinces can provide services to First Nations people both on- and off-reserve without violating constitutional restrictions if the services fall into an area of provincial jurisdiction such as healthcare. The provinces can also use their spending power (i.e., authority to spend money on programs and services within their jurisdiction) for those living on-reserve, and can have a fiduciary responsibility for Indigenous Peoples in honour of the Crown. While the provinces cannot legislate in a way that deters Indianness, they can legislate to ensure Indianness (unless it has to do with Indian lands). Due to provincial jurisdiction of natural resources in Canada, the provinces are involved in Indigenous politics concerning the regulation of natural resources on lands outside of reserves that are the ancestral lands of Indigenous Nations. Where provincial Crown lands and lands reserved for Indians or under Aboriginal title are in conjunction, the province must fulfill obligations to Indigenous Peoples that would otherwise fall to the federal government; this stipulation has led to the involvement of provincial governments in the modern Treaty-making process.

Indigenous Nations and Canadian settler politics are at a crucial juncture of the self-government movement, with court interpretations of Aboriginal rights according to section 35 of the Constitution Act, modern land claims, and the establishment of self-government agreements. However, as Glen Coulthard points out, the Canadian state routinely engages in the politics of recognition, implementing political arrangements that diminish the agency of Indigenous Peoples and entangle them further in the mechanisms of settler colonialism.[91] Given the role of the provinces in Indigenous policy matters and the assimilative nature of settler colonial governance, the narrative of federalism — which ignores these provincial practices — must be addressed for reconciliation.

Jurisdictional Paths of Exploitation

While section 91(24) of the BNA Act seems to clearly define a jurisdictional relationship between the federal government and "Indians, and Lands reserved for the Indians," the historical context shaping this relationship has resulted in provincial influence over Indigenous Peoples as well. In modern Canadian society, section 91(24) has generated multiple interpretations and debate. That said, by limiting the scope of discussion to Canadian federalism and the division of powers between the federal and provincial governments, this debate excludes various arguments about Indigenous autonomy and sovereignty. Historical interpretations of section 91(24) that have framed this jurisdictional debate have limited provincial involvement in Indigenous politics. However, the debate is shifting to include the idea that provinces should be involved, and that they are avoiding their responsibilities to Status First Nations living on-reserve when they are not involved.

No settler colonial government should deprive Indigenous Peoples of political agency; however, while the settler colonial state is operable, it is important that it fulfill its constitutional fiduciary obligations. Every day that provinces are not actively involved in improving the lives of Indigenous Peoples and promoting Indianness is a day that the provinces are failing to meet the evolving mandate of contemporary federalism. The dismissal of provincial jurisdiction through the narrative of federalism is not just a bureaucratic issue but also a direct result of settler colonial narratives that benefit the settler government while marginalizing Indigenous Nations' sovereignty. These narratives, applied through modern governance activities such as jurisdictional ambiguity, have a profound impact on the lives and rights of Indigenous Peoples. The persistence of this dismissal of provincial jurisdiction and federalist practices that ignore Indigenous Peoples' sovereignty perpetuate barriers to reconciliation.

CHAPTER FOUR

EVOLVING FEDERALISM AND IMPLICATIONS FOR INDIGENOUS POLITICAL AGENCY

Canadian federalism has denied Indigenous Nations' sovereignty through the distribution of federal and provincial responsibilities. Yet federalism has also shown flexibility, evolving since Confederation in 1867 from colonial federalism to classic, collaborative, competitive, constitutional, and decentralized types. Is the flexibility of federalism an opportunity to foster better opportunities for reconciliation? Various forms of federalism have emerged that could provide different degrees of self-determination for Indigenous Nations. However, as Martin Papillon argues, although newer approaches to federalism, such as multilevel governance, can offer an alternative to Canadian federalism's dualistic governance, the operators of Canadian federalism continue to be unreceptive to shared and overlapping sovereignty with Indigenous Nations.[1] In many ways, settler society has simply dismissed Indigenous Peoples' sovereignty through the narrative of Canadian federalism. The political subordination of Indigenous governments to the Canadian government is normative, representing clear opportunities for reconciliation.

Federalism in Flux

Canadian nationhood was established in 1867, and at that time, colonial federalism was the entrenched governing model based on the strong central authority of the federal government and the authoritative influence of imperial Britain. Still, by the end of the nineteenth century, Canada was maturing into its nationhood, and the model of classic federalism was adopted, which engaged a more balanced division of powers between the central government and provinces. Later, as the nation endured the rapid social, economic, and political changes from the Great Depression and the post–World War II era, collaborative federalism was developed to enhance cooperation between the federal and provincial governments to meet the changing needs of Canadian society. The political and economic upheavals that shaped the 1960s and '70s were counterbalanced by the regulatory framework of competitive federalism, which remains the dominant approach in Canadian politics — with the exception of constitutional federalism, which punctuated the late 1970s and the '80s during the patriation process of the Constitution Act, 1982. Competitive federalism is often characterized by neoliberal practices such as devolution, shifting responsibilities from a higher to lower level of the state, and privatization, contracting out public services to the private sector. These shifts in Canadian federalism have fundamentally impacted Indigenous Peoples' sovereignty.

Colonial federalism

An early, colonial form of federalism arranged the division of powers so that the federal government was provided with more substantial powers than the provincial governments were. A strong and uniform central government was sought for Canada to avoid the perceived problematic power struggles experienced by the United States' republic model of governance, which at the time had a weaker central government and stronger states.[2] The era of Canadian nation building was focused on accommodating English-French dualism in a single nation.[3]

The emphasis on centralization partly contributed to this arrangement of powers in Canada, situating Indigenous-related policy as a federal mandate. Another determinant was that the federal government was the leading authority over land appropriation during early nationhood development. While federal authority over land was aimed at facilitating settler homesteading and township settlement, an unintended result was a federal monopoly on managing Indigenous policy. Furthermore, under the principle of federal paramountcy, the federal government has traditionally held jurisdiction over matters not explicitly laid out as a responsibility of the provinces. Since initially there was no designated role in Indigenous-related policy for the provinces, federal powers would naturally have assumed any required responsibility.[4]

Thus, without constitutional imperative, the provinces did not have a clear role in Indigenous-related policy, which led the federal government to interpret its role as one of unrestricted authority within this scope of policymaking. This position suited the provinces well: They were required to participate in Indigenous matters only when Treaty negotiations required it (usually at the request of the federal authorities). The provinces understood the federal responsibility to extend to all Indigenous Peoples, even Inuit and Métis, who fell, at this time, outside of the purview of section 91(24) of the BNA Act.[5]

The broader political environment of nation building in the mid- to late nineteenth century was one of immense change with the ongoing construction of the political map and establishment of the nation-state. The Canadian colonial project was preoccupied with the assimilation of Indigenous Peoples. The Canadian government and settler society were impatient about building a country and were not interested in building a framework of equal cohabitation that would require centuries of diplomacy. As historian Sarah Carter explains, Indigenous-related policy was hasty and not given extensive or comprehensive attention.[6] Little thought was given to the notion of sustainable longevity.

Indigenous Peoples across what was becoming Canada had little direct input in the making of the government. As discussed earlier, the work of John Borrows highlighted that some fundamental aspects of Indigenous political practices and legal approaches were incorporated into Canadian governance. In the early years of Confederation, many of the Numbered Treaties were initiated. Official documentation of Indigenous Peoples' opinions from that time, alongside accounts from Indigenous oral traditions, has been examined. Historians Arthur J. Ray, Jim Miller, and Frank Tough relay some of the agency that Indigenous leaders demonstrated during Treaty 4 negotiations in Saskatchewan. While some acts of resistance and agency might be lost to history, records show that these leaders indicated dissatisfaction to the treaty commissioner by withholding pipe ceremony, a customary ceremonial protocol.[7] The leaders confronted the commissioner about their displeasure over the sale of land to the Hudson's Bay Company, asserting their interest in both their ancestral lands and the profits from the sale, viewing it as theft.[8] By withholding pipe ceremony and pressing the commissioner, the Indigenous leaders asserted a position of political hesitancy, negotiation, and independence.

On matters related to governance, Indigenous Peoples received little attention during this era of nation building. As political scientist Peter Russell writes, "Canada's Constitution-makers saw Aboriginal peoples not as 'partners in Confederation' but simply as a subject matter of the new federation's central legislature."[9] The constitutional debates predating the drafting of the BNA Act, 1867, do not include a discussion of Indigenous Peoples, and the index to the Confederation Debates of 1865 include only two insubstantial references to Indigenous Peoples, the first concerning general government and the second regarding jurisdiction.[10] This lack of discussion of Indigenous Peoples' role in the federation showed that Indigenous Peoples would be governed and not govern themselves.

An essential contributor to the settler government jurisdiction over Indigenous-related matters was the societal and institutional racism that shaped the nation-building period. Racism, according to James Frideres and Rene Gadacz, is foundational to any colonial project.[11] Postcolonial theorist Albert Memmi agrees, writing of racism that "it appears not as an incidental detail but as a consubstantial part of colonialism."[12] Sociologists Vic Satzewich and Nikolaos Liodakis explain that "racism was pervasive in early Canada and took a variety of individual and institutional forms" while becoming embedded in Canadian state formation.[13]

As antiracist scholars Enakshi Dua, Narda Razack, and Jody Nyasha Warner explain, Canadian nation building is tied to conceptualizations of race and racism.[14] They argue that Canadian identity was founded on a discourse of whiteness, and this discourse continues to influence how Canadians perceive past and ongoing state formation and function: "National mythologies operate to make Canada a white nation. We are constantly led to believe that Europeans built the nation, and in telling this history, the conquest, genocide, slavery, and continued exploitation of the labor of aboriginal and people of color is suppressed and/or erased."[15] This discourse of race omits the exploitation and marginalization of several groups in Canada's history, including Indigenous Peoples and many other diasporic peoples who have made Canada home. The racism of Canadian nation building contributed to constraints and pressures on Indigenous sovereignty, as Indigenous Peoples were written into the constitutional foundation of the country as a jurisdictional responsibility of the settler colonial state.

Classic federalism

As the federal and provincial governments began to work more closely with one another to achieve responsive and responsible governance, the mode of governance shifted to classic federalism. Yet the notion that the federal government was tasked with the paramount authority of Indigenous Peoples persisted.

In 1887, *St. Catharines Milling and Lumber Co. v. R.* greatly contributed to the modern determination of the division of powers between the provincial and federal governments.[16] This case concerned the provincial regulation of natural resources in the area of Treaty 3 (1873) in Ontario after the Dominion of Canada issued a forestry licence to the St. Catharines Milling and Lumber Company. The Dominion of Canada argued that its authority to license the lands in question derived from section 91(24) of the BNA Act, and that Treaty 3 meant the land was ceded by the First Nations and thus held under federal Crown title.[17] The province argued that section 91(24) referred only to territories designated as Indian reserves and not Treaty lands or Indian title lands, which were regulated by the province through the BNA Act, section 109.[18] The court ruled that Indian title to land was recognized by the Royal Proclamation of 1763, surrendered through Treaty to the Crown, and then passed to the province under the BNA Act.[19] Thus, the lands reserved for Indians, as articulated in section 91(24), remained under the full authority of the provincial Crown.[20] There is no indication that the interests of the First Nations living in the region were taken into account in the court proceedings or case decision. The outcome undercut Indigenous Peoples' agency in these matters.

According to Canadian law, those First Nations who "surrendered" their title could do so only to the federal Crown (a principle of the Royal Proclamation of 1763), not the province. One outcome of the court ruling is that, at varying times, the provinces have come to maintain responsibility for Indian lands. Thus, the federal government maintains authority over Indian lands under the BNA Act's section 91(24), but section 109 also enables the provincial ownership and management of such lands. The federal government must, therefore, consult with the provinces on matters concerning these lands even though the federal government maintains ultimate decision-making power over the sale of these lands. In this way, *St. Catharines Milling* demonstrates the transition from colonial federalism to classic federalism and the beginning of a shift in the balance of provincial and federal powers regarding interactions with Indigenous Peoples.

Classic federalism can be further traced in ensuing court rulings, including *Auditor-General for Quebec v. Auditor-General for Canada* (1920) and *Reference Re: Eskimos* (1939).[21] These rulings demonstrate a growing balance of powers shared with the provinces on Indigenous-related matters. In *Auditor-General for Quebec v. Auditor-General for Canada* (1920), the court ruled that unoccupied reserve lands in Quebec set aside before Confederation did not belong to the province as per section 109 of the BNA Act, but instead were a jurisdiction of the federal government under section 91(24), which the federal government could use to release these lands to the province.[22]

Reference Re: Eskimos (1939) concerned the constitutional status of Inuit and the jurisdictional responsibility for welfare payments to Inuit during the Great Depression. At this time, the federal government provided financial relief to Inuit communities living in northern Quebec and was reimbursed by the provincial government. Under the economic duress of this time, the province of Quebec took the federal Crown to court, arguing that Inuit communities were a federal responsibility under section 91(24) of the BNA Act. The court considered whether Inuit were a federal or provincial responsibility according to the Constitution: Did Inuit have Indian status, thereby establishing a special relationship between Inuit and the federal government? If Inuit were found not to be Indian, or to not have this special relationship, then fiduciary responsibility would belong to the province.[23] The court found, as Peter Kulchyski writes, that "in one law, the bna act, where it says 'indian', it means indian and inuit. In another law, the indian act, where it says 'indian' it means

Burden

In *St. Catharines Milling and Lumber Co. v. R.* (1887), the court ruled that Indian title was a "burden" on Crown title, a deeply colonial understanding of Indigenous Peoples' lands. This means the Crown's title is underlying but still subject to Aboriginal title. Given Indigenous Peoples' pre-existing occupation and use of the land, the Crown is restricted in its land dealings and has a legal obligation to consider Indigenous Peoples' interests. This legal obligation — or burden — must be met in decision-making practices, as established in the *Delgamuukw* (1997) and affirmed in subsequent rulings.[24]

indian and not inuit."[25] This case frames the legal status of Inuit under both federal and provincial jurisdiction. But it was yet another court case where Indigenous Peoples were not present to advocate for themselves.

Collaborative federalism

Collaborative federalism emerged as a response to the changing socioeconomic needs of Canadians during the Great Depression and post–World War II era. Citizen demands for a more proactive government that provided more services led to an increase in the overall size of the bureaucratic government and shifted the function of the state. Collaborative federalism brought more significant pressure from the federal government onto the provincial governments to increase their responsibilities for Indigenous Peoples. In general, the post–World War II period was marked by heightened welfare state policymaking, which included an integration of Keynesian economic strategy into public service delivery to stimulate the economy.

One of the distinguishing features of collaborative federalism from the 1950s to 1970s was the increased federal transfer payments to the provinces to increase their role in the provision of social services for the general population.[26] In this era, as political scientists François Rocher and Miriam Smith demonstrate, federal devolution was also met with federal intervention in provincial matters of jurisdiction.[27] The federal government used fiscal transfers to explicitly shape the scope of provincial programs and policies.

Another outcome of collaborative federalism was a significant increase in the role of provincial governments in Indigenous-centred politics.[28] Previously, the province had acted as an agent of the federal government in regard to First Nations. As the provincial governments expanded the delivery of social services intended to be universal (e.g., family allowances, pensions), provincial provision of services to First Nations also grew.[29]

The federal government had, for some time, demonstrated a clear intention to increase provincial involvement in Indigenous and state relations. One example is the natural resource transfer agreements made with Alberta, Saskatchewan, and Manitoba in 1930, which shifted authority for natural resources from the federal government to the provincial governments (in line with the natural resource management by the eastern provinces described in section 109 of the BNA Act, 1867).

Several hearings held in 1946–48 by a joint committee of the Senate and House of Commons also featured federal advocacy for an increased provincial role.[30] In 1951, at a federal-provincial conference, the provinces gave way to federal pressure and agreed to cover old-age assistance and vision impairment allowance for Indigenous Peoples.[31] As the provinces became more involved in Indigenous-centred governance, the framework for on-reserve service delivery began to change. By the 1960s, joint service delivery activities had grown to require a dedicated federal-provincial division in the federal Department of Indian Affairs.[32] In this same decade, in conjunction with service delivery growth, the provinces also became more active in natural resource and hunting and trapping legislation, which was a "significant departure from past practice."[33]

As the provinces increased service provision, ultra-constitutional practices also grew. Ultra-constitutional practices are nonlegal or ad hoc political arrangements not outlined in the Constitution. Canadian federalism is derived from constitutional parameters as well as the British Westminster parliamentary system. Though Westminster conventions are "crucial components of the Constitution, they are not set out in written form. They are of enduring importance but they are subject over time to gradual change in their interpretation and application."[34] There is a growing gap between the written Constitution and the contemporary conventional practices of federal-provincial relations.[35] Increased provincial involvement in Indigenous-related matters has been tacitly, not necessarily explicitly, accepted by the provinces through policy and program development.[36] The lack of written constitutional entrenchment may contribute to the enduring perception that Indigenous Peoples are a federal jurisdictional matter.

During the era of collaborative federalism, several fiscal and political factors affected the provinces' political motivation and involvement in Indigenous-related matters. Though the federal government pressured the provinces to expand their services to Indigenous Peoples both on- and off-reserve, it did not increase funding to cover rising costs.[37] Thus, by shifting responsibilities to the provinces, the federal government was left in a financially advantageous position.[38] Further, because First Nations people residing on-reserve are exempt from provincial taxation, provinces do not benefit from their tax revenue. As a result, service expansion can pose a significant fiscal strain for the provinces.[39] Since World War II, an increasing number of Status First Nations people have moved off-reserve, in part due to population growth, lack of opportunities and services on the reserve, and changes made to the Indian Act in 1951, whereby they could legally live off-reserve without enfranchisement. Consequently, their use of provincially funded services has risen.

Competitive federalism

In the 1960s, mounting federal pressure for the provinces to take on more responsibilities for Indigenous Peoples signalled a shift to competitive federalism, which carried into the 1980s. This pressure was indicated in a series of federal government policy proposals and government reports, including *A Survey of the Contemporary Indians of Canada* (1966), known as the Hawthorn Report; *Statement of the Government of Canada on Indian Policy, 1969*, known as the White Paper; *Indian Self-Government in Canada: Report of the Special Committee* (1983), known as the Penner Report; *New Management Initiatives: Initial Results from the Ministerial Task Force on Program Review* (1985), produced by the Nielsen Task Force; and an internal document by Indian Affairs entitled "Directional Plan for the 1980s" (1986).[40] Each of these reports recommended a reorganization of relations between the federal government, provincial governments, and Indigenous Nations that in some way would increase provincial activity.

Two reports, the Hawthorn Report (1966) and the Penner Report (1983), recommended enhancing provincial activity in Indigenous-related policy and programming. In taking the position that provincial governments ought to increase their presence in matters pertaining to Indigenous Peoples, the Hawthorn Report, as noted by anthropologist Sally Weaver, "refuted the usual constitutional argument that Indians were the exclusive responsibility of the federal government, thereby leaving the way open for the provinces to deliver programs to Indians."[41] The Penner Report recommended striking a new relationship on the grounds that the inequities that Indigenous Peoples commonly faced were based on the historical system of colonial state relations. The result of the Penner Report's proposed new relationship, according to legal scholar Bruce Rawson, would be self-determination for Indigenous Peoples wherein Indigenous governments would be required to "increase their direct contact with provincial governments and others."[42] Despite a recognition of Indigenous agency, this increased direct contact is simply a shift from federal to provincial jurisdiction, not a genuine enhancement of Indigenous political authority.

The White Paper (1969) and Nielsen Task Force report (1985) made stronger recommendations for enhancing provincial activity. The White Paper proposed the termination of section 91(24) of the BNA Act on the basis that this section limited the participation of Status Indians in settler Canadian society, and it argued that services provided to First Nations ought to be delivered by provincial government agencies that served general Canadian society off-reserve.[43] Indigenous leaders disputed many aspects of the White Paper, but were most strongly opposed to this controversial recommendation because, although section 91(24) entrenches federal jurisdiction and enables and maintains colonial relations, it also preserves in Canadian law a distinction between Indigenous Peoples and settler society. Put another way, section 91(24) can be used by Indigenous Peoples to resist assimilation and retain a diplomatic relationship with the Crown. Indigenous Peoples' opposition to the White Paper and particularly devolution to the provinces made the government pause. Still, the Nielsen Task Force report (1985) later recommended limiting federal spending and transferring responsibilities for on-reserve services to the provinces.[44] Weaver observes that the federal government used the Nielsen Task Force report, which said "programs were largely devised in a vacuum of fiscal concerns," to justify spending cuts.[45] Interestingly, no government solution looked to Indigenous Peoples' sovereignty in this era of competitive federalism (although the Penner Report did call for a constitutional right to self-government).

The state's use of devolution is an attempt to address the outcomes and responsibilities of systemic colonialism. Transferring jurisdiction to the provinces, however, keeps the system of colonialism intact. This approach does not acknowledge or deal with the fundamental challenge that Indigenous Peoples face when their sovereignty has been minimized by colonialism or when their sovereignty challenges the very legitimacy of the colonial state.[46] For example, as Kiera Ladner and Michael Orsini explain, "This transition is not from colonialism to post-colonialism; it is from one form of colonial rule to another 'kinder, gentler' form of colonial management."[47] These authors explain that a serious approach to reshaping Indigenous-state relations would consist of dismantling the colonial bureaucracy that maintains colonial inequity.

The federal pressure to increase the provincial role in Indigenous-related matters was further reinforced by the courts. *Cardinal v. Attorney General of Alberta* (1973) was the first Supreme Court of Canada case to rule on interjurisdictional immunity in relation to section 91(24) of the BNA Act.[48] Interjurisdictional immunity refers to a situation in which legislation from two levels of government cover one matter. If a conflict between federal and provincial legislation emerges, the federal authority is paramount, but if no conflict emerges, the provincial legislation remains in force: It has interjurisdictional immunity. The ruling in *Cardinal* rejected the "enclave doctrine" (the idea that First Nations reserves are only in the federal domain) and concluded that provincial laws can exist on-reserve:[49]

> A Province cannot legislate a subject matter exclusively assigned to the Federal Parliament by s. 91. But it is also well established that Provincial legislation does not necessarily become invalid because it affects something which is subject to Federal legislation.[50]

Thus, as lawyer Albert C. Peeling observes, "provincial legislation may incidentally affect matters assigned exclusively to the federal government, including aboriginal title and rights."[51]

In the *Tsilhqot'in* (2014) decision, the court rejected the application of interjurisdictional immunity. Interjurisdictional immunity prevents provincial laws from applying to federal laws. If this concept was applied to Aboriginal title, it could prevent provincial laws from applying to lands under Aboriginal title — in that section 92 of the Constitution Act, which describes provincial powers, is precluded from being applied to section 91(24).[52] The court argued that a legislative vacuum could arise if interjurisdictional immunity were applied. That said, as Borrows

---

Federal Enclaves?

Cardinal v. Attorney General of Alberta (1973) involved Charlie Cardinal, a Treaty First Nations individual who sold wild game in a reserve community to a non–First Nations person. The province of Alberta alleged that this transaction violated the provincial Wildlife Act. This case examined whether section 91(24) of the BNA Act created a federal enclave (the reserve) where provincial powers did not apply. The court determined that no such enclave exists, and the Wildlife Act did apply to First Nations living in reserve communities.[53]

explains, such a legislative vacuum would not arise if pre-existing and continued Indigenous jurisdiction of Aboriginal title lands was recognized by the courts.[54] In this sense, interjurisdictional immunity offers a clear opportunity for Indigenous sovereignty to be recognized and applied to the Canadian federation.

Constitutional federalism

Constitutional federalism emerged leading up to the patriation of the Constitution in 1982. The process of constitutional patriation contributed to enhancing the role of provinces in matters related to Indigenous Peoples. This enhancement was entrenched in the Constitution and policy shifts at the time. The provinces increased their constitutional presence in Indigenous-centred matters through the amendment process; the Constitution Act, 1982, section 35; and the BNA Act, 1867, section 91(24) (which was reaffirmed in the Proclamation of the Constitution Act, 1982).

The Constitution Act of 1982 undermines Aboriginal rights by enhancing the role of provincial involvement, thus maintaining the colonial federalist system and impacting nation-to-nation diplomacy. While section 35 of the Constitution Act recognizes Aboriginal rights, these Aboriginal rights can now be amended or extinguished through the process of constitutional amendment. A change to the Constitution requires that seven out of ten provinces, with a majority of the country's people — called the 7+50 formula — vote in favour. This amendment process provides the provinces with a possible role in shaping Indigenous-related policies and Aboriginal rights at the constitutional level, a position that Indigenous Peoples oppose.[55] Section 35 guarantees that a constitutional conference will take place in the event of such an amendment, involving representatives from Indigenous Nations. However, Indigenous Nations do not have the right to participate in the constitutional amendment process, as it is primarily a state-centred procedure,[56] which underscores the colonial nature of it.

Additional provincial involvement has been highlighted in the context of constitutional patriation. According to Morse, this process led to a more limited interpretation of section 91(24) by the federal government, necessitating provincial cooperation and active participation.[57] Political scientist Michael Murphy explains that this era of constitutional patriation intensified intergovernmental negotiations regarding Indigenous-related matters.[58] Together, these are significant changes to the constitutionalized role of the provinces in Indigenous-related matters.

In addition to these constitutional mandates, the era of constitutional federalism also saw an enhancement of the policymaking role of the provinces in Indigenous-related matters. For example, during the First Ministers' meetings on patriation, a number of premiers gave speeches that included their analysis of Indigenous-related matters in their provincial policies.[59] On these speeches, William Calder writes, "Although it may be difficult to demonstrate in quantifiable terms, few observers doubt that the aboriginal constitutional discussion process had contributed to a growing provincial involvement in native issues, including Indian self-government issues."[60] The decision-making authority of the provinces in Indigenous-centred politics grew, often in contention with Indigenous Peoples' position on the role of the provinces in matters concerning them.

During the era of constitutional federalism, several changes were made to the approaches to and understandings of Canadian federalism. As Rocher and Smith explain, long-standing understandings of national dualism (English and French) were tested by changes in Canadian society and the Constitution, such as the establishment of the Charter of Rights and Freedoms (1982), as well as broader changes in constitutional conventions arising from institutions and intergovernmentalism.[61] The Charter of Rights and Freedoms is a bill of rights that makes up the first part of the Constitution Act, 1982 (with the remainder including the BNA Act, the principle of equalization payments, and the constitutional amending formula). Rocher and Smith argue that Indigenous nationalism (as well as multiculturalism) has undermined the dualistic approach to Canadian federalism, resulting in an emphasis on multinationalism.[62] During this era, more opportunities emerged for Indigenous Peoples to be involved in state relations, in part due to changes related to Aboriginal self-government. As Ghislain Otis and Martin Papillon write, "Moreover, the insistence on basing discussions on concepts and institutions established in the 1867 Constitution ignores the fact that self-government may require autonomous indigenous polities to straddle categories defined by the constitutional division of powers."[63] Beyond the central state and provinces, this division of powers can include municipal governments as well.

It has been argued that since this era, there are great possibilities for Indigenous governance through the government's negotiation process, which can lead to the development of new governance models.[64] One such model is multilevel governance, an emerging approach to decentralized federalism that provides an alternative to the dualistic nature of Canadian federalism.[65] Multilevel governance occurs in the policy realm, outside of the constitutional and legal realms. According to Papillon, "While they do not alter the formal nature of state authority as defined in the Constitution, multilevel policy exercises are characterized by growing interdependencies between Aboriginal and non-Aboriginal governing actors, leading to a partial displacement of formal rules of authoritative decision-making in favour of joint decision-making processes and negotiated solutions to policy disputes."[66] This alternative approach to Canadian federalism and several others are further explored in Chapter 5. The next section considers additional decentralized federalist measures.

Competitive federalism, intergovernmental relations, and decentralization

The competitive model of Canadian federalism that developed in the 1960s came to take on a decentralizing approach, granting more power to the provinces. One significant aspect of this federalist framework is new public management (NPM), which emerged in the 1980s and its principles have been consistently implemented through neoliberal practices of decentralization over the following decades. Decentralization relies, in part, on intergovernmental relations, allowing new and nontraditional political actors, such as Indigenous Nations and groups, to participate in decision-making and service delivery.

NPM is an administrative practice that many liberal democracies engaged with in the 1980s in response to economic challenges. The intent of NPM was to cut government spending through two main features: (1) retrenching the state and contracting out service delivery to private enterprises or downloading service delivery to other orders of the state and (2) entering into new, unprecedented areas of governance.[67] The NPM approach within Canadian governance is similar to that found in other capitalist democracies: Modern state policy development often occurs alongside or in response to the evolving fluctuations within capitalist markets.[68] This approach, thus, is a broader feature of public administration that is respondent to the market. On retrenching the state, political scientist Andrew Sancton writes, "By any measure,

Canada is a remarkably decentralized federation. Since the 1960s at least, so much of our political activity has been directed at elevating our provincial governments to a status that is fully equal to that of the government of Ottawa."[69] Thus, the provincial role is enhanced in many aspects of governance. On entering into new, unprecedented areas of governance, legal professional Lorne Sossin argues that NPM's governance practices include tying success to the market or equating economic empowerment to political empowerment.[70] NPM has, thus, increased the role of the provinces due to federal activities such as spending cutbacks and devolution, as well as the increased exposure of both provincial and territorial governments to global markets.[71]

The first feature of NPM, the downloading of central government mandates to the provinces, is key to understanding how the provinces behave in these Indigenous matters of governance. This decentralization occurs for two general reasons: provincial interest in expansion and federal pressure to do so. In the first case, the provinces want increased control over land and natural resources.[72] When the provinces actively seek to increase their jurisdictional presence, it is called encroachment. Scholars Menno Boldt and J. Anthony Long write that "they [provinces] are unwilling to assume a significant increase in responsibility for Indians without a satisfactory measure of jurisdiction and management control over Indian peoples and lands."[73] Where the provinces have increased their jurisdiction over land management, they have also taken on increased governance responsibilities for Indigenous Peoples. Morse writes that "protecting provincial jurisdiction came to be seen as a political imperative, while long-standing assimilative impulses were recast as positive efforts to promote fairness for all."[74] The motive for jurisdictional encroachment on land and resource management cannot be separated from assimilative tendencies seeking settler-based benefit at the expense of Indigenous Peoples' livelihood.

In the second case, devolution results from the pressure created when the federal government retrenches from governance activity, leaving vacuums that the provinces must fill. One of the effects of devolution is that jurisdiction becomes unclear or indeterminate. Such indeterminacy arises when jurisdiction is overlapping, which results in the duplication of mandates, or when jurisdictional gaps appear. When a legislative or policy gap arises, there is often no clear mechanism for dealing with the issue, forcing provincial governments to fill the gap.

Attempts to clarify proper jurisdiction are often not successful, explains political scientist Richard Simeon.[75] In such a situation, lawyer Alan Pratt notes, "The inevitable result is of course either the denial of essential social programs or a dramatic increase in the provincial burden for them."[76] The provinces are, in general, reluctant to provide resources or services that may threaten their interest bases, and so any increase in service delivery has occurred with reluctance.[77] Ian G. Scott, then a minister in the Ontario government, writes that "the provinces ... tend historically to read the Constitutional provision both literally when it suits them and broadly when it suits them."[78] Thus, Scott argues, indeterminacy of jurisdiction has increased provinces' responsibilities, but the provinces have also used this indeterminacy to suit their agenda, often deflecting their responsibilities onto the federal government.

These complications concerning jurisdictional indeterminacy arise in Indigenous–Canadian state relations. Scholars Francis Abele and Katherine Graham write, "Federal inaction both prompts pragmatic responses from provincial and territorial governments concerned with meeting their statutory obligations and constrains provincial actions by heightening uncertainty, particularly about the all-important legal and fiscal relationship between the Government of Canada and Aboriginal peoples."[79] When the federal government does not make provisions, the flexible nature of federalism allows the provincial and territorial governments to compensate for the gap in service delivery or avoid doing so.

Radha Jhappan explains how this jurisdictional ambiguity has been used by provincial governments for settler benefit: "The provinces were happy to let responsibility for Aboriginal peoples rest in federal hands, while they enjoyed the economic and other benefits of the lands and resources appropriated from them."[80] Provincial governments often argue that they provide services to citizens equally; they do not provide "special" services to Indigenous Peoples. The internal tug-of-war between willing encroachment and unwilling devolution is evident in on-reserve provincial involvement. The provinces are often uninterested in deepening service delivery costs to Status Indians, which they argue is a federal responsibility. They are, however, interested in maintaining and expanding authority over natural resources as a source of wealth. These resources are often found on reserve lands, Treaty lands, and unceded ancestral lands. Once again, the structure of federalism has enabled the federal government to marginalize Indigenous Peoples' land ownership and sovereignty to create opportunities for the provinces to be involved in the control of Indigenous Peoples' lands. Land management and regulation is a key political incentive for the provinces to increase interaction between themselves and Indigenous Peoples.

These processes of decentralization, including both provincial encroachment and federal devolution, are further evidenced through the courts, which have significantly impacted how the provinces interpret their involvement in Indigenous-related matters in this competitive era of federalism. As scholars Katherine Graham, Frances Abele, and Caroline Dittburner illustrated in the 1990s, "Successive court decisions related to lands and title and to Aboriginal rights more generally made it evident to provincial governments that they could not ignore fundamental issues of lands, resources and governance."[81] In court cases about lands, title, and Aboriginal rights, the courts have found that the provinces cannot ignore and must engage in issues of lands, resources, and governance.[82] Such mechanisms of Canadian law encourage provincial encroachment in Indigenous politics.

Relatively recent court cases *Keewatin* (2014) and *Tsilhqot'in* (2014) have shifted the interpretation of provincial involvement in "Indians, and Lands reserved for the Indians."[83] Briefly, the *Delgamuukw* (1997) ruling clarified that Aboriginal title lands are as much a federal enclave as reserve lands.[84] Thus, provincial governments cannot breach the Indian Act, section 88, which maintains that provinces cannot single out Indians, dampen Indianness, trump federal jurisdiction, or overturn the tenets of Aboriginal rights. In the *Keewatin* decision concerning provincial resource use on Treaty 3 lands in Ontario, the court found that the province has the authority through section 88 to infringe on the Treaty for resource use, but the province then also bears the obligations associated with the duty to uphold the Treaty. The *Tsilhqot'in* decision concerns Aboriginal title in the interior of British Columbia, where Treaties do not exist and ancestral lands were not formally (as perceived by the state) ceded, and the title thus remains unextinguished. The ruling states that Aboriginal title for the Indigenous Nations that do not hold Treaty applies to swaths of lands, not parcels or "dots" of land.

The *Keewatin* and *Tsilhqot'in* cases changed the landscape for provincial activity on Indigenous lands. Legal scholars Nigel Bankes and Jennifer Koshan argue that the *Tsilhqot'in* decision has "eviscerated the lands reserved head of s.91(24)" and dismissed the *Delgamuukw* decision on the division of powers over land, which limits the constitutional protection of Aboriginal title lands afforded by section 91(24) and the jurisdictional immunity provided by *Delgamuukw*.[85] The *Tsilhqot'in* decision does, however, constrain the provinces' control of natural resource development by affirming the strength of Aboriginal title.[86] It can be argued that by strengthening Aboriginal title, the case ruling diminishes both federal and provincial dominion. However, it has been further argued that this case, in some ways, continues to reproduce legal settler colonial narratives that serve settler interests at the expense of Indigenous Peoples' sovereignty.

Looking closely at this ruling, Bankes and Koshan ask several probing questions: Is this limit protection enabled by section 91(24) for the Aboriginal title or "lands reserved" from provincial encroachment through section 88? Or does *Tsilhqot'in* make section 88 obsolete? Although it will take time to test the decision's legal weight concerning the division of powers, Bankes and Koshan argue that *Tsilhqot'in* provides the provinces with new legal parameters: "By focusing on the judicially created justifiable infringement test rather than inapplicability, *Tsilhqot'in* will allow a province to argue the justifiability of the application of its provincial resource laws (e.g. forestry, mining, and oil and gas legislation) to title lands in each and every case rather than dealing with applicability at a more principled level."[87] In this way, the provinces can argue for provincial activity on Aboriginal title lands through the wider subjective and discretionary justification for infringement instead of a narrower proof of justified applicability.

Other scholars similarly argue that *Tsilhqot'in* diminishes the protection that First Nations had from provincial interference.[88] For example, Michael McCrossan and Kiera Ladner argue that *Tsilhqot'in* recognizes Aboriginal title under section 35 of the Constitution Act, 1982, and provides Indigenous Peoples with greater decision-making control over their lands, but does little to shift power from the federal and provincial governments to Indigenous Nations so they can exercise their legal orders (section 35 Aboriginal rights) on their lands.[89] The authors argue that that the court's limited ability to see beyond federal and provincial laws "fundamentally undercuts" Indigenous legal orders, including ancestral legal systems and those written into section 35.[90] Further, the court is unable to fully acknowledge Indigenous legal orders because doing so would expose the illegitimacy of the Crown's sovereignty, which forms the basis for the court's legitimacy. The *Tsilhqot'in* decision continues to favour the powers of the federal and provincial governments at the expense of Indigenous Peoples' Inherent rights.

There are many different aspects of Canadian federalism beyond those mentioned here. Some aspects, such as fiscal federalism or executive federalism, focus on the financial and intergovernmental relations between the federal and provincial governments, which are beyond the scope of this analysis. Others, such as asymmetrical federalism, accommodate political entities by providing access within the federation, though they sustain uneven distributions of power.[91] I conclude this overview of federalism by emphasizing the consequences of the decentralization within competitive federalism. Devolution and encroachment demonstrate settler colonial intent to facilitate settler benefit at the expense of Indigenous Peoples. As Papillon writes, "Not insignificantly, Indigenous people have long been, and continue to be, collateral victims of the competitive nature of Canada federalism."[92]

The prevailing narrative of Canadian federalism reinforces the idea that Indigenous-related matters fall primarily under federal jurisdiction, despite the provinces increasingly asserting their role in these issues. This misconception is largely due to the historical federal monopoly in Indigenous-related policymaking.[93] The ambiguity of contemporary jurisdictional arrangements also contributes to the lack of formal recognition of the governance relationship between the provincial governments and Status First Nations people living on-reserve. Robert Exell writes that the provinces "continue to cling to the notion of federal Constitutional responsibility" regardless of which government level provides the services.[94] This narrative, however, ignores the ongoing processes of devolution and encroachment that are part of contemporary federalism, as well as constitutional and legislative imperatives and Indigenous Peoples' political autonomy.

Opportunities for Indigenous Sovereignty?

Contemporary expressions of federalism that shift and increase provincial activity on First Nations reserves present various opportunities and outcomes for Indigenous Nations and communities across what has become Canada. Leaning on the assumption of federal authority through section 91(24) of the BNA Act, provinces often neglect or deny their involvement in Indigenous politics, despite having constitutional, legislative, and judicial responsibilities to Indigenous Peoples. Political and economic interests can contribute to provincial encroachment and federal devolution. The changing nature of Canadian federalism thus also affects the colonial relationship between Indigenous Peoples and the structures of Canadian governance. Some Indigenous Peoples might argue that the increased involvement of provincial governments threatens their sovereignty and rights. In contrast, others view the provincial government as an important and needed source of funding support.

Any political relationship with the provinces can jeopardize Indigenous sovereignty, which is based on nation-to-nation relationships, as recognized by the Royal Proclamation of 1763 and the Treaties, which were made with the federal Crown. Arguments against devolution are generally based on concerns that provincial relations might dampen federal relations, including fiduciary responsibility, increase assimilation through section 88 of the Indian Act, or impede sovereignty movements. Many Indigenous Peoples understand their sovereignty as better served by negotiating with the federal government.[95] Long and Boldt write that if the relationship between First Nations and the federal government is characterized as "special,"[96] then the relationship between First Nations and the provinces is "tenuous."[97]

When the federal government attempts to transfer responsibility for First Nations to the provinces, significant opposition often emerges from Indigenous communities. A notable example, as discussed, is the White Paper (1969), which proposed federal devolution to the provinces and was met with outrage from Indigenous Peoples.[98] In response, a movement led by Harold Cardinal produced the document *Citizens Plus,* also known as the Red Paper, which countered the White Paper with a series of recommendations developed by Indigenous leadership and communities. This strong opposition forced the Canadian government to withdraw the White Paper. Consequently, the White Paper marked the beginning of a new phase of resistance not only against devolution but also against the suppression of Indigenous rights. This activism ultimately contributed to the inclusion of section 35 recognizing Aboriginal and Treaty rights in the Constitution Act of 1982.[99] Opposition to devolution has played a vital role in advancing the recognition of Aboriginal rights in Canadian law, emphasizing the colonial-based power dynamics between the jurisdiction of the settler colonial state and the rights and sovereignty of Indigenous Peoples.

Indigenous Peoples have voiced concern that increased provincial engagement could endanger their cultural survival. This risk arises when Indigenous Peoples' nationhood — recognized in nation-to-nation relations — is undermined by provincial relations. In response to these concerns, the Penner Report recommended that the federal government use its authority under section 91(24) to completely exempt Indian reserves from provincial laws.[100] Due to the historical pattern of colonial erosion of Indigenous autonomy, Indigenous Peoples are often suspicious of provincial encroachment, or concerned it will jeopardize or even nullify their rights.[101] Arguably, provincial interference could weaken the negotiating power of First Nations and further reduce the federal government's obligations to those living on-reserve or diminish an Indigenous Nation's authority over the reserve's management and band governance.[102] As Calder explains, "A central consideration for Indians was the reduced Indian control implicit in moving from the normal pattern of bilateral relations with the federal government to a tripartite process in which the other two parties (federal government and provinces) had the decisive say on amendments."[103] For instance, some argue that section 88 of the Indian Act weakens the status conferred by section 91(24) of the BNA Act because it allows provincial governments to extend their legislative jurisdiction over First Nations in ways that the Canadian government would not allow in other federally authorized areas.[104] A specific example is the case *Dick v. R.* (1985), which was one of the first instances in which the courts expanded provincial regulatory authority concerning hunting on Treaty lands.[105]

Due to the changing political arrangements resulting from decentralization and concerns for broader Indigenous liberation, Indigenous Peoples' support for provincial involvement in Indigenous-related matters ranges from naught to little. In some instances, Indigenous groups argue that no Canadian government jurisdiction ought to apply as Indigenous Peoples' inherent sovereignty stands.[106] In this sense, Indigenous Peoples "generally 'want out' " of these federalist arrangements.[107] As Murphy explains, "Aboriginal leaders must also contend with the fact that their communities continue to harbour significant levels of mistrust of Canadian governments, and the motivations underlying federal Aboriginal policy."[108] This considerable distrust has built because the provinces and federal government have not historically honoured Treaty rights and Aboriginal rights and title in disputes over hunting, fishing, and gathering.[109] One example is the decades-long *Tsilhqot'in* trials, which demonstrated the province did not honour Indigenous ancestral lands through its enforcement of provincial laws in these areas.

There are Indigenous Nations, including Nations and band governments, that have cooperative political relationships with provincial governments. For instance, some Indigenous groups do enter into tripartite arrangements or double bilateral arrangements, allowing them to establish separate and direct connections with both the province and federal government.[110] In Canada, there are many examples of agreements with provinces, such as benefit-sharing agreements, self-government agreements, or service delivery agreements. Other Indigenous groups are willing to deal with the Crown as a unified entity that includes both the federal and provincial governments.[111] Additionally, some Indigenous groups seek tripartite agreements among Indigenous, provincial, and federal governments to increase fiscal support for projects or other publicly funded initiatives. Furthermore, because provincial governments deliver many services to reserve communities and have jurisdiction over vast amounts of land in Canada through the BNA Act's section 109 and the natural resource transfer agreements of 1930, provincial involvement can be essential for resolving jurisdictional conflicts related to self-government agreements.

In some instances, increased provincial presence in an area traditionally thought to be a federal responsibility might be supported by some Indigenous Nations. In fact, given the constitutional arrangement, provinces must be at the table for some matters of natural resource management. A notable example of a favourable intergovernmental agreement is the Saskatchewan Indigenous Investment Finance Corporation. This Crown corporation of the Saskatchewan government provides investment funding to Indigenous Nations in the province, explicitly targeting the natural resource and agricultural sectors.[112] Increasingly across Canada, these types of investment funds are operating at the federal and provincial levels.

In this era of shifting federalism, some argue that there are Indigenous Nations that have successfully enhanced their decision-making authority and taken on a more prominent role in service delivery through the decentralization of the state. According to Graham, Abele, and Dittburner, the political discourse between the state and Indigenous Peoples has become more institutionalized and formalized over time. This change increases the role and legitimacy of Indigenous governments and enhances their control over implementation of programs.[113] Decentralization has also improved Indigenous governments' capabilities in intergovernmental relations.[114] As a result, inclusion of Indigenous-centred directives in government documents has grown,[115] transforming the relationship between the federal government and Indigenous Peoples from one of "control" to a "government-to-government" relationship.[116] Political scientist Gabrielle A. Slowey argues that devolution benefits Indigenous Peoples by enhancing their decision-making power within communities.[117] Papillon points out the advantages of increased control over programming.[118] For instance, data on the decentralization of health services in Indigenous communities shows that health outcomes improve when these services are under community control, highlighting the effectiveness of Indigenous governance.[119]

The decentralization process in Canadian federalism has expanded the range of variables and actors involved, notably enhancing the role of Indigenous Nations. However, there are still ongoing challenges. Papillon illustrates a central concern: Although decentralization promotes Indigenous decision-making and community-centred service provision, it does not equate to Indigenous sovereignty. He writes, "Without formal status as federal partners, Indigenous peoples have no statutory voice in the shared-rule institutions of the Canadian federation."[120] Additionally, although decentralization can empower Indigenous governments to administer programs, it does not change their legal and constitutional status or the division of powers within the federation.[121] Consequently, Indigenous governments often experience an increased reliance on both federal and provincial governments, as the capacity to deliver services frequently depends on these levels of government, along with their accountability and reporting requirements.[122]

As Canadian federalism evolves, the challenges of indeterminacy resulting from devolution have contributed to new pressures on Indigenous-centred governance matters. The expanding role of provinces, informed by court interpretations and legislation, can lead to overlap that creates double-aspect laws, which in turn limit Indigenous jurisdiction.[123] Cardinal argues that section 91(24) of the BNA Act was intended to protect Indigenous rights from provincial encroachment; however, its enforcement has been weak. Provinces have increasingly applied their statutes to Indigenous Peoples and Indian reserves through provincial game and conservation laws, sometimes superseding Treaty rights.[124] Additionally, funding and service delivery vacuums have arisen, leaving First Nations communities struggling to finance essential services.[125]

A Juncture for Reconciliation

Canadian federalism is flexible and evolving, moving through colonial, classic, collaborative, constitutional, and competitive models, as well as neoliberal practices of decentralization and devolution. These federalist organizations of power show colonial intent, even in the era of devolution. Practices of devolution arguably put decision-making powers more squarely in the hands of Indigenous Nations. Here, the analytical framework of Glen Coulthard's politics of recognition is integral for seeing through the illusionary work of the Canadian state, which has used these types of opportunities to draw Indigenous Peoples further into the state through assimilation tactics.[126] Coulthard explains that the Canadian state has modified relations with Indigenous Peoples from outright assimilation and genocidal tactics to a focus on the *"recognition* and *accommodation"* of Indigenous Peoples' political agency.[127] He writes, "Regardless of this modification, however, the relationship between Indigenous peoples and the state has remained colonial to its foundation."[128] In this evaluation of state-Indigenous relations, the state, intent on a continuation of settler-based interests, animates continued colonial dominance behind a veneer of Indigenous empowerment.

An examination of how settler colonial narratives of federalism overlook provincial responsibilities demonstrates how the provinces evade responsibilities for Indigenous Peoples. Moreover, the default practice of Canadian federalism — to ask if a matter falls under federal or provincial authority — neglects Indigenous Peoples' sovereignty. Changes to federalist power sharing and the increasing involvement of the provinces in Indigenous policy matters — often in ways that favour the provinces — further complicate the path to reconciliation. Yet Indigenous political agency can prevail: Canadian governance is marked by Indigenous sovereignties that are exercised through a variety of political avenues, including Indigenous rights expressions and service delivery.

CHAPTER FIVE

BEYOND SETTLER COLONIAL FEDERALISM

How can those mechanics of federalism that intend colonial domination of Indigenous Peoples be shaped differently in a spirit of reconciliation? There are a range of alternative political arrangements to borrow from, including constitutional politics, domestic and international politics, and Indigenous resurgence movements. By placing the query within broader scholarship, I intend to take up the flexibility of the federalist political system to cover a range of perspectives on how reconciliation might frame federalist power sharing to ensure Indigenous Peoples' autonomy is enhanced, restored, or rebuilt.

Some of the alternative approaches, however, are accommodationist. By this, I mean approaches to the federalist system marked by little to no transformative structural change. These approaches may make (marginally) new and different kinds of space within the political system for continued colonial power relations. In this chapter, I look at three prominent examples: mini-municipalities, adapted federalism, and trilateral federalism. Overall, these alternative political frameworks do little more than reframe colonial oppression and mask ongoing colonial dispossession, as highlighted in Glen Coulthard's critique of the Canadian government and its politics of recognition.[1] There are, however, additional examples that I do not explore. One example is multinational federalism, an approach in which social diversities are considered in the division of powers to empower minority nations and large ethnic groups. Political scientists Alain-G. Gagnon and Arjun Tremblay have explored multinational federalism and the benefits and limitations of its application to support social diversities, finding that multinational federalism has neglected the specific concerns of Indigenous Peoples.[2]

Moving away from accommodationist approaches, I consider perspectives on decolonizing the federalist system. For example, Joyce Green argues that the structure of federalism does not allow meaningful communication between Indigenous governments and provincial and federal governments.[3] She writes, "Canadian federalism permits conversations and negotiations between the national and provincial governments but there are no formalized mechanisms to allow this with Aboriginal governments. This leads to often tense and charged standoffs."[4] In order to ensure political and social change is meaningful, Green argues that the institutions and processes of the Canadian state must be Indigenized as a restructuring mechanism to better support Indigenous Peoples' self-determination. To illustrate a decolonizing approach, I look at the postcolonial potential of Treaty federalism, which is largely championed by Indigenous scholars James (Sákéj) Youngblood Henderson and Kiera Ladner.

Next, I consider some approaches to the federalist power-sharing model and reconciliation that suggest more radical measures of decolonial transformation. For example, international relations scholar Ajay Parasram's concept of pluriversal sovereignties challenges Eurocentric state-centric concepts of sovereignty, making space for Indigenous sovereignties in federalist political contexts.[5] Leanne Betasamosake Simpson similarly emphasizes challenging the Canadian state. She turns to resurgent Indigenous knowledge and political systems to shape relations between Indigenous Peoples and settler society in Canada, with or without the Canadian state.[6] Resurgent politics, she suggests, can exist alongside or replace the systems of the colonial order.

The broad range of perspectives that exist in scholarship is complemented by the political acumen of Indigenous Nations at the community level. In my experience, there is always more fruitful, gritty, alive, and compelling political interpretation and explanation on the ground. Reconciling federalism is a political project reflected in scholarship, community, or the interchange of these locations. I also know that reconciliation can fall short. It can be applied and led by actors with vacuous notions of colonial struggle with little real intention to create positive change. However, I see tremendous effort and funding committed to reconciliation. In this latter sense, reconciliation has some staying power. I hope it holds some normative potential to effect, at minimum, incremental changes to enhance Canadians' understanding of the truth and, preferably, justice for Indigenous Peoples living under settler colonialism.

Accommodationist Models

The historical course of imperial-turned-settler colonial relations has indeed limited Indigenous Peoples' ability to exercise political autonomies, but it has not extinguished Indigenous Inherent rights, section 35 Aboriginal rights, and Treaty rights. The Canadian legal system, despite the burdens of the settler colonial present, continues to recognize and affirm Indigenous Peoples' sovereignty in some ways. Today, Aboriginal rights are understood by the Canadian legal system as unique (*sui generis*), and they are thus protected from interference.[7] Some models for better accommodating Aboriginal rights can be seen as attempting to integrate Indigenous Peoples more fully into the settler colonial present, which often leads to assimilation and the erasure of Indigenous difference. These accommodationist approaches compromise the sovereignty of Indigenous Peoples by subordinating it to the Canadian state. Such models do not move us beyond the framework of settler colonial federalism; rather, they serve as starting points. From here, we can explore alternative understandings that emphasize the agency of Indigenous Nations and envision a decolonial future for Canada.

Three accommodationist models are prevalent in domestic scholarship that proposes alternative federalist relations with Indigenous Peoples. The first model suggests transforming Indigenous reserve communities into "mini-municipalities" within the current federalist mode. This change would presumably advance existing degrees of self-determination by, in part, freeing Indigenous Nations that operate under the close oversight of the Department of Indian Affairs.[8] This concept was introduced in the White Paper (the *Statement of the Government of Canada on Indian Policy, 1969*, discussed in Chapter 4) and appeared again in the proposed First Nations Governance Act, 2002, which sought to convert First Nations communities into municipalities with "limited authority and no autonomous jurisdiction."[9]

Critics of this approach point out that turning Indigenous reserve communities into municipalities is "federalism as usual."[10] It is part of the Canadian government's ongoing effort to assimilate Indigenous Peoples, specifically First Nations. Kiera Ladner and Michael Orsini write that the First Nations Governance Act, "constitutes a new form of colonial rule in which the federal government is dictating, once again, the terms and conditions of Aboriginal governance."[11] This approach fails to acknowledge the realities of First Nations reserve communities, which often have a citizenship base living off-reserve. It also ignores those Métis and Inuit communities that do not operate as reserves. It is not, therefore, a universally applicable approach. In practice, it would place First Nations reserve communities under provincially generated legislation, restricting governance through provincial regulation. Consequently, it would fail to establish an equitable nation-to-nation governance model between Indigenous Nations and the Crown and instead reinforce a power dynamic that perpetuates settler colonial domination over Indigenous Nations, undermining reconciliation efforts.

Adapted federalism is the second accommodationist model of alternative federalist arrangements. This approach is a modest adaptation of Canadian federalism, suggesting that Indigenous Peoples should have a specific designated "new public government," whether a territory or province state.[12] A notable example of this approach is the Nunavut Land Claims Agreement, which was signed in 1993 and helped create the territory of Nunavut in 1999.[13] Although Nunavut is not exclusively designated for Indigenous populations, the population is majority Inuit, and Indigenous leaders describe it as Aboriginal self-government on a territorial scale.

The premise of adapted federalism presents significant improbabilities. Indigenous Peoples and Nations represent small populations, are geographically dispersed across the country, and have different languages, cultures, and other ways of being.[14] The notion of creating an Indigenous-specific public government overlooks Indigenous Peoples' deep connections to ancestral lands and homelands. This approach, furthermore, cannot accommodate the enormous diversity of Indigenous Peoples throughout Canada.[15] It is premised on a Eurocentric and assimilative agenda, which today could be seen as having a genocidal intent to erase and nullify Indigenous difference. Resembling a colonial-minded project, this approach seeks to relocate people, though conceptually rather than physically. This idea has historical parallels with Canada's various forced relocation initiatives, including the Sayisi Dene in Northern Manitoba and the nation-wide reserve system, which have led to human rights violations. Adapted federalism threatens to undermine the Aboriginal rights recognized by the Canadian state.

Finally, a long-standing idea in Canada is trilateral federalism, which involves a third house or order of government in the Canadian federation. An Indigenous third house of government has been proposed several times, including by the Penner Report (1983), the Charlottetown Accord (1992), and the RCAP (1996).[16] In this model, Indigenous Nations would be granted exclusive jurisdiction over certain areas and given substantial political authority.[17]

Advocates argue that this third order of government, with its enhanced political power, would lead to improved socioeconomic conditions for Indigenous Peoples in Canada.[18] This third order of government would create a platform for self-government — an inherent right of Indigenous Peoples that has never been relinquished — that operates alongside federal and provincial governments (nation-to-nation relations). Rather than viewing these provisions as a constitutional basis of federal control, they can be understood as a foothold for securing Indigenous political agency.

Critics argue that trilateral federalism would further envelop Indigenous Peoples in Canadian institutions, rather than acknowledging them as sovereign nations.[19] They contend that this model may lack the legitimacy and political weight necessary to support the political agency of Indigenous Peoples. For example, scholar Meaghan Anne Williams writes, "By 'joining' Canadian federalism, Indigenous Nations in a third-order model would become subject to the Constitution which could, by extension, undermine the legitimacy of their claims to distinctive sovereignty and self-government."[20] These critiques highlight

---

Forced Relocation

The Sayisi Dene are a First Nation who traditionally lived in what is now Northern Manitoba and Northwest Territories and followed the caribou migration. In 1956, the Canadian government relocated them to Churchill, Manitoba, disrupting their long-standing connection to their ancestral territory and way of life as caribou hunters. This move forced them into state dependency. In the 1970s they returned to their ancestral territories at Tadoule Lake, working diligently to reclaim their self-sufficiency through hunting and other ancestral practices. By 1995, they had successfully taken over healthcare, education, and other community service delivery from the Department of Indian Affairs.[21]

significant concerns for the viability and effectiveness of trilateral federalism and efforts to reconcile the power imbalances within the Canadian federalist structure.

Does the federalist system provide a mechanism in settler Canadian law to implement the existing right of Indigenous sovereignty to support a third order of government? There are arguments on both sides. Francis Abele and Michael J. Prince argue it does not because, for example, the Constitution Act, 1982, section 35 does not recognize an Indigenous order of government.[22] The RCAP takes a differing position: "We have come to the conclusion that the inherent right of self-government is one of the 'existing Aboriginal and Treaty rights' recognized and affirmed by section 35 of the Constitution Act, 1982."[23] The RCAP explains that, in federalist systems of governance, the provincial and federal levels of government are autonomous, and the federal government cannot derogate provincial laws. For the RCAP, this model offers a framework for Indigenous self-government, where autonomous levels of government can coexist side-by-side or nation-to-nation, as they did in the early years of imperial colonialism. The RCAP further states, "So the federal/provincial relationship provides a model for many of the features that would characterize a sound relationship between Aboriginal governments and federal and provincial governments.[24] However, the RCAP's position has been critiqued by those arguing it perpetuates self-administration instead of establishing a stronger derivative of self-government.[25]

Legal scholar Brian Slattery further argues that section 91(24) of the BNA Act provides a legal authority for settler Canada to recognize Aboriginal self-governments in the Canadian state.[26] He demonstrates that the existing sovereign status of Indigenous Peoples, as recorded by various Treaties and the Royal Proclamation of 1763, is built into the BNA Act, 1867, section 91(24) and the Canadian Constitution Act, 1982, section 35. Slattery argues that the Treaties and the Royal Proclamation recognize Indigenous Peoples' Inherent rights; this recognition does not petrify and is carried forward.[27] These founding documents were used to develop the BNA Act, section 91(24); thus, it stands to reason that this entrenched sovereignty is also built into section 91(24). The Constitution Act, 1982, section 35 "recognizes and affirms existing Aboriginal rights."[28] This extension of recognized sovereignty opens a legal doorway for Indigenous self-government.

Some members of Indigenous communities suggest that Indigenous governments have the potential to develop into or scaffold such a third order of government. For example, federal Indigenous political institutions exist, including the Assembly of First Nations, Métis National Council, and Inuit Tapiriit Kanatami, with similar political organizations at the provincial level where appropriate. In a sense, these political organizations are structured in a federated model. Yet for a third order of government to be feasible, it is not enough for it to be provided for in the Constitution, whether through section 35 or section 91(24), or to have a federated model in place. Genuine political will from Indigenous Peoples and the settler state and society is also essential for its success.

These accommodationist approaches show how domestic political theory has attempted to mitigate the colonial oppression of Indigenous peoples. However, these approaches would result in opportunities for cooptation and continued colonial exploitation. Arguably, adding a third order of government could produce transformative change in the federation; whether this change would support the political autonomy of sovereignty that Indigenous Peoples envision remains unclear. Overall, these approaches tell us very little about how to mitigate settler colonial narratives with tangible opportunities for reconciliation.

Treaty Federalism

One alternative to the current jurisdictional arrangement in Canada is Treaty federalism, a unique approach to governance premised on the Treaties and federalism. This constitutional arrangement does not, importantly, demand that Indigenous Peoples surrender to the colonial order and instead respects their unique (*sui generis*) and independent legal orders — which are distinct and do not derive from Canadian colonial systems.[29] This emphasis on respect for Indigenous legal orders is central to Treaty federalism.

Treaty federalism, as explained by Henderson, is a postcolonial framework for Indigenous–settler state governance relations that can mitigate the settler state's basic equation of settler benefit at Indigenous expense. In this framework, Henderson writes, Indigenous Peoples in Canada "affirm the right to *sui generis* orders and kinship bonds, treaty federalism and its shared subjecthood, and the ability of these rights and powers to converge with older colonial powers in dynamic modern reconciliations to create a postcolonial society."[30] Postcolonialism is often misunderstood as meaning the colonial presence is abolished. In fact, postcolonial theory reveals that the colonial presence is never fully vanquished: Elements remain that can never be fully mitigated — or removed — from the decolonized political unit's language, culture, and political institutions.[31] Instead, postcolonialism refers to the elimination of external colonial dominance, while an internal colonial presence remains, which is the focus of resistance and abolition.

Treaty federalism is a postcolonial approach because it brings together — "converges" — both Indigenous and settler understandings of law in a way that is not premised on colonial exploitation, despite the presence of the colonial order. In this way, Treaty federalism is deeply rooted in Indigenous Peoples' concepts of political organization and also based on the Canadian legal system. Treaty federalism is grounded in Indigenous concepts of federalism and constitutionalism, which predate European occupation. These concepts can be illustrated by the Haudenosaunee (Hodinohso:ni) Nation, or the Iroquois Confederation, which had a well-developed federal system of governance that influenced the development of the US federation.[32] They can also be illustrated by Cree/nēhiyawēwin oral histories of Treaty with the Crown.[33] Across the Canadian Prairies, Indigenous Nations understand Treaty as continuing "as long as the sun shines, the waters flow, and the grass grows."[34] This statement points to the ongoing and evolving status of Treaty. Indigenous Nations across what has become Canada have oral histories that similarly demonstrate these kinds of precontact political orders. Treaty federalism is fundamentally based on these long-standing *sui generis* Indigenous legal orders.[35]

Postcolonialism or Anticolonialism?

Postcolonialism is a theoretical analysis of imperial colonial powers. Decolonization — in the sense of colonized territories gaining independence from colonial powers — occurred at various times across the globe. As nations established their independence, it became apparent that remnants of colonial order persisted in government structures, economic systems, social orders, and cultural domains. Postcolonialism explores the consequences of decolonization, including ongoing power structures of inequality. It differs from anticolonialism, which refers to political action that operates independently of colonial structures or systems. Anticolonialism empowers Indigenous Peoples to enact political decision-making without colonial influences; it is an expression of political agency through Indigenous difference, influenced by ancestral knowledge systems.

Treaty federalism is based, too, on the Canadian legal system because it is premised primarily on Treaty relations, which Ladner explains are the "foundational law" in Canada[36] given their place in the Constitution and thus federalism. Treaties can be understood as a diplomatic mechanism that allows Canada to exist; thus, they form the basis of Canadian laws.[37] Today there is growing appreciation for the overwhelming evidence that the Canadian state and Crown have not lived up to their Treaty obligations.[38] Scholars such as Sheldon Krasowski demonstrate that the settler society and state have come to misinterpret Treaty as a surrender of Indigenous lands instead of an agreement for sharing land and resources for equal benefit, with evidence that the settler state deliberately engaged in manipulation as part of an extinguishment policy designed to undermine Indigenous sovereignty and exploit lands for settler gains.[39] In fact, Krasowski's work shows that the surrender clause in Treaties, whereby Indigenous Peoples allegedly ceded their land, was not discussed in negotiations. Indigenous oral histories are testimony to the promises made during Treaty negotiations, often described as the "spirit and intent of the Treaties," that are not reflected in the written records.[40] In fact, Treaty Commissioner Alexander Morris, who negotiated Treaties 3 to 6 and renegotiated Treaties 1 and 2, noted these inconsistencies in his personal journal, and his assistant (secretary) made note of them as well.[41] As Indigenous scholar Sharon Venne writes, "Actually, all of North America is Indigenous land. At the time of the treaty making, Indigenous Peoples never gave up the land."[42] Even with this ongoing colonial legacy of neglect, the Treaties remain foundational to Canada, and the political obligations under these agreements remain.

Traditionally used in both Indigenous and Euro-Canadian political systems, treaties are governance and diplomatic practices embedded in normative political systems. Henderson explains that the Treaty rights of Indigenous Peoples, based on Indigenous customary laws and traditions, are independent of common law but vested in Canada's constitutional order.[43] Therefore, Treaty federalism is built on Indigenous legal tradition, and because the Crown recognizes Treaties, Treaty federalism can work with Canadian constitutionalism and common law. Abele and Prince further demonstrate that the constitutional underpinnings of Canadian federalism support Treaty federalism, with the Treaty of Niagara of 1764 as an example of Treaty federalism in practice.[44] The Two-Row Wampum Belt of the Treaty of Niagara illustrates the concept of

Treaty federalism in that it depicts the European powers and Indigenous Nations on distinct paths but existing side-by-side. As civil servant Liam Nohr states, "At its foundation, treaty federalism acknowledges that before and after contact with settlers, Indigenous Peoples retained their sovereignty and nationhood through negotiated treaties."[45]

As an approach to Indigenous-state governance relations, Treaty federalism renews the nation-to-nation relationship. According to Ladner, "Treaty federalism is an agreed on framework for the mutual coexistence of two sovereign entities within the same territory."[46] It affirms Indigenous autonomy by recognizing that Indigenous Nations are sovereign nations that exercised self-government prior to the Canadian state (as captured by the Royal Proclamation of 1763). Abele and Prince explain that Treaty federalism acknowledges the historical nature of Indigenous Nations' sovereignty and distinct approaches to culture and governance.[47] Through this model of federalism, Indigenous Nations maintain their sovereignty: "A First Nation does not 'join' federalism, instead it is a sovereign nation that has relations with the Crown in Canada, and this relationship is defined by a treaty."[48]

Treaty federalism presents a powerful framework for fostering reconciliation within the context of the Canadian settler colonial narrative. By reaffirming pre-existing Indigenous sovereignties through Treaties in settler states,[49] for example, this approach can enable "reciprocal processes of external recognition with Indigenous legal orders."[50] Consequently, the Canadian state is provided with another opportunity to recognize Indigenous political orders within a federalist structure. Ultimately, Treaty federalism revives the nation-to-nation diplomacy outlined in the Royal Proclamation of 1763, the Treaties, the BNA Act of 1867, and the Constitution Act of 1982, promoting mutual recognition rather than political dispossession and subjugation.[51]

In practice, Treaty federalism requires an investment in political administration and institutional development to support it.[52] Williams outlines four operational components to support Treaty federalism, including Aboriginal electoral districts and reserved legislative seats, an Aboriginal Lands and Treaty Tribunal, a House of First Peoples, and intergovernmental relations and multilevel governance.[53] For Williams, these pieces alone will not necessarily bring about postcolonial or reconciliatory change, but they support Indigenous decision-making. In this discussion of operational components, we see elements of postcolonialism: The state has a legal framework to support Treaty federalism, but institutional infrastructure is also required. This infrastructure could be built from anticolonial frameworks, but Coulthard's warning about the cooptation of the Canadian state through recognition politics arises. Ultimately, this warning is central to Williams' insistence that the architecture of Treaty federalism be constructed under Indigenous Peoples' guidance.

Additional challenges to the implementation of Treaty federalism are a reminder that this approach does not offer a clear-cut road to reconciliation. Treaty, according to Mills, is "arguably the most complex kind of model for indigenous-settler reconciliation because of its myriad usages."[54] Treaty is understood in different ways: It can be a contract between communities, or a form of interacting relationships.[55] Contracts are static and can have power differentials, whereas relationships are ever-evolving and ought to be based on mutual needs and interests. The Canadian settler project often reverts to an understanding of Treaty as a surrender of Indigenous lands, whereas Indigenous Peoples understand Treaty as a formalized relationship of coexistence. Conflicting understandings of Treaty in Canada and the long history of the settler state not meeting its Treaty obligations are a challenge to Treaty federalism and reconciliation efforts.

Another challenge to Treaty federalism is the lack of political will to support it across the Canadian government and much of Canadian society.[56] As mentioned, it will require extensive resources such as time, finances, and new administrative infrastructure. Nohr and others remind us that institutional change must be accompanied by societal structural changes, too: "Reconciliation through the bounds of Constitutional change must be accommodated with societal change."[57] Without social and political support, Treaty federalism is largely unachievable.

Some critics of Treaty federalism have argued that multilevel governance would be a more suitable approach for addressing Indigenous-settler relations. Multilevel governance is arguably a federalist system that brings more actors — including community-based voices and non-state actors — into decision-making practices to mitigate conflict, whereas Treaty federalism may be understood as a top-down governance approach.[58] Multilevel governance is evident in land claims, self-government agreements, court rulings on duty to consult, and the growth of federal, provincial, and Indigenous collaborative processes.[59]

It is based on power divisions between vertical levels of government, which enhances autonomous decision-making at the community level. Multilevel governance "seeks to manage conflict by explicitly recognizing and protecting national identities, mainly through the territorial division of multiple nations within a single state."[60] However, critics argue that while multilevel governance recognizes and accommodates diversity, it does not adequately support Indigenous autonomy.[61] Additionally, a multinational approach can promote a pan-Indigenous view, which oversimplifies and minimizes the distinct identities of different Indigenous Peoples. By recognizing national identities, this framework also has the potential to undermine the role of provinces, thereby weakening their position within the federation.[62]

Another alternative to Treaty federalism is interstate federalism. This approach organizes relations between different orders of government, includes formal interactions between government officials, and ensures the provinces remain strong players in the federation.[63] It is understood by some to support Indigenous Nations in government-centred decision-making processes. Papillon writes that "Indigenous policy is now a multiactor and multilevel affair,"[64] a development that increased under Justin Trudeau's Liberal government.[65] At this time, intergovernmental relations have undeniably strengthened the presence of Indigenous Nations in various state decision-making forums. However, although interstate federalism increases the involvement of Indigenous Peoples in decision-making, it does so without providing a formal status to them as partners in the federation, limiting Indigenous Nations' roles in shared-rule governance.[66]

Ultimately, the greatest challenge for the implementation of Treaty federalism is working with the Canadian state in ways that do not oppress Indigenous Peoples or co-opt its potential. Critics have argued that Treaty federalism would bring Indigenous Nations and the provinces into more deeply enmeshed relationships with the settler state.[67] A similar critique is made of trilateral federalism and the third order of government. Moreover, Nohr explains that the diversity of Indigenous Peoples limits the possibilities of Treaty federalism.[68] Not all Indigenous Peoples in Canada are in a Treaty relationship with the Crown. And when the province replaces the Crown at the negotiating table, it complicates and strains the self-determination of Indigenous Nations. Additionally, jurisdictional football can occur as powers change from federal to provincial orders — one order of government refuses responsibility and kicks it to a different order of government, which also refuses to accept it and tosses it back to the original governing order, and so on. These kinds of tactics related to jurisdictional delineations — which "remain as acute as before"[69] — can have deleterious impacts on Indigenous Nations.

While federalism has been conceived to dispossess Indigenous Peoples of decision-making powers within the colonial state, some argue that the Treaties provide opportunities to exercise Indigenous agency within the federalist system. Williams, for example, has argued that the Treaty relationship is a foundational element of the Canadian state's approach to reconciliation.[70] Henderson and Ladner argue that Treaty federalism is crucial for Indigenous agency. Certainly, Treaty federalism demonstrates the ongoing morass of the legacy of colonialism in the federalist system but also possible opportunities for postcolonial change.

Multiplural Sovereignty

Multiplural or pluriversal sovereignty is an approach that could be used to navigate reconciliation in the Canadian federalist model because it makes space for nonstate actors' sovereignty. Multiplural sovereignty conceptualizes different sovereign actors exerting their autonomous agency within an overarching shared political region. As Parasram describes it, "Pluri-versal sovereignty, I argue, describes enactments of sovereignty that emerge out of practices that may overlap with uni-versal sovereignty, but cannot be reduced to state territoriality and norms of land ownership."[71] In this approach, the capacity for self-determination is not hindered by the presence of other actors' expressions of agency. It is this shared autonomy among many actors that holds the potential for decolonization for Indigenous Peoples within the Canadian federalist model.

A central feature of multiplural sovereignty is that it disturbs the state-centric approach of the Westphalian international system through its inclusion of nonstate actors. The conceptualization of the state as the sovereign is a core understanding of the Westphalian international system. Accordingly, the state is the only political unit that holds sovereignty and is the central political actor in the international system. No political unit or actor is higher or has more authority than the state, and all internal or domestic units or actors are lesser than the state. Further, the legitimacy of the state is established through recognition by external states and internal actors. This model generally has no space for nonstate actors to hold sovereignty.

As a Eurocentric state model, the Westphalian international system relies on various colonial logics that are complicit with the erasure of Indigenous Peoples' political practices.[72] Eurocentric notions of state sovereignty, as Parasram writes, shape ideas of "land, property, and law" intersecting with racism.[73] We have looked at these intersections of Eurocentric racism as related to contact and Indigenous dispossession through federalist jurisdiction making. Indigenous scholar Katherine Walker (Okanese First Nation) argues that "colonial notions of sovereignty" have excluded Indigenous Peoples from Canadian federalism while maintaining "only two Constitutionally recognized levels of government" (federal and provincial), which continues today under the growing presence of intergovernmentalism.[74] Multiplural sovereignty challenges the Eurocentricism at the heart of the sovereign state.[75]

The state-centric approach is a relatively modern political conception. It developed through colonial expansion, in part supporting these practices of rule, domination, and exploitation. Importantly, early imperial colonial projects relied on multiplural legal structures or legalities of entanglement: "Here and elsewhere, imperial and local legalities overlapped, and imperial subjects navigated the different bodies of norms and jurisdictions, often choosing sites and norms beneficial for them individually and creating 'relational fields' of law along the way."[76] Thus, even as state-centric sovereignty evolved, there was recognition of Indigenous sovereignty and mutual sovereign coexistence. Scholar Stuart Christie describes this overlap and coexistence: "Once exercised by lawful sovereigns, even originally 'foreign' entitlements and languages have been welcomed, so long as they serve the local community (or sovereign) interest, however lawfully appointed custodians of a given tribe or band view it."[77] Colonial states have, as an example, varied in their recognition and respect for Indigenous Peoples' agency; there are long-standing forms of recognition of *sui generis* Indigenous legal orders, which are understood as distinct from the Canadian state.[78]

Scholars and grassroots advocates are increasingly pushing against a state-centric understanding of state sovereignty. As Sheryl R. Lightfoot explains, theorists are increasingly moving away from the Westphalian notion of sovereignty. Lightfoot writes, "I argue that some Indigenous practices of self-determination are actively decolonial and are ushering in a broadening and reshaping of its meaning that breaks through the strict, static state-centric construction of Westphalian sovereignty in order to make room for more nuanced, flexible, dynamic and negotiated forms."[79] This shift away from state-centric notions of sovereignty entails ongoing negotiation and engagement between peoples and states.

Indigenous Peoples have long asserted agency within the international system, significantly impacting the concept of state-centric sovereignty. One example is the achievement of UNDRIP. Changing pressures on the international system allow for a diverse range of political actors to participate at the global level, from individuals to multinational corporations and intergovernmental bodies. Parasram, for example, understands pluriversal sovereignty as creating space for practices of sovereignty that do not translate directly into the state-centric approach and instead exceed these reductive definitive parameters.[80] Indigenous sovereignty practices are grounded in culture, free from external interference, derived from the collective will of the community, situated in language and political application, and relational and fluid. Ultimately, these expressions of sovereignty not only disrupt state-centric notions of sovereignty but can also challenge the supreme sovereignty of the state: "The survival and resurgence of Indigenous legal orders and Constitutional traditions in Canada, as elsewhere in the world, disrupt the normative hegemony of the liberal state and articulate a Constitutionalism that accounts for a plurality of laws."[81]

A multiplural sovereignty approach could address the oppression that federalist jurisdiction imposes in settler colonial contexts. However, the constitutional founding of settler states typically sidelines Indigenous Peoples and their interests, posing a real challenge for multiplural sovereignty.[82] Although the sovereignty of Indigenous Peoples is not externally recognized (given with the restrictions of the Westphalia state model), they assert rights or political authority independent of the state,[83] as supported by the understanding of Indigenous rights as *sui generis*. Further, international law affirms Indigenous Peoples as distinct peoples with the right to self-determination or self-government. Under domestic laws though, this is interpreted as a right to "internal self-governance" within existing nation-states.[84] There are contemporary examples of multiplural sovereignty wrapped into constitutional orders. For instance, Ecuador's 2008 Constitution states that the country is a "plurinational" state and affirms the sovereignty of the Indigenous Peoples, Afro-descendent groups, and ecosystems (giving these legally enforceable rights) to challenge the hegemony of the state.[85] This declaration of a plurinational state was championed by the Confederation of Indigenous Nationalities of Ecuador and resulted from decades of advocacy by Indigenous and Afro-descendant communities. Similar conceptual language related to pluriculturalism was included in the 1988 Constitution, yet it did not result in concrete policy changes, only multicultural recognition.[86] The Confederation of Indigenous Nationalities of Ecuador continues to critique the state and explore plurinational solutions to give legal backing to Indigenous sovereignties. How does this plurinationalism work? Scholars Christine Keating and Amy Lind explain that the state supports "intercultural dialogue," which is "state-enabled, not state-centered," and not imposed by political actors.[87] They also describe limitations to these changes but explain that Ecuador's plurinationalism is an ongoing project that, while continuing to raise questions and even fall short of expectations, is a victory for Indigenous Peoples' struggle for self-determination.[88]

Examples of multiplural sovereignty can also be found in Canada. Scholars Keith Culver and Michael Giudice argue that multiplural sovereignty can be evidenced in how the Canadian state and Indigenous legal orders are increasingly entangled. Changes in how the judiciary understands Indigenous legal orders are shifting the Canadian legal landscape from a "supremacy-claiming systematicity view" to a "government-to-government" partnership between state (federal and provincial) governments and Indigenous governments.[89] Christie, on the other hand, notes that practices of multiplural sovereignty have long been exercised by Indigenous Nations throughout what has become Canada.[90] Drawing from Indigenous literatures, Christie describes the complexities of navigating Indigenous sovereignties in settler colonial Canada to demonstrate how Indigenous political practices amount to "plural sovereignties."

The Mi'kmaw lobster fisheries are one tangible example of multiversal sovereignty in the Mi'kma'ki territory in the Maritimes of Canada.[91] In September 2020, Sipekne'katik First Nation, which represents one of the districts of Mi'kma'ki, set up a lobster fishing operation under both their sovereign laws and their Treaty rights with the Crown. The competition that the fishery brought to the broader sector was met with racist and violent resistance from settler fishers and the state.[92] The federal government responded by shutting down the Sipekne'katik fishery, which Parasram argues was done under the pretence that the lobster stock was under threat. The real issue, he points out, was that Sipekne'katik sovereignty and Treaty rights posed a threat to Canadian state sovereignty and unbridled settler privilege: "Rather than addressing the problem as one between two sovereign nations, the government of Canada tries to subsume Mi'kmaq sovereignty into its uni-versal lens."[93] This example of colonial control diminishes Aboriginal rights (as per section 35 of the Constitution Act, 1982), Treaty rights (affirmed in the Constitution and, in this case, the Supreme Court of Canada[94]), Indigenous rights (affirmed in UNDRIP), and specific practices of Mi'kmaw sovereignty from across Mi'kma'ki.

The implications of Eurocentric state-centric understandings of sovereignty for Indigenous Peoples' sovereignties are evident in the real world. The concept of multiversal or pluriversal sovereignty challenges the colonial foundation of state-centric sovereignty. My interpretation of the theory related to multiplural sovereignty and Indigenous Peoples' agency is that Indigenous Peoples are increasingly taking a global view of sovereignty. This perspective may be influenced by the political power outlined in UNDRIP or the rise of internet and social media communications that connect Indigenous Peoples' struggles transnationally. Although there is a tension in this approach, given that Indigenous knowledges are specific to place, there is also a benefit in how Indigenous liberation movements adapt, expand, and consolidate political power for change in response to one another. I also think that this global scope is a theoretical prescription that will eventually revert to a localized nature. In many ways, the theories of multiplural sovereignty remain shaped by local contexts. For example, Indigenous theorists, whose work is considered next, ensure that this tethering to localized knowledges remains.

Indigenous Resurgences

Indigenous resurgence, a relatively new field of scholarship, is a testament to the enduring resilience of Indigenous ancestral knowledges. It is deeply rooted in the intergenerational and relational knowledge systems that thrive within Indigenous Nations and are often transmitted through oral traditions and ceremonial practices. These ancestral knowledges, far from being relics of the past, are contemporary sources of resistance to colonial dispossession and assimilation, offering robust alternatives to settler colonial paths. International relations scholar Justin de Leon writes, "Resurgence emphasizes internal revitalization that is cognizant, but not dependent upon, exogenous conditions."[95] Thus, Indigenous resurgent movements are not subservient to colonial conditions but rather are acutely aware of the constraints and destructive processes of the colonial order and work to counteract their influence.

Much like anticolonialism, Indigenous resurgence movements do not rely on the colonial order, because they are oriented to knowledge systems and practices that predate and are independent of the colonial order. When I was a doctoral student, Dr. Kiera Ladner (Cree) emphasized to me that Indigenous scholarship — what makes it into books and other publications — has often originated with or been sourced from the Indigenous thought leaders within community. What follows is a brief introduction to some key Indigenous thought leaders who have significantly contributed to Indigenous resurgence theory. These thought leaders not only have shaped my understanding of Indigenous resurgence but also feel like familiar voices from my community, as their teachings reflect those shared by various Knowledge Keepers and thought leaders from whom I have learned. These perspectives can help us explore the question: How can we reshape the mechanics of federalism, originally designed for the colonial domination of Indigenous Peoples, in a spirit of reconciliation?

Michi Saagiig Nishnaabeg activist and scholar Leanne Betasamosake Simpson has written extensively on radical resurgence. She demonstrates that the primary experience of Indigenous Peoples in settler colonial Canada is continual dispossession and disappearance.[96] Resurgence, then, is a reattachment to what is central amid varied and complex practices of dispossession and disappearance: Resurgence is built from the foundations of Indigenous difference. This difference includes the distinct knowledge systems of Indigenous Peoples as they relate to specific relationships with lands, peoples, and more-than-humans. Simpson writes:

> To me, Indigenous nationhood is a radical and complete overturning of the nation-state's political formations. It is a vision that centers our lives around our responsibility to work with our Ancestors and those yet unborn to continuously give birth to a spectacular Nishnaabeg present. This is a manifesto to create networks of reciprocal resurgent movements with other humans and non-humans radically imagining their ways out of domination, who are not afraid to let those imaginings destroy the pillar of settler colonialism.[97]

In Simpson's work, Indigenous sovereignty is a practice or way of being grounded in ancestral knowledge systems that is also mindful of future generations. It connects the human experience to broader environments, including human and nonhuman relatives. Simpson emphasizes that dreaming — projecting future possibilities — is essential to concretizing what Indigenous Peoples seek in liberation from settler colonial oppression. She outlines a resurgence movement that is place-based and situated in ancestral knowledges, which are integral to framing reconciliation practices. Reconciling or reforming federal power-sharing systems by reorienting Indigenous political practices can empower Indigenous communities.

Glen Coulthard (Yellowknives Dene) has written extensively on grounded normativity, which, like Simpson's work, is based on situated knowledges. I have written elsewhere in this book about his impactful work on rejecting Canada's politics of recognition, or settler colonial tactics of ongoing Indigenous assimilation. In Coulthard's work, place (land, and relationships with land) is essential to decolonization because it holds relations and ways of knowing:

> I call this place-based foundation of Indigenous decolonial thought and practice grounded normativity, by which I mean the modalities of Indigenous land-connected practices and longstanding experiential knowledge that inform and structure our ethical engagements with the world and our relationships with human and non-human others over time.[98]

In this framing, we can understand Indigenous resurgence through long-standing relations with place — lands, humans, and more-than-humans — and the knowledge systems that support these relations. This place-based foundation is grounded normativity. Coulthard applies the concept to the politics of resistance related to the Yellowknives Dene Nation, yet we get a sense that grounded normativity can be fostered by any system of Indigenous knowledge that is distinct and unique as understood through specific place-based and relational knowledges. Here we see decolonial action — for some a critical component of reconciliation — in placed-based knowledges.

Métis scholar Zoe Todd explores the relational nature of Treaties with respect to ecologies. She writes about Treaty 6 territory and "fish philosophy," which connects Indigenous sovereignties to fish relatives, demonstrating how to live collectively and ethically.[99] This philosophy reflects a Métis legal order that shapes her responsibilities toward fish, water, and the more-than-human beings that inhabit Treaty 6 territory.[100] Todd's work highlights that relational responsibilities are foundational to Indigenous understandings of Treaty relations.

From Todd's perspective, relational ties to lands, waters, and more-than-humans are rooted in specific places through the networks of rivers, linking the past to the future. This work demonstrates how advocates for recontextualizing Treaty relationship through Indigenous resurgences can reframe the concept of reconciliation. Todd's "fish philosophy" offers a theoretical framework that examines the interconnectedness of Indigenous Peoples and ecologies as a foundation of legal orders that should be central to reconciliation.

Next, Heidi Kiiwetinepinesiik Stark (Turtle Mountain Ojibwe) has articulated the political resurgence of the Anishinaabe Nation. Much like Simpson and Coulthard, Stark describes Indigenous resurgence as a decolonial strategy to transform or dismantle power relations that give priority to settler benefit: "Indigenous resurgence literature calls on us to be attentive to how power structures and determines which narratives, modes of understanding our world and the web of relationships in operation, are given primacy."[101]

In the Anishinaabe political approach, nationhood is a flexible mechanism that can adjust to changing environments.[102] Describing Indigenous governance through the example of the Anishinaabe, Stark notes that "a dense web of clans, kinship ties, and loyalties to non-Anishinaabe nations existed within nationhood, not as forces that opposed it."[103] This description of Indigenous governance is transnational, with Indigenous Nations operating in an interstellar system of collective relationality understood to function as an international system.[104] Along with Indigenous Peoples' specific relationship to lands, peoples, and more-than-humans, this collectivity can inform reconciliatory approaches through multiplural sovereignty approaches.

Métis scholar Daniel Voth has written on the need for Métis and First Nations peoples to rekindle kinship ties to overcome political issues that generate social discord as an approach to decolonizing settler colonial politics in Canada.[105] He explains how relations with place can support the restoration of kinship. Focusing on the historical Red River area in what is now Manitoba, he "provides insights into the way the land and waters convey invitations to other beings, and explores what political values and activities those invitations have the power to encourage."[106]

Voth's work offers a crucial reanimation of past (and, in many ways, ongoing) kinship, or relational interconnections, that can animate decolonial resistance. As an example of kinship ties in the area in which I write, Treaty 4 in southern Saskatchewan, people commonly understand that the Métis Nation was historically referred to by the Cree or nêhiyawak Nation as otipemisiwak, or "the people who own themselves." As Michel Hogue demonstrates, this term reflects a long history of kinship ties and political regard between the Métis and First Nations, which some say continue to run deep in the region.[107] Voth makes a necessary interjection by calling for Indigenous Peoples to restore and honour these kinship ties as a step closer to reconciliation of Indigenous social relational structures.

Finally, Anishinaabe scholar Aaron Mills has developed a large body of resurgence work related to Anishinaabe laws. Reconciliation, for Mills, must be connected to the "earthway."[108] His multilayered work builds on the common distinction in Canadian scholarship between European or Western thought and Indigenous knowledges. He captures the diametrical difference through the *sovereignty thesis* — a Western notion that humans are separate from nature and are the only beings with autonomy — and the *humility thesis* — the Indigenous perspective that humans are interrelated with all living beings.[109] For Mills, the sovereignty thesis forces disconnect, whereas the humility thesis is steeped in relationships.

The colonial status quo does not provide a path forward for reconciliation: We must reconfigure the existing power structure to avoid reification of colonial inequity. Mills posits that a reconciliatory path forward requires us to ask different questions. For instance, he writes:

> Despite the enormous impact respect for the principle of Constitutional dialogue would have on Canada's colonial status quo, it remains a minimalist, negative principle. It tells us only how *not* to place the rocks, so as to avoid crushing one another. It says nothing about how the remaining rocks *should* be placed and so offers no clear way forward. It remains for me to clarify which positive conditions enable a genuine dialogue, and to identify obstacles to their realization.[110]

By applying Mills' Anishinaabe approach to reconciliation, we can reframe our pursuit to better reconfigure power relations. For Mills, the humility thesis can guide us in exploring relationships: How can we understand Canadian federalism through the lens of mutual benefit and coexistence? Does a focus on relationality alter the federalist approach that grants the settler state jurisdiction over Indigenous Peoples? Furthermore, does reframing discussions of reconciliation and federalism generate political interest in "how the remaining rocks *should* be placed"? Mills argues that these questions transform understandings of how power and social dynamics relate, from hierarchical to mutual recognition: can this similarly influence the political discussion on reconciliation?

Let's consider these Indigenous resurgence manifestos in response to my question: How can we reshape the mechanics of federalism, originally designed for the colonial domination of Indigenous Peoples, in a spirit of reconciliation? We have seen how Indigenous resurgence can guide the process of reconciliation. Indigenous knowledges are rooted in specific places and ancestral traditions; therefore, reconciliation efforts should be tailored to the unique locations of place and colonial or decolonial experiences of Indigenous Nations. Indigenous resurgence movements seek to dismantle colonial structures and advocate for multiplural sovereignty and renewed Treaty relationships. Consequently, reconciliation efforts should embrace a multifaceted approach that understands Indigenous political autonomy as sovereign. A strong emphasis on the truth component of reconciliation is required: Learning about and deeply understanding the ongoing colonial injustices and inequities that subordinate Indigenous Peoples' political authority is needed to address the issues through structural change. Indigenous resurgence movements also emphasize the importance of restoring relational Treaties and kinship practices to address power imbalances. Reconciliation efforts should aim to eliminate socially reproduced power differentials and challenge the status quo. Lastly, Indigenous resurgence movements encourage us to ask new questions about the issues we want to address, steering us away from colonial logics and toward Indigenous-centred solutions.

The Indigenous resurgence theorists considered here have all animated how grounded ancestral knowledge systems — relational to place, lands, other Indigenous Nations, and more-than-human beings — are practised with mindfulness for future generations. They remind us that Canadian federalism was built with the intent of Indigenous dispossession and settler benefit, but all structures can be rebuilt with different intent. As Simpson has written, "If we experience settler colonialism as a structure made up of processes, when the practices of settler colonialism appear to shift, it can appear to present an opportunity to do things differently, to change our relationship to the state."[111] Approaches to Indigenous resurgence take up Indigenous political orders to shift power inequities and create opportunities to do things differently. These Indigenous resurgences shed some light on different reconciliatory paths forward.

Exploitation or Liberation? Navigating Reconciliation in Federalism

To effectively pursue reconciliation within Canada's federal political framework, it is crucial to analyze previous reform efforts to address how the agency of Indigenous Peoples has been marginalized by jurisdictional powers. These powers were shaped by the settler colonial pursuit of dispossession — to generate settler benefit at the expense of Indigenous Peoples. Federal and provincial jurisdiction have been shaped by narratives of settler colonialism, excluding Indigenous Peoples' sovereignty and masking the uneven power relations at the centre of the federalist division of powers.

This final chapter considered the situation of federalism, power, and dispossession as one that offers opportunities for reconciliation. The reconfiguration of federalism is not a new topic — alternative measures have previously been imagined — nor is it a simple fix — many of these measures have been abandoned as impossible to implement or criticized as recolonizing. No approach to reconciliation will be effective without situating Indigenous resurgence movements and ancestral knowledge systems and political actions as a starting reference.

POSTSCRIPT

INDIGENOUS SOVEREIGNTIES AND THE SUSTAINABILITY OF RECONCILIATION

Reconciliation efforts cannot dismiss the influence of settler colonial narratives and mechanics of dispossession built into the structure of federalism. These narratives ensure that any disruption to settler colonial sovereignties that Indigenous Peoples present are simply "folded back" into the Canadian myth, subsumed by and reifying colonial dominance.[1] That is a clear impediment to reconciliation, as is the broader lack of political will for change. These obstacles render reconciliation unsustainable: It cannot achieve change while subservient to the colonial order.

Indigenous Peoples' agency is never fully extinguished in any colonial project. This could be, as John Borrows explains, because the Canadian state has integrated Indigenous legal orders and political practices into its settler colonial frameworks.[2] Or, as scholar Russell Barsh shows, it may stem from the way Indigenous cultures are foundational to Canada's broader national consciousness.[3] Or still, as postcolonial theorist Edward Said has demonstrated, the colonial presence cannot sustain itself without the existence of colonized people to define and uphold the colonial order.[4]

Another way to understand how Indigenous Peoples' agency continues despite colonization is more straightforward: Indigenous ways of knowing and being just never went away. They were hard-fought and fiercely protected. Even when made illegal, these practices remained, often going underground. Ancestral knowledges were passed orally through storytelling and held in languages. Music and dance were hidden but never left quiet. The settler colonial presence circumscribed Indigenous Peoples' autonomy, but it could never be vanquished. And so, Indigenous difference persists.

Federalism, however, effectively prevents Indigenous Peoples from fully exercising their *sui generis* legal orders. Alternative frameworks have been developed, but they continue to face a challenge that is summed up well by Meaghan Anne Williams: "Growth in the perspectives of *who* is party to our federal arrangement has not yet led to a change in *how* the federal arrangement is structured."[5] This critique echoes many I have heard in Indigenous communities. Colonial structures continue to undermine the sovereignty of Indigenous Peoples, regardless of the approach taken. The question of whose power will be circumscribed by any decolonial activity — Indigenous or settler? — ultimately falls to Indigenous Peoples. In settler colonial contexts, maintaining Indigenous difference relegates communities to the margins, whether they choose this positioning intentionally or it occurs against their will.

To centre Indigenous difference — which has always been central to assimilative and genocidal agendas — is to build a structure framed not by colonial dominance but by Indigenous nationhood. Indigenous knowledges exist in relation to specific places and are a means of approaching relations of power in differing ways. Indigenous resurgences are grounded in ancestral knowledge systems that emphasize the interconnectedness of place, lands, Indigenous Nations, and more-than-human beings as well as mindful practice for future generations. These resurgences can stand alone or intertwine political efforts with other visions of liberation from settler colonial Canada, including trilateral federalism, interstate federalism, Treaty federalism, or multi-plural sovereignties.

There is no clear path for reconciliation. Indigenous liberation movements are complex and varied, focusing on reconciliatory, decolonial, postcolonial, or anticolonial terrain. Although reconciliation on its own does not necessarily ensure the kind of justice related to colonial inequities that many would like to see, it does provide opportunities for change. These opportunities, in turn, support the sustainability of broader Indigenous liberation movements. By promoting Indigenous sovereignties, reconciliation strengthens the foundation of the federalist structure, paving the way for more sustainable reconciliation efforts.

This book examined a range of possible alternatives to Canada's federalist political system, because colonialism and its undoing are not straightforward. The revolutionary theory of the global political movement of postcolonialism has demonstrated just this. Pivotal theorists such as Edward Said, Frantz Fanon, and Albert Memmi have shown, across different colonial liberation projects including Palestine, Algeria, and Tunisia, that the cessation of colonial occupation does not mean an immediate or untarnished liberty from colonial presence.[6] As international relations scholar Somdeep Sen writes, "The presence/absence of the colonizer is an insufficient marker of liberation."[7] Decolonial countries remain marked by a colonial occupation that persists, overtly and covertly and to varying degrees, in remnants across sociocultural, political, and economic spheres.

While Canada is distinct from the locations that these postcolonial theorists describe, they provide important reminders that undoing the grasp of colonial power is not straightforward: For this reason, thinking through reconciliation in Canada should not be expected to be straightforward. Real-life experiences show that colonial occupation and Indigenous Peoples' liberation are not mutually exclusive. Put another way, there can be and often is overlap. Surely, liberation movements can be mapped over colonial occupations, starting as dreams, ideologies, or calls for change and then carrying over into the postcolonial reality to confront and challenge the ongoing legacies of colonial power and dispossession. Postcolonial theory demonstrates that analysis alone cannot eradicate colonialism; practical and tangible changes must also be made. In Canada, land claims, self-governing agreements, and economic development projects shape decolonial and postcolonial expressions alongside the "everyday acts of resistance"[8] from community and individuals demonstrating collective opposition to colonial exploitation and dispossession.

In Canada, reconciliation occurs squarely within the settler colonial present. As Kiera Ladner and Michael Orsini remind us, Canada was never meant to be a decolonial state; instead, it was envisioned by the British Crown as a continuously tethered British subject of imperial operations. They write:

> More than a century ago, Prime Minister John A. Macdonald argued that the *Indian Act* political system of elected band councils would accustom "Indians to the modes of government prevalent in the white communities surrounding them" and would "thus tend to prepare them for earlier amalgamation with the general population of the country."[9]

The federalist system of power sharing fundamentally failed to establish a jurisdictional framework that recognizes the sovereignty of Indigenous Peoples, despite existing Treaty commitments and constitutional and judicial recognition. The underlying aim of this system is colonial assimilation — what many now identify as a genocidal intent to erase Indigenous identities for the broader benefit of the settler project. When left unchallenged, this structure amounts to a form of colonial violence,[10] intertwining the narrative of federalism with the marginalization of Indigenous political agency in Canada.

As I conclude, I am left with an earlier question: How much can we truly expect from reconciliation when we seek real change, not a metaphor?[11] Despite its limitations, reconciliation in Canada holds the potential to bring about transformative decolonial change. This potential is rooted in how Canadian political systems operate; they are flexible, they change to meet sociopolitical evolutions, and they have a foundation in Indigenous political practices. When a system such as federalism perpetuates settler colonial dispossession, it becomes a crucial part of the national conversation on reconciliation. Ignoring the role of federalism in perpetuating settler colonialism risks obstructing any meaningful and sustainable advancements in our efforts toward reconciliation.

ENDNOTES

Preface

1. Niigaan Sinclair, *Wînipêk: Visions of Canada From an Indigenous Centre* (Toronto: McClelland & Stewart, 2024).
2. Howard Adams, *Prison of Grass: Canada From the Native Point of View* (Toronto: General Publishing, 1975).
3. Marie Battiste, "Micmac Literacy and Cognitive Assimilation," in *Indian Education in Canada: The Legacy*, ed. Jean Barman, Yvonne Herbert, and Don McCaskell (Vancouver: UBC Press, 1986), 23–44.

Chapter One

1. Office of the Treaty Commissioner, "Statement of Treaty Issues: Treaties as a Bridge to the Future" (Saskatoon: Office of the Treaty Commissioner, 1998), 12.
2. Gregory Younging, *Elements of Indigenous Style: A Guide for Writing By and About Indigenous Peoples* (Edmonton: Brush Education, 2018), 81.
3. The Canadian Press, "Justin Trudeau Vows to End First Nations Reserve Boil-Water Advisories Within 5 Years," *CBC News*, October 5, 2015, cbc.ca/news/politics/canada-election-2015-justin-trudeau-first-nations-boil-water-advisories-1.3258058.
4. National Inquiry Into Missing and Murdered Indigenous Women and Girls, *Reclaiming Power and Place: The Final Report of the National Inquiry Into Missing and Murdered Indigenous Women and Girls*, Vol. 1a (Vancouver: Privy Council Office, 2019), mmiwg-ffada.ca/wp-content/uploads/2019/06/Final_Report_Vol_1a-1.pdf.
5. Mary Jane McCallum and Adele Perry, *Structures of Indifference: An Indigenous Life and Death in a Canadian City* (Winnipeg: University of Manitoba Press, 2018).
6. Eve Tuck and K. Wayne Yang, "Decolonization Is Not a Metaphor," *Decolonization: Indigeneity, Education & Society* 1, 1 (2013).
7. Tony Ballantyne, *Orientalism and Race: Aryanism in the British Empire* (New York: Palgrave Macmillan, 2002).
8. Benedict Anderson, *Imagined Communities: Reflections on the Origin and Spread of Nationalism* (New York: Verso Books, 2006).
9. Paulette Regan, *Unsettling the Settler Within: Indian Residential Schools, Truth Telling, and Reconciliation in Canada* (Vancouver: UBC Press, 2010).
10. Elizabeth Furniss, "Pioneers, Progress and the Myth of the Frontier: Landscape of Public History in Rural British Columbia," *BC Studies* 115 and 116 (Autumn/Winter 1997/98).

11 Olive Patricia Dickason, *The Myth of the Savage and the Beginnings of French Colonialism in the Americas* (Edmonton: University of Alberta Press, 1984).
12 George A. MacLean, Duncan R. Wood, and Lori Turnbull, *Politics: An Introduction*, 3rd ed. (Don Mills, ON: Oxford University Press, 2020).
13 Thomas Biersteker and Cynthia Weber, "The Social Construction of State Sovereignty," in *State Sovereignty as a Social Construct*, ed. Thomas Biersteker and Cynthia Weber (New York: Cambridge University Press, 1996), 14; Ajay Parasram, "Pluriversal Sovereignty and the State of IR," *Review of International Studies* 49, 3 (2023).
14 Lorenzo Veracini, *Settler Colonialism: A Theoretical Overview* (New York: Palgrave Macmillan, 2010), 53.
15 James M. Blaut, *The Colonizer's Model of the World: Geographical Diffusionism and Eurocentric History* (New York: The Guilford Press, 1993); Ballantyne, *Orientalism and Race*.
16 Jennifer Reid, "The Doctrine of Discovery and Canadian Law," *Canadian Journal of Native Studies* XXX, 2 (2010).
17 Reid, "Doctrine of Discovery."
18 Veracini, *Settler Colonialism*.
19 Veracini, *Settler Colonialism*, 53.
20 Emma Battell Lowman and Adam J. Barker, *Settler Identity and Colonialism in the 21st Century* (Winnipeg: Fernwood Publishing, 2015), 55.
21 Battell Lowman and Barker, *Settler Identity and Colonialism*, 53–55.
22 Manu Vimalassery, "The Wealth of the Natives: Toward a Critique of Settler Colonial Political Economy," *Settler Colonial Studies* 3, 3–4 (2013); Veracini, *Settler Colonialism*, 55–61.
23 Arthur J. Ray, Jim Miller, and Frank Tough, *Bounty and Benevolence: A Documentary History of Saskatchewan Treaties* (Montreal: McGill-Queen's University Press, 2002).
24 Battell Lowman and Barker, *Settler Identity and Colonialism*, 49.
25 Veracini, "Colonialism, Frontiers, Genocide"; Vimalassery, "Wealth of the Natives."
26 McCallum and Perry, *Structures of Indifference*.
27 United Nations, "Definitions of Genocide and Related Crimes," n.d., un.org/en/genocide-prevention/definition.
28 Kiera L. Ladner, "Treaty Federalism: An Indigenous Vision of Canadian Federalisms," in *New Trends in Canadian Federalism*, 2nd ed., ed. Francois Rocher and Miriam Smith (Peterborough: Broadview Press, 2003), 168–69; John Borrows, "Indigenous Legal Traditions in Canada," *Washington University Journal of Law & Policy* 19 (2005): 180; Alex Marland and Jared J. Wesley, *Inside Canadian Politics*, 2nd ed. (Don Mills, ON: Oxford University Press, 2020).
29 Borrows, "Indigenous Legal Traditions," 178.
30 John Borrows, *Canada's Indigenous Constitution* (Toronto: University of Toronto, 2010), 8.
31 Jodi A. Byrd, "Colonialism's Cacophony: Natives and Arrivants at the Limits of Postcolonial Theory" (PhD Dissertation, the University of Iowa, 2002), v.
32 Brenna Bhandar, "Anxious Reconciliation(s): Unsettling Foundations and Spatializing History," *Environment and Planning. D, Society & Space* 22, 6 (2004): 838.
33 Bhandar, "Anxious Reconciliation(s)," 837.

34 John L. Tobias, "Protection, Civilization, Assimilation: An Outline History of Canada's Indian Policy," in *As Long as the Sun Shines and Water Flows: A Reader in Canadian Native Studies,* ed. Ian L. Getty and Antoine S. Lussier (Vancouver: UBC Press, 1983), 40–49; Hugh E. Q. Shewell, *Enough to Keep Them Alive: Indian Welfare in Canada 1873–1965* (Toronto: University of Toronto Press, 2004), 95.
35 Allyson Stevenson, *Intimate Integration: A History of the Sixties Scoop and the Colonization of Indigenous Kinship* (Toronto: University of Toronto Press, 2021); Sarah Carter, *Lost Harvests: Prairie Indian Reserve Farmers and Government Policy* (Montreal and Kingston: McGill-Queen's University Press, 1990); James Daschuk, *Clearing the Plains: Disease, Politics of Starvation, and the Loss of Aboriginal Life* (Regina: University of Regina Press, 2013).
36 Sunera Thobani, *Exalted Subjects: Studies in the Making of Race and Nation in Canada* (Toronto: University of Toronto Press, 2007), 172.
37 Thobani, *Exalted Subjects,* 172.
38 Battell Lowman and Barker, *Settler Identity and Colonialism,* 79–84.
39 Byrd, "Colonialism's Cacophony."
40 Lorenzo Veracini, *The Settler Colonial Present* (New York: Palgrave Macmillan, 2015), 43–44.
41 Corwin Aragon and Alison M. Jaggar, "Agency, Complicity, and the Responsibility to Resist Structural Injustice," *Journal of Social Philosophy* 49, 3 (2018): 449.
42 Regan, *Unsettling the Settler Within,* 176; Leslie Thielen-Wilson, "Troubling the Path to Decolonization: Indian Residential School Case Law, Genocide, and Settler Illegitimacy," *Canadian Journal of Law and Society* 29, 2 (2014): 181.
43 Battell Lowman and Barker, *Settler Identity and Colonialism,* 91.
44 Tuck and Yang, "Decolonization Is Not a Metaphor."
45 McCallum and Perry, *Structures of Indifference.*
46 Michel Hogue, *Métis and the Medicine Line: Creating a Border and Dividing a People* (Regina: University of Regina Press, 2015).
47 Thielen-Wilson, "Troubling the Path to Decolonization."
48 Rosemary Nagy, "The Truth and Reconciliation Commission of Canada: Genesis and Design," *Canadian Journal of Law and Society* 29, 2 (2014); Dylan Robinson and Keavy Martin, "Introduction: The Body Is a Resonant Chamber," in *Arts of Engagement: Taking Aesthetic Action In and Beyond the Truth and Reconciliation Commission of Canada,* ed. Dylan Robinson and Keavy Martin (Waterloo: Wilfrid Laurier University Press, 2016), 5–6.
49 Rosemary Nagy, "The Scope and Bounds of Transitional Justice and the Canadian Truth and Reconciliation Commission," *International Journal of Transitional Justice* 7, 1 (2013).
50 Nagy, "Truth and Reconciliation Commission of Canada," 216.
51 Mayo Moran, "The Role of Reparative Justice in Responding to the Legacy of Indian Residential Schools," *University of Toronto Law Journal* 64, 4 (2014); Nagy, "Truth and Reconciliation Commission."
52 Moran, "Role of Reparative Justice"; Kent Roach, "Blaming the Victim: Canadian Law, Causation, and Residential Schools," *University of Toronto Law Journal* 64, 4 (2014).
53 Truth and Reconciliation Commission of Canada, *The Final Report of the Truth and Reconciliation Commission of Canada, Volume 1: Summary, Honouring the Truth, Reconciling for the Future* (Toronto: James Lorimer & Company, 2015), 25–35; Robinson and Martin, "Introduction."

54 Government of Canada, "Backgrounder - Truth and Reconciliation Commission's Sixth National Event," modified September 18, 2013, canada.ca/en/news/archive/2013/09/backgrounder-truth-reconciliation-commission-sixth-national-event.html.
55 Truth and Reconciliation Commission of Canada, *Final Report, Volume 1: Summary*, 25–29.
56 David Gaertner, " 'Aboriginal Principles of Witnessing' and the Truth and Reconciliation Commission of Canada," in *Arts of Engagement: Taking Aesthetic Action In and Beyond the Truth and Reconciliation Commission of Canada*, ed. D. Robinson and K. Martin (Waterloo: Wilfrid Laurier University Press, 2016), 145.
57 Truth and Reconciliation Commission of Canada, *The Final Report of the Truth and Reconciliation Commission of Canada* (Montreal: McGill-Queen's University Press, 2015).
58 Truth and Reconciliation Commission of Canada, *The Final Report of the Truth and Reconciliation Commission of Canada: Canada's Residential Schools: Reconciliation, Volume 6* (Montreal: McGill-Queen's University Press, 2015), 17.
59 Leslie Young, "What You Need to Know About the Liberal Election Platform," *Global News*, October 5, 2015, globalnews.ca/news/2259367/what-you-need-to-know-about-the-liberal-election-platform; Corey Snelgrove and Matthew Wildcat, "Political Action in a Time of Reconciliation," in *Indigenous Resurgence in an Age of Reconciliation*, ed. Heidi Kiiwetinepinesiik Stark, Aimée Craft, and Hokulani K. Aikau (Toronto: University of Toronto Press, 2023), 157.
60 Indigenous Watchdog, "Canada Says That 85% of the TRC Calls to Action Are Either Complete or Well Under Way. Really?," n.d., indigenouswatchdog.org/2024/01/18/canada-says-that-85-of-the-trc-calls-to-action-are-either-complete-or-well-under-way-really.
61 Eva Jewell and Ian Mosby, *Calls to Action Accountability: A 2023 Status Update on Reconciliation* (Yellowhead Institute, 2023), 2, yellowheadinstitute.org/wp-content/uploads/2023/12/YI-TRC-C2A-2023-Special-Report-compressed.pdf.
62 Riley Yesno, "Is Reconciliation Dead? Maybe Only Government Reconciliation Is," *Toronto Star*, February 19, 2020, thestar.com/opinion/contributors/2020/02/19/is-reconciliation-is-dead-maybe-only-government-reconciliation-is.html.
63 Matt James, "A Carnival of Truth? Knowledge, Ignorance and the Canadian Truth and Reconciliation Commission," *International Journal of Transitional Justice* 6, 2 (2012); Jeff Corntassel and Cindy Holder, "Who's Sorry Now? Government Apologies, Truth Commissions, and Indigenous Self-Determination in Australia, Canada, Guatemala, and Peru," *Human Rights Review* 9, 4 (2008).
64 Gaertner, "Aboriginal Principles of Witnessing."
65 Liam Midzain-Gobin and Heather A. Smith, "Debunking the Myth of Canada as a Non-Colonial Power," *American Review of Canadian Studies*, 50, 4 (2020): 489.
66 Jo-Ann Episkenew, *Taking Back Our Spirits: Indigenous Literature, Public Policy, and Healing* (Winnipeg: University of Manitoba Press, 2009); Laura Mudde, "Framing the Truth and Reconciliation Commission Process in Canada: A Media Analysis of Settler Colonial Rhetoric and Colonial Denial, 2003–2016," *Journal of Critical Race Inquiry* 7, 2 (2020).
67 Glen S. Coulthard, *Red Skin White Masks: Rejecting the Colonial Politics of Recognition* (Minneapolis: University of Minnesota Press, 2014), 106.
68 Damien Short, "Reconciliation and the Problem of Internal Colonialism," *Journal of Intercultural Studies* 26, 3 (2005): 268.

69   David Garneau, "Imaginary Spaces of Conciliation and Reconciliation: Art, Curation, and Healing," in *Arts of Engagement: Taking Aesthetic Action In and Beyond the Truth and Reconciliation Commission of Canada*, ed. D. Robinson and K. Martin (Waterloo: Wilfrid Laurier University Press, 2016); David MacDonald, "Paved With Comfortable Intentions: Moving Beyond Liberal Multiculturalism and Civil Rights Frames on the Road to Transformative Reconciliation," in *Pathways to Reconciliation: Indigenous and Settler Approaches to Implementing the TRC's Calls to Action*, ed. Aimée Craft and Paulette Regan (Winnipeg: University of Manitoba Press, 2020).
70   Snelgrove and Wildcat, "Political Action."
71   Snelgrove and Wildcat, "Political Action," 169.
72   Snelgrove and Wildcat, "Political Action," 161.
73   Aimée Craft and Paulette Regan, eds., *Pathways to Reconciliation: Indigenous and Settler Approaches to Implementing the TRC's Calls to Action* (Winnipeg: University of Manitoba Press, 2020).
74   Jewell and Mosby, "Calls to Action Accountability," 2.
75   Truth and Reconciliation Commission of Canada, *Final Report*, 17.
76   Emily Grafton and Jérôme Melançon, "The Dynamics of Decolonization and Indigenization in an Era of Academic 'Reconciliation,' " in *Indigenizing the Canadian Academy: Critical Reflections*, ed. Sheila Cote-Meek and Taima Moeke-Pickering (Toronto: Canadian Scholars' Press, 2020).
77   Tuck and Yang, "Decolonization Is Not a Metaphor."
78   Treaty Land Sharing Network, n.d., "Connecting Farmers and Indigenous Land Users," treatylandsharingnetwork.ca.
79   Battell Lowman and Barker, *Settler Identity and Colonialism*, 61, 68.
80   Truth and Reconciliation Commission of Canada, *Final Report, Volume 1: Summary*, 326.
81   Martin Papillon, "Nation to Nation? Canadian Federalism and Indigenous Multi-Level Governance," in *Canadian Federalism: Performance, Effectiveness, and Legitimacy*, 4th ed., ed. Herman Bakvis and Grace Skogstad (Toronto: University of Toronto Press, 2020), 404.
82   Tobias, "Protection, Civilization, Assimilation," 39.
83   Audra Simpson, "On Ethnographic Refusal: Indigeneity, 'Voice', and Colonial Citizenship," *Junctures* 9 (2007): 76.
84   Alan Pratt, "Federalism in the Era of Aboriginal Self-Government," in *Aboriginal Peoples and Government Responsibility: Exploring Federal and Provincial Roles*, ed. C. David (Ottawa: Carleton University Press, 1989), 23; Pamela D. Palmater, *Beyond Blood: Rethinking Indigenous Identity* (Saskatoon: Purich, 2011).
85   Menno Boldt and J. Anthony Long, eds., *The Quest for Justice: Aboriginal Peoples and Aboriginal Rights* (Toronto: University of Toronto Press, 1985), 50.
86   Pratt, "Federalism in the Era," 23.
87   Reference as to Whether "Indians" Includes in s. 91 (24) of the B.N.A. Act Includes Eskimo Inhabitants of the Province of Quebec, [1939] SCR 104; *Daniels v. Canada* (Indian Affairs and Northern Development), 2013 FC 6, [2013] 2 FCR 268; *Daniels v. Canada* (Indian Affairs and Northern Development), 2016 SCC 12, [2016] 1 SCR 99.
88   Robin Jarvis Brownlie, *A Fatherly Eye: Indian Agents, Government Power, and Aboriginal Resistance in Ontario, 1918–1939* (Toronto: Oxford University Press, 2003), xxi–xxii.

89 Patricia Monture-Angus, *Thunder in My Soul: A Mohawk Woman Speaks* (Black Point: Fernwood Publishing, 1995), 2.
90 Harold Cardinal, "Indian Nations and Constitutional Change," in *Governments in Conflict? Provinces and Indian Nations in Canada*, ed. J. Anthony Long and Menno Boldt (Toronto: University of Toronto Press, 1988), 84.
91 Brownlie, *Fatherly Eye*, xxii.
92 James Sákéj Youngblood Henderson, "Sui Generis and Treaty Citizenship," *Citizenship Studies*, 6, 4 (2002).
93 Jeff Corntassel, "Re-Envisioning Resurgence: Indigenous Pathways to Decolonization and Sustainable Self-Determination," *Decolonization: Indigeneity, Education & Society* 1, 1 (2012).
94 Corntassel, "Re-Envisioning Resurgence," 92.
95 United Nations, *United Nations Declaration on the Rights of Indigenous Peoples* (United Nations: 2007), un.org/development/desa/indigenouspeoples/wp-content/uploads/sites/19/2018/11/UNDRIP_E_web.pdf.
96 United Nations, *Declaration on the Rights of Indigenous Peoples*, 7.
97 Corinne Lennox and Damien Short, "Introduction," in *Handbook of Indigenous Peoples' Rights*, ed. Corrine Lennox and Damien Short (New York: Routledge, 2016), 1.
98 Sheryl R. Lightfoot, "Decolonizing Self-Determination: Haudenosaunee Passports and Negotiated Sovereignty," *European Journal of International Relations* 27, 4 (2021): 973.
99 Arthur Manuel and Ronald M. Derrickson, *Unsettling Canada: A National Wake-up Call*, 2nd ed. (Toronto: Between the Lines, 2015), 53.
100 Lightfoot, "Decolonizing Self-Determination."
101 Joyce Green, "The Complexity of Indigenous Identity Formation and Politics in Canada: Self-Determination and Decolonization," *International Journal of Critical Indigenous Studies* 2, 2 (2009), 42.
102 Erin Hanson, "Constitution Express," *Indigenous Foundations*, n.d., indigenousfoundations.arts.ubc.ca/constitution_express.
103 James Frideres, *First Nations in the Twenty-First Century* (Toronto: University Press, 2012), 153.
104 Heidi Kiiwetinepinesiik Stark, "Nenabozho's Smart Berries: Rethinking Tribal Sovereignty and Accountability," *Michigan State Law Review* 2 (2013).
105 Parasram, "Pluriversal Sovereignty," 356.
106 Rashwet Shrinkhal, " 'Indigenous Sovereignty' and Right to Self-Determination in International Law: A Critical Appraisal," *AlterNative* 17, 1 (2021): 72.
107 Shrinkhal, "Indigenous Sovereignty," 72.
108 Taiaiake Alfred, *Peace, Power, Righteousness: An Indigenous Manifesto*, 2nd ed. (Oxford University Press, 2009), 79.
109 Gerald R. Alfred, *Peace, Power, Righteousness: An Indigenous Manifesto* (Toronto: Oxford University Press, 1999), 59.
110 Dale Turner, *This Is Not a Peace Pipe: Towards a Critical Indigenous Philosophy* (Toronto: University of Toronto Press, 2006), 325.
111 Parasram, "Pluriversal Sovereignty," 356.
112 Blaut, *Colonizer's Model of the World*; Ashcroft, Griffiths, and Tiffin, *Post-Colonial Studies*.
113 Bill Ashcroft, Gareth Griffiths, and Helen Tiffin, *Post-Colonial Studies: The Key Concepts* (London, UK: Routledge, 2000), 84–85.

114 Biersteker and Weber, "Social Construction," 14; Audra Simpson, "The Sovereignty of Critique," *South Atlantic Quarterly* 119, 4 (2020).
115 Parasram, "Pluriversal Sovereignty," 367.
116 Simpson, "Sovereignty of Critique," 688–91.
117 Louis Henkin (1995), as quoted in Shrinkhal, "Indigenous Sovereignty," 72.
118 Paul Muldoon, "Divided Against Itself: Plural Sovereignties and the Australian State," in *The Oxford Handbook of Australian Politics*, ed. Jenny M. Lewis and Anne Tiernan (Oxford University Press, 2020), 186.
119 Parasram, "Pluriversal Sovereignty," 358.
120 Justin de Leon, "Theorising From the Land: House or Tipi of IR?," *Millennium Journal of International Studies* 50, 3 (2023): 767.
121 Parasram, "Pluriversal Sovereignty," 357; Ajay Parasram, *Pluriversal Sovereignty and the State: Imperial Encounters in Sri Lanka* (Manchester: Manchester University Press, 2023).
122 Stuart Christie, *Plural Sovereignties and Contemporary Indigenous Literature* (New York: Palgrave Macmillan, 2009), 1.
123 Stark, "Nenabozho's Smart Berries," 342.
124 Ludvig Beckman, Kirsty Gover, and Ulf Mörkenstam, "The Popular Sovereignty of Indigenous Peoples: A Challenge in Multi-People States," *Citizenship Studies* 26, 1 (2022): 3.
125 Stark, "Nenabozho's Smart Berries," 342.
126 By place I mean all the relations as conceptualized through lands, waterways, and skies and more-than-humans such as animals, birds, water life, and so on.
127 De Leon, "Theorising From the Land," 774.
128 Sarah Hunt, "Ontologies of Indigeneity: The Politics of Embodying a Concept," *Cultural Geographies* 2, 1 (2014): 31.
129 As quoted in Stark, "Nenabozho's Smart Berries," 343.
130 Parasram, "Pluriversal Sovereignty," 356.
131 Shrinkhal, "Indigenous Sovereignty," 71.
132 Federico Lenzerini, 2006, as quoted in Shrinkhal, "Indigenous Sovereignty," 74.
133 Battell Lowman and Barker, *Settler Identity and Colonialism*, 55.
134 The Constitution Act, 30 & 31 Victoria, c. 3, 1867 (UK).
135 Henderson, "Sui Generis"; Ladner, "Treaty Federalism."
136 Coulthard, *Red Skin White Masks*.
137 Leanne Betasamosake Simpson, *Dancing on Our Turtle's Back: Stories of Nishnaabeg Re-Creation, Resurgence and a New Emergence* (Winnipeg: ARP Books, 2011); Leanne Betasamosake Simpson, *As We Have Always Done: Indigenous Freedom Through Radical Resistance* (Minneapolis: University of Minnesota Press, 2020).
138 Tuck and Yang, "Decolonization Is Not a Metaphor."

Chapter Two

1 Arthur Manuel and Ronald Derrickson, *The Reconciliation Manifesto: Recovering the Land and Rebuilding the Economy* (Toronto: James Lorimer & Company, 2017), 18.
2 Anderson, *Imagined Communities*.

3   Raven's Canoe exhibit at the Museum of Civilization, as quoted in Julia Emberley, "(Un)Housing Aboriginal Possessions in the Virtual Museum: Cultural Practices and Decolonization in Civilization.Ca and *Reservation X*," *Journal of Visual Culture* 5, 3 (2006): 397.
4   Adams, *Prison of Grass*; Veracini, "Colonialism, Frontiers, Genocide."
5   Coll Thrush, *Native Seattle: Histories From the Crossing-Over Place* (Seattle: University of Washington Press, 2007).
6   Ashcroft, Griffiths, and Tiffin, *Post-Colonial Studies*, 28.
7   Gayatri C. Spivak, "Can the Subaltern Speak?," in *Colonial Discourse and Postcolonial Theory: A Reader*, ed. P. Williams and L. Chrisman (Hertfordshire, UK: Harvester Wheatsheaf, 1994).
8   Emma LaRocque, *When the Other Is Me: Native Resistance Discourse 1850–1990* (Winnipeg: University of Manitoba Press, 2011).
9   Drew C. Bednasek and Anne M. C. Godlewska, "The Influence of Betterment Discourses on Canadian Aboriginal Peoples in the Late Nineteenth and Early Twentieth Centuries: The Influence of Betterment Discourses on Canadian Aboriginal Peoples," *The Canadian Geographer* 53, 4 (2009).
10 Veracini, *Settler Colonialism*, 41.
11 Regan, *Unsettling the Settler Within*, 83–110.
12 Regan, *Unsettling the Settler Within*, 101.
13 Paul Litt, "Settler Colonial Theory and Canadian Cultural Nationalism," *Settler Colonial Studies* 13, 3 (2023): 446.
14 Papillon, "Nation to Nation?," 400.
15 Michel Foucault, *The History of Sexuality: Volume 1; An Introduction*, translated by Robert Hurley (New York: Pantheon Books, 1978).
16 David Campbell and Roland Bleiker, "Poststructuralism," in *International Relations Theories*, 4th ed., ed. Tim Dunne, Milja Kurki, and Steve Smith (Don Mills, ON: Oxford University Press, 2016).
17 Amy Lonetree, *Decolonizing Museums: Representing Native American in National and Tribal Museums* (Chapel Hill: University of North Carolina Press, 2012).
18 Regan, *Unsettling the Settler Within*, 84.
19 Veracini, "Colonialism, Frontiers, Genocide"; McCallum and Perry, *Structures of Indifference*.
20 Chelsea Vowel, *Indigenous Writes: A Guide to First Nations, Metis, and Inuit Issues in Canada* (Winnipeg: Highwater Press, 2016), 121.
21 Aaron James Mills, "Miinigowiziwin: All That Has Been Given for Living Well Together One Vision of Anishinaabe Constitutionalism" (Phd Dissertation, University of Victoria, 2019), 2; Kara Granzow, *Invested Indifference: How Violence Persists in Settler Colonial Society* (Vancouver: UBC Press, 2020); Veracini, "Colonialism, Frontiers, Genocide."
22 National Inquiry Into Missing and Murdered Indigenous Women and Girls, *Reclaiming Power and Place*.
23 Truth and Reconciliation Commission of Canada, *Final Report: Reconciliation*, Volume 6, 17.
24 Manuel and Derrickson, *Reconciliation Manifesto*, 25.
25 Jean M. O'Brien, *Firsting and Lasting: Writing Indians Out of Existence in New England* (Minneapolis, MN: University of Minnesota Press, 2010).
26 O'Brien, *Firsting and Lasting*, xiii.
27 Thrush, *Native Seattle*.

28. James Joseph Buss, *Winning the West With Words: Language and Conquest in the Lower Great Lakes* (Norman: University of Oklahoma Press, 2011).
29. Patrick Wolfe, "Settler Colonialism and the Elimination of the Native," *Journal of Genocide Research* 8, 4 (2006).
30. Wolfe, "Settler Colonialism," 402.
31. Wolfe, "Settler Colonialism," 388.
32. Wolfe, "Settler Colonialism," 397.
33. Peter Kulchyski, *Unjust Relations: Aboriginal Rights in Canadian Courts* (Don Mills, ON: Oxford University Press, 1994), 4.
34. Wolfe, "Settler Colonialism," 393.
35. Lorenzo Veracini, "Settler Collective, Founding Violence and Disavowal: The Settler Colonial Situation," *Journal of Intercultural Studies* 29, 4 (2008): 363–79.
36. Michael McCrossan and Kiera L. Ladner, "Eliminating Indigenous Jurisdictions: Federalism, the Supreme Court of Canada, and Territorial Rationalities of Power," *Canadian Journal of Political Science* 49, 3 (2016): 422.
37. McCrossan, "Contaminating and Collapsing Indigenous Space," 35.
38. McCrossan, "Contaminating and Collapsing Indigenous Space," 31.
39. Ashcroft, Griffiths, and Tiffin, *Post-Colonial Studies,* 40–41.
40. Ashcroft, Griffiths, and Tiffin, *Post-Colonial Studies,* 111.
41. James S. Frideres and René R. Gadacz, *Aboriginal Peoples in Canada* (Toronto: Pearson Canada, 2012), 1–24.
42. Edward Said, *Orientalism* (New York: Vintage Books, 1994); Albert Memmi, *The Colonizer and the Colonized* (Boston: Beacon Press, 1993); Frantz Fanon, *The Wretched of the Earth,* translated by Richard Philcox (New York: Grove Press/Atlantic, 1963).
43. Patrick Wolfe, *Settler Colonialism and the Transformation of Anthropology: The Politics and Poetics of an Ethnographic Event* (New York: Cassell, 1999), 1.
44. See Memmi, *The Colonizer*; Linda Tuhiwai Smith, *Decolonizing Methodologies: Research and Indigenous Peoples* (New York: Zed Books, 1999).
45. Wolfe, *Settler Colonialism*.
46. Vimalassery, "Wealth of the Natives."
47. James Rodger Miller, "The Royal Proclamation – 'The Indians' Magna Carta'?," *Active History,* September 30, 2013, activehistory.ca/2013/09/the-royal-proclamation-the-indians-magna-carta.
48. John Milloy, "Indian Act Colonialism: A Century of Dishonour, 1869–1969" (Ottawa: National Centre for First Nations Governance, 2008); Shewell, *Enough to Keep Them Alive*; Ray, Miller, and Tough, *Bounty and Benevolence*.
49. Michael Asch, "The Dene Economy," in *Dene Nation: The Colony Within,* ed. Mel Watkins (Toronto: University of Toronto Press, 1977); Peter Kulchyski, *The Red Indians: Aboriginal Resistance to Capitalism in Canada Now and Then* (Winnipeg: Arbeiter Ring Publishing, 2008); Monture-Angus, *Thunder in My Soul*.
50. Daschuk, *Clearing the Plains*.
51. Gina Starblanket and Dallas Hunt, *Storying Violence: Unravelling Colonial Narratives in the Stanley Trial* (Winnipeg: ARP Books, 2020).
52. Sharon Venne, "Understanding Treaty 6: An Indigenous Perspective," in *Aboriginal and Treaty Rights in Canada: Essays on Law, Equality, and Respect for Difference,* ed. Michael Asch (Vancouver: UBC Press, 1997); John Borrows, "The Durability of Terra Nullius: Tsilhqot'in Nation V British Columbia," *UBC Law Review* 48, 3 (2015).

53 Patrick Macklem, Indigenous Difference and the Constitution of Canada (Toronto: University of Toronto Press, 2001), 85–86.
54 Venne, "Understanding Treaty 6," 185.
55 Borrows, "Durability of Terra Nullius," 702.
56 Paul Patton, "Reconciliation, Aboriginal Rights and Constitutional Paradox in Australia," *Australian Feminist Law Journal* 15, 1 (2001): 32.
57 Buss, *Winning the West with Words*; O'Brien, *Firsting and Lasting*; Thrush, *Native Seattle*.
58 Bhandar, "Anxious Reconciliation(s)," 837.
59 BC Treaty Commission, *A Lay Person's Guide to Delgamuukw* (BC Treaty Commission, 1999), bctreaty.ca/wp-content/uploads/2022/12/delgamuukw.pdf.
60 *Delgamuukw v. British Columbia*, [1997] 3 SCR 1010.
61 Minnawaanagogiizhigook (Dawnis Kennedy), "Reconciliation Without Respect? Section 35 and Indigenous Legal Orders," in *Indigenous Legal Traditions*, ed. Law Commission of Canada (Vancouver: UBC Press, 2007), 90.
62 BC Treaty Commission, *Lay Person's Guide*, 62; Michael McCrossan, "Contaminating and Collapsing Indigenous Space: Judicial Narratives of Canadian Territoriality," *Settler Colonial Studies* 5, 1 (2015): 21.
63 Michael McCrossan, "Contaminating and Collapsing Indigenous Space: Judicial Narratives of Canadian Territoriality," *Settler Colonial Studies* 5, 1 (2015): 21.
64 McCrossan, "Contaminating and Collapsing Indigenous Space," 28.
65 McCrossan, "Contaminating and Collapsing Indigenous Space," 20.
66 Bhandar, "Anxious Reconciliation(s)," 839.
67 Kate Brown, "Gridded Lives: Why Kazakhstan and Montana Are Nearly the Same Place," *American Historical Review* 106, 1 (2001): 17.
68 Truth and Reconciliation Commission of Canada, *Final Report, Volume 1: Summary*, 49.
69 Daschuk, *Clearing the Plains*.
70 See Macklem, *Indigenous Difference*, 113.
71 Bill Chapel, "The Vatican Repudiates 'Doctrine of Discovery,' Which Was Used to Justify Colonialism," *NPR*, March 30, 2023, npr.org/2023/03/30/1167056438/vatican-doctrine-of-discovery-colonialism-indigenous.
72 Borrows, "Durability of Terra Nullius."
73 Mills, "Miinigowiziwin," 123.
74 Renee Hulan and Renate Eigenbrod, ed., *Aboriginal Oral Traditions: Theory, Practice, Ethics* (Winnipeg: Fernwood Publishing, 2008).
75 Marsha C. Bol, *North, South, East, West: American Indians and the Natural World* (Boulder, CO: Roberts Rinehart Publishers, 1998); Leo Pettipas, *"Other Peoples' Heritage": A Cross-Cultural Approach to Museum Interpretation* (Winnipeg: Association of Manitoba Museums, 1994); O'Brien, *Firsting and Lasting*.
76 Borrows, "Durability of Terra Nullius," 714; Alan Hanna, "Making the Round: Aboriginal Title in the Common Law from a Tsilhqot'in Legal Perspective," *Ottawa Law Review* 45 (2015): 368.
77 Hanna, "Making the Round," 368; Brenda Gunn, "Case Note: *Tsilhqot'in Nation v British Columbia* 2014 SCC 44," *Indigenous Law Bulletin* 8, 14 (2014): 27.
78 Royal Commission on Aboriginal Peoples, *Report of the Royal Commission on Aboriginal Peoples: Volume 1: Looking Forward, Looking Back* (Ottawa: Minister of Supply and Services Canada, 1996), 34, publications.gc.ca/collections/collection_2016/bcp-pco/Z1-1991-1-1-eng.pdf.

79 Borrows, "Durability of Terra Nullius," 702.
80 Bhandar, "Anxious Reconciliation(s)," 840.
81 *Tsilhqot'in Nation v. British Columbia*, 2014 SCC 44, [2014] 2 SCR 7.
82 Borrows, "Durability of Terra Nullius"; Nigel Bankes and Jennifer Koshan, "Tsilhqot'in: What Happened to the Second Half of Section 91(24) of the Constitution Act, 1867?," *University of Calgary Faculty of Law Blog on Developments in Alberta Law,* July 7, 2014, ablawg.ca/2014/07/07/tsilhqotin-what-happened-to-the-second-half-of-section-9124-of-the-constitution-act-1867.
83 Bhandar, "Anxious Reconciliation(s)."
84 Bhandar, "Anxious Reconciliation(s)," 832.
85 Borrows, "Durability of Terra Nullius," 726.
86 *Guerin v. The Queen,* [1984] 2 SCR 335; Tanisha Salomons and Erin Hanson, "Guerin Case," *Indigenous Foundations,* n.d., indigenousfoundations.arts.ubc.ca/guerin_case.
87 John Borrows, *Drawing Out Law: A Spirit's Guide* (Toronto: University of Toronto Press, 2010), 59.
88 Marie Battiste and James (Sákéj) Youngblood Henderson, *Protecting Indigenous Knowledge and Heritage: A Global Challenge* (Saskatoon: Purich, 2000); Thomas King, "Godzilla vs. Post-Colonial," in *New Contexts of Canadian Criticism,* ed. A. Heble, D.P. Pennee, and J.R. Struthers (Peterborough: Broadview Press, 1997); Tasha Hubbard, "Voices Heard in the Silence, History Held in the Memory: Ways of Knowing Jeanette Armstrong's 'Threads of Old Memory,' " in *Aboriginal Oral Traditions: Theory, Practice, Ethics,* ed. Renee Hulan and Renate Eigenbrod (Halifax: Fernwood Books, 2008).
89 James Anaya, "Statement of Special Rapporteur to UN Permanent Forum on Indigenous Issues, 2012," May 15, 2012, unsr.jamesanaya.org/?p=668.

Chapter Three

1 This section offers a general overview of the political concept of federalism in Canada. For more, see Jennifer Smith, *Federalism* (Vancouver: UBC Press, 2004); Marland and Wesley, *Inside Canadian Politics.*
2 Smith, *Federalism,* 8.
3 Dara Lithwick, *A pas de deux: The Division of Federal and Provincial Legislative Powers in Sections 91 and 92 of the Constitution Act, 1867* (Library of Parliament, 2015), publications.gc.ca/collections/collection_2016/bdp-lop/eb/YM32-5-2015-128-eng.pdf.
4 Peter Hogg, *Constitutional Law of Canada* (Toronto: Thomson Canada, 2004), 294.
5 Radha Jhappan, "The Federal-Provincial Power-Grid and Aboriginal Self-Government," in *New Trends in Canadian Federalism,* ed. François Rocher and Miriam Smith (Toronto: Broadview Press, 1995), 163.
6 David C. Hawkes, ed., *Aboriginal Peoples and Government Responsibility: Exploring Federal and Provincial Roles* (Ottawa: Carleton University Press, 1989).
7 Anthony J. Hall, *The American Empire and the Fourth World* (Montreal & Kingston: McGill-Queen's University Press, 2003), 321–22.
8 Truth and Reconciliation Commission of Canada, *Final Report, Volume 1: Summary,* 326.
9 John Borrows, "Wampum at Niagara: The Royal Proclamation, Canadian Legal History, and Self-Government," in *Aboriginal and Treaty Rights in Canada: Essays*

on Law, Equality, and Respect for Difference, ed. Michael Asch (Vancouver: UBC Press, 1997), 156.
10 Claire Breay, *Magna Carta: Manuscripts and Myths* (London, UK: British Library Publishing Division, 2011).
11 Frances Abele and Michael J. Prince, "Four Pathways to Aboriginal Self-Government in Canada," *American Review of Canadian Studies* 36, 4 (2006), 569.
12 Borrows, "Durability of Terra Nullius," 735.
13 Borrows, "Wampum at Niagara," 159–60.
14 Borrows, "Wampum at Niagara," 161.
15 Bol, *North, South, East, West*, 67; J.C.H. King, *First Peoples, First Contacts: Native Peoples of North America* (Cambridge: Harvard University Press, 1999), 50.
16 Borrows, "Wampum at Niagara," 155.
17 John Borrows, *Aboriginal Legal Issues: Cases, Materials & Commentary* (Markham: LexisNexis Canada, 2007), 159.
18 Kulchyski, *Unjust Relations*, 8; Kulchyski, *Red Indians*, 24; James B. Waldram, *As Long as the Rivers Run: Hydroelectric Development and Native Communities in Northern Manitoba* (Winnipeg: University of Manitoba Press, 1988), 27.
19 Brenna Bhandar, *Colonial Lives of Property: Law, Land, and Racial Regimes of Ownership* (Durham: Duke University Press), 3.
20 Clifford Atleo and Jonathon Boron, "Land Is Life: Indigenous Relationships to Territory and Navigating Settler Colonial Property Regimes in Canada," *Land* 11 (2022): 609.
21 Shewell, *Enough to Keep Them Alive*, 8.
22 Irene Spry and Bennett McCardle, *The Records of the Department of the Interior and Research Concerning Canada's Western Frontier of Settlement* (Regina: Canadian Plains Research Center, 1993).
23 Shewell, *Enough to Keep Them Alive*; Tobias, "Protection."
24 Macklem, *Indigenous Difference*.
25 Kiera L. Ladner and Michael McCrossan, "The Road Not Taken," in *Contested Constitutionalism: Reflections on the Canadian Charter of Rights and Freedoms*, ed. James B. Kelly and Christopher P. Manfredi (Vancouver: UBC Press, 2009), 263–83.
26 Kulchyski, *Unjust Relations*, 6.
27 As quoted in Emily Grafton, "Reserved Responsibilities: A Comparative Analysis of Settler Colonial Narratives of Canadian Federalism and Province Jurisdictional Responsibility for Status First Nations Peoples Living on-Reserve in Manitoba, British Columbia, and the Northwest Territories" (PhD Dissertation, University of Manitoba, 2017), 75.
28 Bonita Lawrence, *"Real" Indians and Others: Mixed-Blood Urban Native Peoples and Indigenous Nationhood* (Lincoln: University of Nebraska Press, 2004); Palmater, *Beyond Blood*.
29 Carter, *Lost Harvests*, 24–25.
30 Tobias, "Protection," 129.
31 *Daniels v. Canada* (Indian Affairs and Northern Development), 2013 FC 6, [2013] 2 FCR 268; *Daniels v. Canada* (Indian Affairs and Northern Development), 2016 SCC 12, [2016] 1 SCR 99; *Reference as to Whether "Indians" Includes in s. 91 (24) of the B.N.A. Act Includes Eskimo Inhabitants of the Province of Quebec*, [1939] SCR 104.
32 Palmater, *Beyond Blood*; Lawrence, *"Real" Indians and Others*.
33 Boldt and Long, *Quest for Justice*; Lawrence, *"Real" Indians and Others*; Palmater, *Beyond Blood*.

34 Tobias, "Protection," 127.
35 Kent McNeil, "The Meaning of Aboriginal Title," in *Aboriginal and Treaty Rights in Canada: Essays on Law, Equality, and Respect for Difference*, ed. Michael Asch (Vancouver: UBC Press, 1997), 148.
36 Neal McLeod, *Cree Narrative Memory: From Treaties to Contemporary Times* (Saskatoon: Purich, 2007), 57.
37 Macklem, *Indigenous Difference*, 88.
38 E. Richard Atleo, *Tsawalk: A Nuu-Chah-Nulth Worldview* (Vancouver: UBC Press, 2004), 63.
39 Michael Asch and Norman Zlotkin, "Affirming Aboriginal Title: A New Basis for Comprehensive Claims," in *Aboriginal and Treaty Rights in Canada: Essays on Law, Equality, and Respect for Difference*, ed. Michael Asch (Vancouver: UBC Press, 1997), 214–15.
40 Hogg, *Constitutional Law*, 597.
41 Miller, "Royal Proclamation."
42 Macklem, *Indigenous Difference*, 88.
43 Macklem, *Indigenous Difference*, 87.
44 Hanna, "Making the Round," 368; Gunn, "Case Note," 27.
45 Asch, "Dene Economy," 55–56.
46 Brian Slattery, "The Hidden Constitution," *American Journal of Comparative Law* 32, 2 (1984).
47 Diana Ginn, "Indian Hunting Rights: *Dick v. R., Jack and Charlie v. R.* and *Simon v. R.*," *McGill Law Journal* 31, 4 (1986), 529.
48 Albert C. Peeling, *Provincial Jurisdiction After Delgamuukw* (Vancouver: Continuing Legal Education, 1998), 3.
49 Douglas Sanders, "The Constitution, the Provinces, and Aboriginal Peoples," in *Governments in Conflict? Provinces and Indian Nations in Canada*, ed. J. Anthony Long and Menno Boldt (Toronto: University of Toronto Press, 1989), 155–56.
50 Bradford Morse, "Government Obligations, Aboriginal Peoples and Section 91(24)," in *Aboriginal Peoples and Government Responsibility: Exploring Federal and Provincial Roles*, ed. David C. Hawkes (Ottawa: Carleton University Press, 1989), 71.
51 Hogg, *Constitutional Law*, 602–605; Sanders, "The Constitution," 169.
52 Ginn, "Indian Hunting Rights," 531.
53 Milloy, "Indian Act Colonialism," 216–17.
54 Tobias, "Protection."
55 Shewell, *Enough to Keep Them Alive*, 205.
56 Macklem, *Indigenous Difference*, 157; Hogg, *Constitutional Law*, 602–605.
57 Hogg, *Constitutional Law*, 605; *Delgamuukw v. British Columbia*, [1997] SCR 1010.
58 Thomas Isaac, Heather Weberg, and Jeremy Barretto, "Provincial Jurisdiction Confirmed Regarding Treaty Rights – Supreme Court of Canada's Keewatin Decision," *Legal Monitor Worldwide*, July 15, 2014, lexology.com/library/detail.aspx?g=673c4da2-2f16-4e70-88a7-71ed8bff6e53.; *Tsilhqot'in Nation v. British Columbia*, 2014 SCC 44, [2014] 2 SCR 7; Borrows, "Durability of Terra Nullius," 735.
59 Kulchyski, *Unjust Relations*, 9.
60 Macklem, *Indigenous Difference*, 144–45.
61 Pratt, "Federalism in the Era," 22.
62 Macklem, *Indigenous Difference*, 116.

63 Papillon, "Nation to Nation?," 402.
64 Pratt, "Federalism in the Era," 22.
65 Frideres and Gadacz, *Aboriginal Peoples*, 5.
66 Papillon, "Nation to Nation?," 403.
67 First Nations Child and Family Caring Society of Canada, *Back-to-Basics Approach for Improving Outcomes Under Jordan's Principle* (First Nations Child and Family Caring Society of Canada, 2023), fncaringsociety.com/sites/default/files/2023-05/Back%20to%20Basics%20Approach%20EN_3.pdf.
68 Timothy S. McCabe, *The Honour of the Crown and Its Fiduciary Duties to Aboriginal Peoples* (Markham: LexisNexis, 2008), 277.
69 Morse, "Government Obligations," 86.
70 Hogg, *Constitutional Law*, 601.
71 McCabe, *Honour of the Crown*, 240.
72 Borrows, "Durability of Terra Nullius," 735.
73 McCabe, *Honour of the Crown*, 243.
74 McCabe, *Honour of the Crown*, 242–43.
75 Martin Papillon, "Adapting Federalism: Indigenous Multilevel Governance in Canada and the United States," paper presented at the American Political Science Association Annual Meeting, Toronto, September 3–6, 2009, 4, papers.ssrn.com/sol3/papers.cfm?abstract_id=1450913.
76 Kent McNeil, "Aboriginal Title and Section 88 of the 'Indian Act,' " *University of British Columbia Law Review* 34, 1 (2000).
77 McCabe, *Honour of the Crown*, 249.
78 Jhappan, "Federal-Provincial Power-Grid," 169.
79 Andrew R. Thompson, "Resource Rights," *The Canadian Encyclopedia*, last edited December 16, 2013, thecanadianencyclopedia.ca/en/article/resource-rights.
80 *Yukon Northern Affairs Program Devolution Transfer Agreement*, October 29, 2001, between the Government of Canada and the Government of the Yukon, publications.gc.ca/collections/Collection/R2-184-2001E.pdf; *Northwest Territories Lands and Resources Devolution Agreement*, June 25, 2013, between the Government of Canada, the Government of the Northwest Territories, the Inuvialuit Regional Corporation, the Northwest Territory Métis Nation, the Sahtu Secretariat Incorporated, the Gwich'in Tribal Council, and the Tłı̨chǫ Government, eia.gov.nt.ca/sites/eia/files/final-devolution-agreement.pdf; *Nunavut Lands and Resources Devolution Agreement*, January 18, 2024, between The Government of Canada as represented by the Minister of Northern Affairs, The Government of Nunavut as represented by the Premier, and Nunavut Tunngavik Incorporated as represented by the President, rcaanc-cirnac.gc.ca/eng/1702495657169/1702495761711.
81 *Grassy Narrows First Nation v. Ontario (Natural Resources)*, 2014 SCC 48, [2014] 2 SCR 447; Isaac, Weberg, and Barretto, "Provincial Jurisdiction Confirmed," 3.
81 Papillon, "Nation to Nation?," 402.
82 E. Bruce Mellett, "Supreme Court Decision in Keewatin Confirms Provincial Ability to Take Up Treaty Lands," *Bennett Jones blog*, July 11, 2014, bennettjones.com/Blogs-Section/Supreme-Court-Decision-in-Keewatin-Confirms-Provincial-Ability-to-Take-up-Treaty-Lands.
83 Papillon, "Nation to Nation?," 402.
84 Brady Lang, "Sask. Portraying 'Totally False' Depiction of Crown Land Auction Sales, Groups Say," *CTV News*, March 16, 2023, ctvnews.ca/regina/article/sask-portraying-totally-false-depiction-of-crown-land-auction-sales-groups-say.

85 Lang, "Sask. Portraying 'Totally False' Depiction"; Mah Noor Mubarik, "Sask. NDP MLA Calls for Province to Halt Sale of Crown Lands," *CBC News,* October 21, 2021, cbc.ca/news/canada/saskatchewan/sask-crown-land-1.6220441.
86 Mubarik, "Sask. NDP MLA."
87 Mubarik, "Sask. NDP MLA."
88 *Saskatchewan Treaty Land Entitlement Framework Agreement,* September 22, 1992, between Her Majesty the Queen in Right of Canada, as represented by the Prime Minister of Canada and the Minister of Indian Affairs and Northern Development; the Entitlement Bands; and Her Majesty the Queen in Right of Saskatchewan, as represented by the Premier of Saskatchewan and the Minister responsible for the Indian and Metis Affairs Secretariat, publications.saskatchewan.ca/#/products/67033.
89 Great Britain Colonial Office, "Copies or Extracts of Correspondence Since 1st April 1835, Between The Secretary of State for the Colonies and the Governors of the British North American Provinces, Respecting the Indians in those Provinces" (London, 1839), 34.
90 Great Britain Colonial Office, "Copies or Extracts," 8.
91 Coulthard, *Red Skin White Masks.*

Chapter Four

1 Martin Papillon, "Federalism From Below? The Emergence of Aboriginal Multilevel Governance in Canada: A Comparison of the James Bay Crees and Kahnawá:ke Mohawks" (PhD Dissertation, University of Toronto, 2008), 31.
2 Wyatt A. Tilby, *The English People Overseas: British North America 1763–1867* (New York: Houghton Mifflin Company, 1912).
3 Meaghan Anne Williams, "The Same River, Together: Theorizing and Assessing Shared Rule in Treaty Federalism" (Phd Dissertation, Univ ersity of Toronto, 2023), 63.
4 Morse, "Government Obligations," 64–65.
5 Morse, "Government Obligations," 65–66.
6 Carter, *Lost Harvests.*
7 Ray, Miller, and Tough, *Bounty and Benevolence,* 107.
8 Ray, Miller, and Tough, *Bounty and Benevolence,* 109.
9 Peter Russell, *Recognizing Aboriginal Title: The Mabo Case and Indigenous Resistance to English-Settler Colonialism* (Toronto: University of Toronto Press, 2005), 101.
10 Murray A. Lapin, *Index to Parliamentary Debates on the Subject of the Confederation of the British North American Provinces* (Ottawa: King's Printer and Controller of Stationary, 1951), 3 and 1029.
11 Frideres and Gadacz, *Aboriginal Peoples,* 8–10.
12 As quoted in LaRocque, *When the Other Is Me,* 9.
13 Vic Satzewich and Nikolaos Liodakis, *'Race' and Ethnicity in Canada: A Critical Introduction* (Don Mills, ON: Oxford University Press, 2010), 42.
14 Enakshi Dua, Narda Razack, and Jody Nyasha Warner, "Race, Racism, and Empire: Reflections on Canada," *Social Justice* 32, 4 (2005).
15 Dua, Razack, and Warner, "Race, Racism, and Empire," 4.
16 *St. Catharines Milling and Lumber Co. v. R.*, [1887] 13 SCR 577.
17 Kulchyski, *Red Indians,* 49.

18 *St. Catharines Milling and Lumber Co. v. R.*, [1887] 13 SCR 577; Kulchyski, *Red Indians*, 49; Hogg, *Constitutional Law*, 598.
19 Royal Proclamation, 1763; Kulchyski, *Unjust Relations*.
20 Hogg, *Constitutional Law*, 598.
21 *Auditor-General for Quebec v. Auditor-General for Canada* (1920), [1921] 1 AC 401; Reference as to Whether "Indians" Includes in s. 91 (24) of the B.N.A. Act Includes Eskimo Inhabitants of the Province of Quebec, [1939] SCR 104.
22 McNeil, "The Meaning," 150.
23 Kulchyski, *Unjust Relations*.
24 Erin Hanson, "Aboriginal Title," Indigenous Foundations, n.d., indigenousfoundations.arts.ubc.ca/aboriginal_title.
25 Kulchyski, *Red Indians*, 67. The capitalization in the quotation reflects the original source.
26 Sanders, "The Constitution."
27 François Rocher and Miriam Smith, "The Four Dimensions of Canadian Federalism," in *New Trends in Canadian Federalism*, ed. François Rocher and Miriam Smith (Peterborough: Broadview Press, 2003), 9.
28 Morse, "Government Obligations," 63; Leroy Little Bear, "Section 88 of the Indian Act and the Application of Provincial Laws to Indians," in *Governments in Conflict? Provinces and Indian Nations in Canada*, ed. J. Anthony Long and Menno Boldt (Toronto: University of Toronto Press, 1988), 175; Jhappan, "Federal-Provincial Power-Grid," 167.
29 J. Anthony Long and Menno Boldt, eds., *Governments in Conflict? Provinces and Indian Nations in Canada* (Toronto: University of Toronto Press, 1988), 3.
30 Shewell, *Enough to Keep Them Alive*, 260–321.
31 Shewell, *Enough to Keep Them Alive*.
32 Long and Boldt, *Governments in Conflict*, 4.
33 Morse, "Government Obligations," 72.
34 Kenneth Kernaghan, "East Block and Westminster: Conventions, Values, and Public Service," in *The Handbook of Canadian Public Administration*, ed. Christopher Dunn (Don Mills, ON: Oxford University Press, 2002), 104.
35 Rocher and Smith, "Four Dimensions."
36 Pratt, "Federalism in the Era," 21.
37 Pratt, "Federalism in the Era," 50; Sanders, "The Constitution," 159–60.
38 Ian G. Scott and Timothy J.S. McCabe, "The Role of the Provinces in the Elucidation of Rights," in *Governments in Conflict? Provinces and Indian Nations in Canada*, ed. J. Anthony Long and Menno Boldt (Toronto: University of Toronto Press, 1988), 65.
39 Pratt, "Federalism in the Era," 50.
40 William Calder, "The Provinces and Indian Self-Government in the Constitutional Forum," in *Governments in Conflict? Provinces and Indian Nations in Canada*, ed. J. Anthony Long and Menno Boldt (Toronto: University of Toronto Press, 1988), 75; H.B. Hawthorn, ed., *A Survey of the Contemporary Indians of Canada: Economic, Political, Educational Needs and Policies; Part 1* (Ottawa: Indian Affairs Branch, 1966), publications.gc.ca/collections/collection_2014/aadnc-aandc/R32-1267-1-1-eng.pdf; Indian Affairs and Northern Development, *Statement of the Government of Canada on Indian Policy, 1969* (Ottawa: Queen's Printer, 1969), publications.gc.ca/collections/collection_2014/aadnc-aandc/R32-2469-eng.pdf; Special Committee on Indian Self-Government, *Indian Self-Government in*

Canada: Report of the Special Committee (Ottawa: Queen's Printer for Canada, 1983), publications.gc.ca/site/eng/9.872084/publication.html; Erik Nielsen, *New Management Initiatives: Initial Results from the Ministerial Task Force on Program Review* (Ottawa: The Task Force, 1985).

41 Sally Weaver, "The Hawthorn Report: Its Use in the Making of Canadian Indian Policy," in *Anthropology, Public Policy and Native Peoples in Canada*, ed. Noel Dyck and James B. Waldram (Montreal: McGill-Queen's University Press, 1993), 6.

42 Bruce Rawson, "Federal Perspectives on Indian-Provincial Relations," in *Governments in Conflict? Provinces and Indian Nations in Canada*, ed. J. Anthony Long and Menno Boldt, 23–30 (Toronto: University of Toronto Press, 1988), 28.

43 Pratt, "Federalism in the Era," 43.

44 Long and Boldt, *Governments in Conflict*, 9; Weaver, "Hawthorn Report," 92.

45 Sally M. Weaver, "Indian Policy in the New Conservative Government, Part II: The Nielsen Task Force in the Context of Recent Policy Initiatives," *Native Studies Review* 2, 2 (1986): 31.

46 Papillon, "Federalism From Below?," 33.

47 Kiera L. Ladner and Michael Orsini, "The Persistence of Paradigm Paralysis: The First Nations Governance Act as the Continuation of Colonial Policy," in *Reconfiguring Aboriginal-State Relations*, ed. Michael Murphy (Montreal & Kingston: McGill-Queen's University Press, 2003), 196.

48 Nigel Bankes, "Delgamuukw, Division of Powers and Provincial Land and Resource Laws: Some Implications for Provincial Resource Rights," *UBC Law Review* 32 (1998): 338; Cardinal v. Attorney General for Alberta (1973), [1974] SCR 695.

49 Bankes, "Delgamuukw," 339.

50 *Cardinal v. Attorney General for Alberta* (1973), [1974] SCR 695.

51 Peeling, *Provincial Jurisdiction*, 2.

52 Borrows, "Durability of Terra Nullius," 734–35.

53 *Cardinal v. Attorney General for Alberta* (1973), [1974] SCR 695.

54 Borrows, "Durability of Terra Nullius," 738.

55 Long and Boldt, *Governments in Conflict*, 45; Morse, "Government Obligations," 79; Scott and McCabe, "Role of the Provinces," 65.

56 Bhandar, "Anxious Reconciliation(s)," 833.

57 Morse, "Government Obligations," 76.

58 Michael Murphy, ed., *Reconfiguring Aboriginal-State Relations, Canada: The State of the Federation 2003* (Kingston: Queen's University, 2003), 21.

59 Sanders, "The Constitution," 170.

60 Calder, "Provinces and Indian Self-Government," 81.

61 Rocher and Smith, "Four Dimensions."

62 Rocher and Smith, "Four Dimensions," 28.

63 Ghislain Otis and Martin Papillon, eds., *Fédéralisme et gouvernance autochtone / Federalism and Aboriginal Governance* (Quebec City: Presses de l'Université Laval, 2013), 16.

64 Michael Coyle, "Establishing Indigenous Governance: The Challenge of Confronting Mainstream Cultural Norms," in *Fédéralisme et gouvernance autochtone / Federalism and Aboriginal Governance*, ed. Ghislain Otis and Martin Papillon (Quebec City: Presses de l'Université Laval, 2013).

65 Papillon, "Federalism From Below?," 31.

66 Papillon, "Federalism From Below?," ii.

67 Christopher Dunn, ed. *A Handbook of Canadian Public Administration* (Don Mills, ON: Oxford University Press, 2002), ix–xi.
68 Alasdair Roberts, "A Fragile State: Federal Public Administration in the Twentieth Century," in *The Handbook of Canadian Public Administration*, ed. Christopher Dunn (Don Mills, ON: Oxford University Press, 2002).
69 Andrew Sancton, "Provincial and Local Public Administration," in *The Handbook of Canadian Public Administration*, ed. Christopher Dunn (Don Mills, ON: Oxford University Press, 2002), 249.
70 Lorne Sossin, "Democratic Administration," in *The Handbook of Canadian Public Administration*, ed. Christopher Dunn (Don Mills, ON: Oxford University Press, 2002), 86.
71 Nelson Wiseman, "Provincial Political Cultures," in *Provinces: Canadian Provincial Politics*, ed. Christopher Dunn (Peterborough: Broadview Press, 1996), 58.
72 Long and Boldt, *Governments in Conflict*, 5.
73 Long and Boldt, *Governments in Conflict*, 46.
74 Morse, "Government Obligations," 72.
75 Richard Simeon, "Federalism and Intergovernmental Relations," in *The Handbook of Canadian Public Administration*, ed. Christopher Dunn (Don Mills, ON: Oxford University Press, 2002), 214.
76 Pratt, "Federalism in the Era," 23.
77 Long and Boldt, *Governments in Conflict*, 57, 127.
78 Ian G. Scott, "Respective Roles and Responsibilities of Federal and Provincial Governments Regarding the Aboriginal Peoples of Canada," in *Aboriginal Peoples and Government Responsibility: Exploring Federal and Provincial Roles*, ed. David C. Hawkes (Ottawa: Carleton University Press, 1989), 353.
79 Frances Abele and Katherine Graham, "High Politics Is Not Enough: Services for Aboriginal Peoples in Alberta and Ontario," in *Defining the Responsibilities: Federal and Provincial Governments and Aboriginal Peoples*, ed. David C. Hawkes (Ottawa: Carleton University Press, 1989), 144.
80 Jhappan, "Federal-Provincial Power-Grid," 167.
81 Katherine Graham, Frances Abele, and Caroline Dittburner, *Soliloquy and Dialogue: The Evolution of Public Policy Discourse on Aboriginal Issues* (Ottawa: Canada Communications Group, 1996), xi.
82 Kerry Wilkins, "Dancing in the Dark: Of Provinces and Section 35 Rights After 2010," *Supreme Court Law Review* 54, 1 (2011): 533.
83 *Grassy Narrows First Nation v. Ontario (Natural Resources)*, 2014 SCC 48, [2014] 2 SCR 447; *Tsilhqot'in Nation v. British Columbia*, 2014 SCC 44, [2014] 2 SCR 7.
84 *Delgamuukw v. British Columbia*, [1997] 3 SCR 1010.
85 Bankes and Koshan, "Tsilhqot'in," 1.
86 Bankes and Koshan, "Tsilhqot'in," 2.
87 Bankes and Koshan, "Tsilhqot'in," 2.
88 Borrows, "Durability of Terra Nullius," 737; McCrossan and Ladner, "Eliminating Indigenous Jurisdictions," 416–17.
89 McCrossan and Ladner, "Eliminating Indigenous Jurisdictions," 416–17.
90 McCrossan and Ladner, "Eliminating Indigenous Jurisdictions," 412.
91 Grace Skogstad and Herman Bakvis, "Conclusion: Taking Stock of Canadian Federalism," in *Canadian Federalism: Performance, Effectiveness, and Legitimacy*, 3rd ed., ed. Herman Bakvis and Grace Skogstad (Toronto: University of Toronto Press, 2012), 340.

92   Papillon, "Nation to Nation?," 402.
93   Morse, "Government Obligations," 64–67.
94   Robert Exell, "British Columbia and the Native Community," in *Governments in Conflict? Provinces and Indian Nations in Canada*, ed. J. Anthony Long and Menno Boldt (Toronto: University of Toronto Press, 1988), 96.
95   Long and Boldt, *Governments in Conflict*.
96   Kulchyski, *Unjust Relations*, 7; Boldt and Long, *Quest for Justice*, 50.
97   Long and Boldt, *Governments in Conflict*, 3.
98   Indian Affairs and Northern Development, *Statement of the Government of Canada on Indian Policy, 1969*.
99   Turner, *This Is Not a Peace Pipe*, 13.
100 Long and Boldt, *Governments in Conflict*, 8.
101 Long and Boldt, *Governments in Conflict*, 5; Alan Cairns, *Citizens Plus: Aboriginal Peoples and the Canadian State* (Vancouver, UBC: 2000), 90.
102 Cairns, *Citizens Plus*, 90; Calder, "Provinces and Indian Self-Government," 76; Long and Boldt, *Governments in Conflict*, 58.
103 Calder, "Provinces and Indian Self-Government," 76.
104 Long and Boldt, *Governments in Conflict*, 6–7.
105 Dianna Ginn, "Indian Hunting Rights."
106 Hawkes, *Aboriginal Peoples and Government Responsibility*, 360.
107 Martin Papillon, "Indigenous Peoples and Federalism: In or Out?," in *Teaching Federalism: Multidimensional Approaches*, ed. John Kincaid and J. Leckrone (Elgar Online, 2023), 213.
108 Murphy, *Reconfiguring Aboriginal-State Relations*, 5.
109 Long and Boldt, *Governments in Conflict*, 6.
110 Morse, "Government Obligations," 79.
111 Hawkes, *Aboriginal Peoples and Government Responsibility*, 361.
112 Saskatchewan Indigenous Investment Finance Corporation, "Programs," n.d., siifc.ca/program.
113 Martin Papillon, "Canadian Federalism and the Emerging Mosaic of Aboriginal Multilevel Governance," in *Canadian Federalism: Performance, Effectiveness, and Legitimacy*, 3rd ed., ed. Herman Bakvis and Grace Skogstad (Toronto: University of Toronto Press, 2012), 296.
114 Papillon, "Canadian Federalism," 297.
115 Graham, Abele, and Dittburner, *Soliloquy and Dialogue*, xii.
116 Abele and Prince, "Four Pathways."
117 Gabrielle A. Slowey, *Navigating Neoliberalism: Self-determination and the Mikisew Cree First Nation* (Vancouver: UBC Press, 2008).
118 Papillon, "Canadian Federalism," 296.
119 Sam Halabi, "The Role of Provinces States and Territories in Shaping Federal Policy for Indigenous Peoples' Health," *American Review of Canadian Studies*, 49, 2 (2019); 236.
120 Papillon, "Nation to Nation?," 401.
121 Papillon, "Canadian Federalism," 296
122 Papillon, "Canadian Federalism," 296.
123 Long and Boldt, *Governments in Conflict*, 7.
124 Harold Cardinal, *The Unjust Society: The Tragedy of Canada's Indians* (Edmonton: Hurtig, 1969), 46.

125 Josée Lavoie, "Community Healing and Aboriginal Self-Government," in *Aboriginal Self-Government in Canada*, ed. Yale Belanger (Saskatoon: Purich, 2008), 192.
126 Coulthard, *Red Skin White Masks*.
127 Coulthard, *Red Skin White Masks*, 6.
128 Coulthard, *Red Skin White Masks*, 6.

Chapter Five

1 Coulthard, *Red Skin White Masks*.
2 Alain-G. Gagnon and Arjun Tremblay, "Introduction: Puzzles of Multinational Federalism," in *Federalism and National Diversity in the 21st Century*, ed. Alain-G. Gagnon and Arjun Tremblay (Cham, Switzerland: Springer International Publishing AG, 2020), 2–5.
3 Joyce Green, *Self-Determination, Citizenship, and Federalism: Indigenous and Canadian Palimpsest* (Regina: Saskatchewan Institute of Public Policy, 2003), 333.
4 Green, *Self-Determination*, 333.
5 Parasram, "Pluriversal Sovereignty."
6 Simpson, *As We Have Always Done*.
7 Henderson, "Sui Generis," 423.
8 Abele and Prince, "Four Pathways," 572.
9 Ladner and Orsini, "Persistence of Paradigm Paralysis," 197.
10 Abele and Prince, "Four Pathways."
11 Ladner and Orsini, "Persistence of Paradigm Paralysis," 193.
12 Abele and Prince, "Four Pathways."
13 *Agreement Between the Inuit of the Nunavut Settlement Area and Her Majesty The Queen in Right of Canada*, May 25, 1993, between the Inuit of the Nunavut Settlement Area as represented by the Tungavik Federation of Nunavut and Her Majesty The Queen in Right of Canada, publications.gc.ca/collections/Collection/R32-134-1993E.pdf; Abele and Prince, "Four Pathways," 574.
14 Papillon, "Nation to Nation?," 405; Papillon, "Canadian Federalism," 284.
15 Abele and Prince, "Four Pathways," 575.
16 Michael Morden, "Indigenizing Parliament: Time to Re-Start a Conversation," *Canadian Parliamentary Review*, 39, 2 (2016): 26; Abele and Prince, "Four Pathways," 576–78; Henderson, "Sui Generis," 428.
17 Williams, "The Same River, Together," 211.
18 Abele and Prince, "Four Pathways," 579; Bhandar, "Anxious Reconciliation(s)," 837.
19 Morden, "Indigenizing Parliament," 24.
20 Williams, "The Same River, Together," 72.
21 Ila Bussidor and Üstün Bilgen-Reinart, *Night Spirits: The Story of the Relocation of the Sayisi Dene* (Winnipeg: University of Manitoba Press, 1997).
22 Abele and Prince, "Four Pathways," 579.
23 Royal Commission on Aboriginal Peoples, *Report*, 647.
24 Royal Commission on Aboriginal Peoples, *Report*, 647.
25 Ladner, "Treaty Federalism," 183–84.
26 Slattery, "Hidden Constitution."
27 Slattery, "Hidden Constitution," 367.

28 Slattery, "Hidden Constitution," 386.
29 Henderson, "Sui Generis."
30 Henderson, "Sui Generis," 417.
31 Foundational to my understanding of postcolonialism are the following works: Memmi, *The Colonizer*; Fanon, *Wretched*; Said, *Orientalism*; Homi K. Bhabha, *The Location of Culture* (London and New York: Routledge, 1994); Spivak, "Can the Subaltern Speak?"
32 Ladner, "Treaty Federalism," 168–69.
33 Sharon Venne, "Treaties Made in Good Faith," in *Natives and Settlers Now and Then*, ed. Paul W. DePasquale (Edmonton: University of Alberta Press, 2007).
34 Venne, "Treaties Made," 1.
35 Henderson, "Sui Generis."
36 Ladner, "Treaty Federalism," 173.
37 Michael Asch, *On Being Here to Stay: Treaties and Aboriginal Rights in Canada* (Toronto: University of Toronto Press, 2014).
38 Sheldon Krasowski, *No Surrender: The Land Remains Indigenous* (Regina: University of Regina Press, 2019); John Borrows and Michael Coyle, *The Right Relationship: Reimaging the Implementation of Historical Treaties* (Toronto: University of Toronto Press, 2017); Kulchyski, *Red Indians*.
39 Krasowski, *No Surrender*; Peter Kulchyski, *Like the Sound of a Drum: Aboriginal Cultural Politics in Denendeh and Nunavut* (Winnipeg: University of Manitoba Press, 2005), 89.
40 Kulchyski, *Unjust Relations*, 9.
41 Alexander Morris, *The Treaties of Canada* (Toronto: Belfords, Clarke & Co., 1880; Markham, ON: Fifth House Publishers, 1991), citations refer to the Fifth House edition; Ray, Miller, and Tough, *Bounty and Benevolence*, 111–12.
42 Venne, "Treaties Made," 2.
43 Henderson, "Sui Generis," 428.
44 Abele and Prince, "Four Pathways."
45 Liam Nohr, "Reconciliatory Federalism: A Nation-To-Nation Relationship Under Critical Evaluation," *Federalism-E* 24, 1 (2023): 3.
46 Ladner, "Treaty Federalism," 178.
47 Abele and Prince, "Four Pathways," 579–80.
48 Katherine Walker, "Treaty Federalism: Building a Foundation for Duty to Consult in Saskatchewan" (Master's thesis, University of Saskatchewan, 2010), 13–14.
49 Beckman, Gover, and Mörkenstam, "Popular Sovereignty," 5.
50 Kelty McKerracher, "Relational Legal Pluralism and Indigenous Legal Orders in Canada," *Global Constitutionalism* 12, 1 (2023): 152.
51 Martin Papillon, "The Two Faces of Treaty Federalism," in *Canadian Politics*, ed. James Bickerton and Alain-G. Gagnon, 7th ed. (University of Toronto Press, 2019): 8–10.
52 Abele and Prince, "Four Pathways," 579–83.
53 Williams, "The Same River, Together."
54 Mills, "Miinigowiziwin," 230.
55 Mills, "Miinigowiziwin," 230.
56 Abele and Prince, "Four Pathways," 587–88; Ladner and Orsini, "Persistence of Paradigm Paralysis."
57 Nohr, "Reconciliatory Federalism," 5.
58 Papillon, "Nation to Nation?"; Nohr, "Reconciliatory Federalism."

59 Papillon, "Nation to Nation?," 407.
60 Williams, "The Same River, Together," 68.
61 Williams, "The Same River, Together," 71.
62 Williams, "The Same River, Together," 69.
63 Marland and Wesley, *Inside Canadian Politics*, 514.
64 Papillon, "Nation to Nation?," 419.
65 Papillon, "Nation to Nation?," 415.
66 Papillon, "Nation to Nation?," 401.
67 Papillon, "Nation to Nation?," 405.
68 Nohr, "Reconciliatory Federalism," 6.
69 Papillon, "Nation to Nation?," 402.
70 Williams, "The Same River, Together," 17.
71 Parasram, "Pluriversal Sovereignty," 357.
72 Parasram, "Pluriversal Sovereignty," 359–62.
73 Parasram, "Pluriversal Sovereignty," 60.
74 Walker, "Treaty Federalism," 11.
75 Parasram, "Pluriversal Sovereignty," 356.
76 Nico Krisch, "Framing Entangled Legalities Beyond the State," in *Entangled Legalities Beyond the State*, ed. Nico Krisch (New York: Cambridge University Press, 2021), 9.
77 Christie, *Plural Sovereignties*, 6.
78 McKerracher, "Relational Legal Pluralism," 145.
79 Lightfoot, "Decolonizing Self-Determination," 972–73.
80 Parasram, "Pluriversal Sovereignty," 359.
81 McKerracher, "Relational Legal Pluralism," 134.
82 Beckman, Gover, and Mörkenstam, "Popular Sovereignty," 2–3.
83 Beckman, Gover, and Mörkenstam, "Popular Sovereignty," 14.
84 Beckman, Gover, and Mörkenstam, "Popular Sovereignty," 4.
85 Christine Keating and Amy Lind, "Plural Sovereignty and La Familia Diversa in Ecuador's 2008 Constitution," *Feminist Studies* 43, 2 (2017).
86 Keating and Lind, "Plural Sovereignty," 295.
87 Keating and Lind, "Plural Sovereignty," 299.
88 Keating and Lind, "Plural Sovereignty," 301.
89 Keith Culver and Michael Giudice, "Entanglement of State and Indigenous Legal Orders in Canada," in *Entangled Legalities Beyond the State*, ed. Nico Krisch (Cambridge, University Press, 2021), 377–78.
90 Christie, *Plural Sovereignties*.
91 Parasram, "Pluriversal Sovereignty," 362.
92 Parasram, "Pluriversal Sovereignty," 363.
93 Parasram, "Pluriversal Sovereignty," 364.
94 *R. v. Marshall*, [1999] 3 SCR 456.
95 De Leon, "Theorising From the Land," 772.
96 Simpson, *As We Have Always Done*, 40–45.
97 Simpson, *As We Have Always Done*, 10.
98 Coulthard, *Red Skin White Masks*, 13.
99 Zoe Todd, "Fish, Kin and Hope: Tending to Water Violations in *Amiskwaciwâskahikan* and Treaty Six Territory," *Afterall: A Journal of Art Context and Enquiry* 43 (2017): 103.
100 Todd, "Fish, Kin and Hope," 106.

101 Stark, "Nenabozho's Smart Berries," 13.
102 Heidi Kiiwetinepinesiik Stark, "Marked by Fire: Anishinaabe Articulations of Nationhood in Treaty Making with the United States and Canada," *American Indian Quarterly* 36, 2 (2012): 122.
103 Stark, "Marked by Fire," 122–23.
104 Mills, "Miinigowiziwin," 227.
105 Daniel Voth, "Her Majesty's Justice Be Done: Métis Legal Mobilization and the Pitfalls to Indigenous Political Movement Building," *Canadian Journal of Political Science* 49, 2 (2016): 243–66.
106 Daniel Voth, "Invitations from the Land and Waters: Lessons From the Peace of Fort Garry," *Canadian Journal of Urban Research* 29, 1 (2020): 94.
107 Hogue, *Métis and the Medicine Line*.
108 Mills, "Miinigowiziwin," 192.
109 Mills, "Miinigowiziwin," 197.
110 Mills, "Miinigowiziwin," 194.
111 Simpson, *As We Have Always Done*, 46.

Postscript

1 Bhandar, "Anxious Reconciliation(s)," 831.
2 Borrows, "Indigenous Legal Traditions."
3 Russell Barsh, "Aboriginal Peoples and Canada's Conscience," in *Hidden in Plain Sight: Contributions of Aboriginal Peoples to Canadian Identity and Culture*, ed. David Newhouse, Cora Voyageur, and Dan Beavon (Toronto: University of Toronto Press, 2005).
4 Said, *Orientalism*.
5 Williams, "The Same River, Together," 73.
6 Said, *Orientalism*; Fanon, *Wretched*; Memmi, *The Colonizer*.
7 Somdeep Sen, *Decolonizing Palestine: Hamas Between the Anticolonial and Postcolonial* (Ithaca, NY: Cornell University Press, 2020), 133.
8 Jeff Corntassel, Taiaiake Alfred, Noelani Goodyear-Kaʻōpua, Noenoe K. Silva, Hokulani Aikau, and Devi Mucina, eds., *Everyday Acts of Resurgence: Peoples, Places, Practices* (Olympia, WA: Daykeeper Press, 2018).
9 Ladner and Orsini, "Persistence of Paradigm Paralysis," 197.
10 Bhandar, "Anxious Reconciliation(s)," 840.
11 Tuck and Yang, "Decolonization Is Not a Metaphor."

INDEX

Abele, Francis, 92–3, 98–9, 106, 109–10
Aboriginal title, 75
    contested concepts of, 47, 65–6
    legal cases on, 49, 68, 71–2, 82, 87–8, 93–4
    terra nullius versus, 48, 51–3
"Aboriginal," use of term, 25
accommodationist governance models, 101–4, 107
Adams, Howard, 5
adapted federalism, 101, 104–5
agency, Indigenous,
    assertions of, 51, 53, 79, 115
    complicity in eroding, 16, 36–7, 54–5, 75, 123, 127
    concepts of, 26, 103, 124
    federalism denial of, 6–11, 42, 57, 61, 81, 103–4
    models to support, 103, 105, 108, 113
    nation-to-nation relations affirming, 24, 27
    provincial authority undermining, 67–8, 73, 86
    settler acknowledgement of, 51–2, 59–60, 85–6, 100, 114
    sovereignty as collective, 32–4, 113, 117
Alberta, 18, 72, 83, 87
Anaya, James, 27, 54
ancestry/ancestral knowledge,
    Indigeneity/Indianness and, 24, 67
    Inherent rights and, 26, 46, 62–3
    land rights/guardianship based on, 46, 49–52, 65, 75, 92–4
    resurgence/resistance revival of, 36, 54, 79, 108, 117–19, 122–5
    settler colonial undermining of, 14, 43–4, 62–4, 72, 98, 104–5
    shared Métis, 1–4
    traditional/legal practices according to, 8, 44, 54, 59

animus manendi, 12
Anishinaabe Nation,
    resurgence, 120–2
    scholars, 1, 13, 27, 30, 48, 51, 121
anticolonialism, 31, 108, 111, 118, 125
Aragon, Corwin, 16
assimilation, 4
    "Aboriginal"/Indian status and, 25, 64
    accommodationism and, 100, 103
    devolving responsibility to provinces, 68, 74–5, 91, 96
    discourse to conceal, 10, 27, 39–40
    dispossession and, 10, 13–15, 31, 43–6, 118
    enfranchised, 63–4
    genocidal, 15–18, 40, 43–4, 104, 127
    Indigenous resistance to, 54, 86, 118–19, 125
    settler state policies of, 6, 13, 15, 24, 61
    as stage of settler colonial expansion, 15, 79
    tactics of, 10, 13, 17–18, 66
Atleo, Clifford, 60
Atleo, E. Richard, 65
Auditor-General for Quebec v. Auditor-General for Canada, 82
Australia, 21, 43–4
autonomy, Indigenous,
    concept of, 26–7
    Crown negotiation of, 58
    Indigenous rights upheld by, 8, 32–4, 53
    governance models upholding, 106–7, 110–13
    reconciliation recognition of, 29, 122
    resistance/resurgence movements and, 101, 124
    settler colonial theft/denial of, 8, 15, 23, 95–7, 103
    state sovereignty versus, 29, 31–3, 54, 89, 107

Ballantyne, Tony, 8
Bankes, Nigel, 93–4
Barker, Adam J., 12, 33
Barsh, Russell, 124
Battell Lowman, Emma, 12, 33
Battiste, Marie, 5
Beckman, Ludvig, 32
Bhandar, Brenna, 49, 52–3, 60
  paradox of iterability, 14, 50
Boldt, Menno, 91, 96
Boron, Jonathan, 60
Borrows, John, 87–8
  on Doctrine of Discovery/*terra nullius*, 48, 51–2
  on Indigenous legal traditions, 13–14, 79, 124
Boushie, Colten, 47
British Columbia, 18, 27–8, 72
  court cases, 49, 52–3, 93
British North America Act, 1867 (BNA Act),
  as Canada's first constitutional document, 9, 56, 80
  Indigenous marginalization through, 35, 57–8, 61, 69, 82–3
  provincial jurisdiction vis-à-vis, 68–72, 75, 79, 81, 86–8, 96–100
  section 91(24) (on "special relationship"): 24, 63–6, 68–72, 79, 106, 110
  section 109: 72, 81
  settler land dispossession through, 57–8, 61, 72, 81
Brown, Kate, 50
Buss, James Joseph, 43
Byrd, Jodi, 14

Calder, William, 89, 97
Calls to Action,
  No. 45: 23, 58, 60
  release of and inaction on, 19–22
Canada,
  as federation, 26, 56–7, 90–1, 105–7, 110–11
  Indigenous basis of, 1, 14, 28, 51, 61, 109
  as peacekeeper, 10, 16, 40
  reconciliation, stance on, 17–22, 52, 126
  as settler colonial state, 6, 12–15, 46, 118, 126
  as UNDRIP signatory, 27

capitalism, 12, 40, 48, 90
Cardinal, Harold, 25, 96, 99–100
Cardinal v. Attorney General of Alberta, 87
Carter, Sarah, 15, 79
Christie, Stuart, 31, 114, 116
Citizens Plus (Red Paper), 96
classic federalism, 77–8, 81–3
Coffey, Wallace, 32–3
collaborative federalism, 78, 83–4
colonial federalism, 77–82, 88
colonial order(s),
  exposing weaknesses in, 21, 102, 118, 124
  imperial, *see* imperial colonialism
  treaty federalism amid, 107–8
colonization, 7
  justifications for, 30–1, 45–6
  TRC Report on, 19, 50
competitive federalism, 77–8, 85–8, 90, 93–5, 100
complicity, structural, 16, 31, 37, 60, 114
Confederation, 35
  Indigenous involvement in, 1, 23, 79–80
  provincial jurisdiction in, 72, 74, 82
  Treaty making amid, 46, 79–80
Confederation of Indigenous Nationalities of Ecuador, 116
Constitution Act, 1982: 66, 78, 89
  on Aboriginal and Treaty rights, 8, 17, 29, 110
  on federal/provincial powers, 9, 56–7, 87–8
  Indianness and, 25, 63–4
  see also section 35 (Constitution Act, 1982)
constitutional federalism, 77–8, 88–90, 93–5, 100
Constitution Express, 28
Corntassel, Jeff, 27, 29, 33
Coulthard, Glen,
  on grounded normativity, 119–20
  on politics of recognition, *see* politics of recognition
courts,
  Aboriginal rights cases in, 14–15, 58, 63–4, 75
  Aboriginal title cases in, 47–9, 51–2, 81–2, 93–4

on duty to consult, 52, 72, 111
on federal enclaves, 87, 93
fiduciary responsibilities established
    via, 25-6, 81-3
Indigenous sovereignty versus, 29, 50,
    94-5
interjurisdictional immunity in, 87-8,
    94
provincial authority cases in, 68-72, 81,
    87, 93, 97-9
reconciliation efforts via, 6, 17-18
settler colonial narratives reinforced in,
    44, 47-8, 50-3
state/Crown sovereignty reinforced in,
    14, 44, 50, 82
Supreme, *see* Supreme Court of Canada
Cree Nation, 70
    language terms, 4, 64, 108, 121
    scholars, 21, 25, 44, 47-8, 73, 118
Crown, the,
    court rulings/federalism reinforcing
        sovereignty of, 14-15, 30, 44, 52-3,
        94, 126
    fiduciary responsibilities, 61-2, 65,
        72-4, 82, 109
    Indigenous resistance/resurgence
        versus, 17, 86, 98
    lands, 64, 71-3, 75, 81
    "special relationship" with Indigenous
        Peoples, 13, 23-5, 68-9, 82, 96
    sui generis Indigenous rights versus, 26,
        52, 58-63, 104, 116
    treaty federalism and, 108-10, 112
Culver, Keith, 116

Daniels v. Canada: 25, 63-4
Daschuk, James, 15, 46-7
decentralized federalism, 77, 90-1
decolonization, 102, 113
    cognitive, 5, 27-8
    concepts of, 7-8, 22, 108
    as distinct from reconciliation, 8, 22-3
    land restitution as central to, 22-3, 119,
        121
de Leon, Justin, 32, 118
Delgamuukw v. British Columbia, 50
    on Aboriginal title, 49, 51, 65-8, 71, 82,
        93-4
Derrickson, Ronald, 28, 38, 42

dialectic tension, Indigeneity and, 4-5, 14
discourse(s),
    betterment, 39-42
    cacophonous, 14
    concept of, 41
    national, 43, 57, 99
    power relations and, 39-43, 80
    rights, 27, 62, 99
disease, European-derived, 15, 43, 50
dispossession, Indigenous,
    federalism aim of settler benefit and,
        7-10, 16, 38-9, 42, 101, 113-14
    Indigenous resistance to, 34, 36, 51-2,
        118, 126
    jurisdictional challenges and, 57, 60, 66
    narratives reinforcing, 34-5, 38-43,
        50-2, 66
    processes of, 13, 15, 23, 46-7, 123
    reconciliation efforts and, 20-2, 27, 66,
        110, 123-4, 127
Dittburner, Caroline, 93, 98-9
doctrine of discovery,
    aim of dispossession, 11-12, 47-50
    persistence of, 48-9, 53-4
    rejection of, 23, 51
domination, settler colonial,
    downplaying/obscuring of, 14, 21
    historical framework of, 12-16, 35, 114
    Indigenous resistance to, 17, 21, 36,
        118-19
    structural, 43, 45, 104
Dominion of Canada, 94
    extractive economic basis for, 12, 58-9,
        81
Dua, Enakshi, 80
duty to consult, 52, 72, 111

economic structures/systems,
    collaborative federalism and, 78, 83
    Indigenous, 6, 24, 27, 61, 66, 108
    Indigenous marginalization/erasure in,
        3, 12-13, 16, 34, 39, 49
    jurisdictional disagreements in, 12, 96,
        105
    reconciliation efforts and, 6, 38, 126
    settler colonial, 1, 8, 11-12, 15, 45-7
education, 3, 6-7
    enfranchisement loss of status via, 24, 63
    First Nations-delivered, 105

Elders, teachings of, 4, 6, 32, 47
erasure, Indigenous,
   enfranchisement and, 63
   narratives to reinforce, 12, 34, 38–40, 43–4, 50–1, 54
   resistance to, 6, 127
   settler colonial state processes of, 6, 14, 57, 80, 103–4, 114
Eurocentrism,
   concept of, 30
   Indigenous sovereignty and, 29–31, 33, 102
   in land dispossession, 47–9, 51, 65–6
   in state models/systems, 104, 114, 117

Fanon, Frantz, 45, 126
federalism,
   adapted, 101, 104–5
   aim of settler benefit, 7–10, 16, 38–9, 42, 113–14
   alternatives to, 9, 11, 77, 90, 107
   classic, 77–8, 81–3
   collaborative, 78, 83–4
   colonial, 77–82, 88
   competitive, 77–8, 85–8, 90, 93–5, 100
   concept of, 9, 56
   constitutional, 77–8, 88–90, 93–5, 100
   decentralized, 77, 90–1
   denial of Indigenous agency, 5–11, 42, 57, 61, 81, 103–4
   enabling Indigenous dispossession, 8–10, 13–15, 75–6, 101
   Indigenous legal foundations in, 13–15, 79, 124
   interstate, 112, 125
   as limiting reconciliation, 5, 9, 22–3, 34, 37–8, 100, 124–7
   multinational, 101
   as political system of governance, 8–10, 13–15, 69, 78
   politics of recognition and, 101, 111
   power relations, 8–11, 35, 40–1, 57, 81, 127
   power-sharing models, 101–2, 107–8, 110–13, 119–22
   settler decision-making authority in, 35, 40–1, 48–9, 54–6, 80–1, 90–7
   treaty, 36, 102, 107–13, 125
   trilateral, 101, 105–7, 112
   undermining self-determination, 8–10, 35, 77
First Nations Governance Act, 103–4
Foucault, Michel, 41
Frideres, James, 69, 80
fur trade, 1–2, 15, 49

Gadacz, Rene, 69, 80
Gagnon, Alain-G., 101
genocide, Indigenous, 42
   IRS system and, 7, 13, 15, 17
   logics/narratives supporting, 44, 80, 100, 104, 125, 127
governance,
   accommodationist models of, 101–4, 107
   devolution to provinces, 35, 48–9, 54–5, 75–6, 84, 90–7
   federalist, *see* federalism
   federal responsibilities under, 40–1, 69
   Indigenous, 51, 59, 99–100, 106–8, 120
   multilevel, 11, 77, 90, 110–12, 115
   nation-to-nation relations in, 59–60, 72–3, 109–10
   new public management (NPM) and, 90–1
Graham, Katherine, 92–3, 98–9
Great Depression, 78, 82–3
Green, Joyce, 28–9, 102

Hall, Anthony J., 58
Haudenosaunee (Hodinohso:ni) Nation, 60
   governance system, 13, 28, 108
Hawthorn Report (*A Survey of the Contemporary Indians of Canada*), 85
healthcare,
   inequitable access to, 7, 13, 70
   jurisdictional responsibility for, 56, 69–70, 74, 105
Henderson, James (Sákéj) Youngblood, 102, 107, 109, 113
Hogg, Peter, 65, 70–1
Hogue, Michel, 17, 121
housing, 60–1, 69
Hudson's Bay Company, 2, 12, 50, 58, 79
humility thesis, 121
Hunt, Dallas (*Storying Violence*), 47
Hunt, Sarah, 32

hunting,
    ancestral practices of, 2, 105
    Indigenous rights for, 23, 73, 68, 98
    legislation, 67–8, 84, 97–8
imperial colonialism, 10, 108
    concept of, 11, 30, 45
    Indigenous sovereignty versus, 103, 106, 114
    settler colonialism versus, 12, 44–6, 54, 62
imperialism,
    cognitive, 5
    narratives reinforcing, 24, 33, 77, 126
    religious justifications for, 10–11, 30
    see also imperial colonialism
Indian Act, 54
    elimination of Indian status/identity via, 13, 24, 63–4, 85, 126
    "Indian," definition in, 24–5, 64, 82–3
    provincial jurisdiction vis-à-vis, 67–8, 71, 93–7
    section 88: 49, 67–8, 74, 93–4, 96–7
Indian Affairs, 103
    jurisdiction/service provision, 68–70, 84–5, 105
    land appropriation via, 53, 61
Indianness,
    Indian Act section 88 and, 67–8, 74, 93–4
    restricted provincial jurisdiction, 67–8, 71–2, 74–6, 93
    use of term, 67
    see also "Indian," use of term; Indigeneity
Indian Residential Schools Settlement Agreement (IRSSA), 18
Indian residential school (IRS) system, stories/legacies of, 16–18
    Survivors/Intergenerational Survivors of, 6, 17–18, 21
    TRC/reconciliation work on, 6, 18–21, 61
    violence of, 7, 13, 15, 17–18, 54
Indian status,
    Indian Act elimination of, 24, 63
    Indigenous identity and, 24–6, 64, 85
    provincial/federal jurisdiction and, 55–7, 69, 75, 82–6, 92, 95–7
"Indian," use of term, 24–5, 64, 82–3

Indigeneity,
    authentic versus state-generated, 24–5, 63, 66–7
    dialectic tension in, 4–5, 14
    see also Indianness
Indigenous difference,
    concept of, 6, 67
    decolonization/reconciliation centring, 6–7, 17, 108, 118, 124–5
    settler desire/tactics to erase, 13–14, 10, 25, 44, 103–4
Indigenous legal orders/traditions, 51, 94
    Canadian federalism basis in, 13–15, 79, 124
    multiplural sovereignty and, 114–16
    as *sui generis*, 107–8, 114–15, 125
    treaty federalism and, 107–10
Indigenous sovereignty, 29, 34
    concepts of, 30–3, 119–20, 122
    liberatory, 31–3, 115–16, 125
    recognition of, 10, 31–2, 59, 65, 88, 110, 114
    settler colonial denial of, 13, 48–50, 57–8, 80, 96, 109
    state sovereignty versus, 30–3, 99–102, 105–6, 122
    see also sovereignty
"Indigenous," use of term, 25–6
inequities,
    decision-making structures sustaining, 2, 85–6
    embeddedness of colonial, 6–7, 41, 85–6
    federalism producing/maintaining, 34, 41
    Indigenous resistance and resurgence to counter, 121–3
    limited possibilities to overcome, 5, 125
    narratives concealing power, 35, 37–8
    reconciliation aims to alleviate, 6–8, 19, 41, 121–2
Inherent rights,
    concept of, 26–7
    as *sui generis*, 26, 29, 32, 63, 115
institutions,
    decolonizing/Indigenous, 8, 102, 107
    Indigenous presence in, 24, 89, 99, 102
    power relations/racism in, 8, 40–1, 80, 105, 110–11
    settler colonial narratives in, 54–5, 108

Intergenerational Survivors, 6, 17–19, 21
interjurisdictional immunity, 87–8, 94
interstate federalism, 112, 125
Inuit, 13, 107
    fiduciary/jurisdictional obligations to, 25, 63–4, 69, 79, 82–3, 104
    TRC Report experiences, 19
Iroquois Confederacy, 13, 108

Jaggar, Alison M., 16
Jhappan, Radha, 57, 71–2, 92
Jordan's Principle, 70
jurisdiction, 23
    alternatives to current, 112, 114–15
    concept of, 56
    denial of Indigenous agency/sovereignty in, 8–10, 37–8, 44, 50, 86, 103, 127
    devolution of, 35, 48–9, 54–7, 75–6, 83–4, 90–7
    disagreements/ambiguity over, 12, 35, 54–5, 65–6, 91–3, 112–13
    federal, 9–10, 35, 56–8, 61–7
    fiduciary responsibilities, 25, 70–2, 74–6, 78
    Indigenous, 49, 62, 75–6, 87–8, 105
    on-reserve, 67, 69, 84, 86, 95
    provincial, 57, 66–8, 71–5, 91–3, 97–9
    racism contributing to historical, 8, 80–3, 95–7, 123
    shared, 8, 56, 74, 87, 113
    transfer of, 70, 73–4, 86–7
    ultra vires, 69, 71
    see also interjurisdictional immunity

Keating, Christine, 116
Keewatin (Grassy Narrows First Nation v. Ontario [Natural Resources]), 72, 93
kinship relations, 46
    Indigeneity and, 24, 64
    resistance/resurgence movements honouring, 17, 120–2
    sui generis rights and, 26, 107, 120
Knowledge Keepers, 4, 33–4, 46, 118
Koshan, Jennifer, 93–4
Krasowski, Sheldon, 109
Kulchyski, Peter, 44, 82

Ladner, Kiera, 103–4, 118
    settler state versus Indigenous legal orders, 44, 86, 94
    on treaty federalism, 102, 109–10, 113
land(s),
    acknowledgements, 7, 39
    claims, *see* land claims
    Crown, 64, 71–3, 75, 81
    defence, 17, 49
    Indigenous presence on/relations with, 6, 9, 26, 38, 47, 51–2, 82
    narratives to justify dispossession, 10–12, 44–51, 61–6, 72, 114
    ownership disputes, 45–9, 51–2, 60, 63–6, 81
    provincial authority over, 71, 91, 93–4, 98
    return, 7, 22–3, 119, 121
    rights/guardianship based on, 46, 49–52, 65, 75, 92–4
    Royal Proclamation ambiguity on, 58–61
    theft of Indigenous, 8, 15, 39, 44–5, 78–9, 81
    violence to acquire, 11, 13, 46–7
    see also Aboriginal title; *terra nullius*; Treaty Land Entitlement
land claims, 75, 104
    alternative governance systems and, 109, 111, 113
    regulatory authority in, 23, 72–3, 126
LaRocque, Emma, 39
Legislative Assembly, Manitoba, working at, 1–2, 73
Lenzerini, Federico, 33
liberation, Indigenous,
    aspects of, 46, 119
    changes in governance and, 35–6, 117, 126
    notions of sovereignty versus, 28, 30–1
    reconciliation vis-à-vis, 21, 125
    settler colonial governments versus, 5, 97, 126
Lightfoot, Sheryl R., 27–8, 114–15
Liodakis, Nikolaos, 80
Litt, Paul, 40
logic of elimination, 43–4, 49
Long, J. Anthony, 91, 96

Manitoba, 18, 70–2, 83, 104–5, 121; *see also* Winnipeg
Manuel, Arthur, 28, 38, 42
mapping, settler colonial, 39, 79
marginalization, Indigenous,
   economic, 3, 34, 92–3
   narratives reinforcing, 34–5, 39, 54–5, 76, 80, 127
   settler colonial legislation/processes and, 46, 66, 92, 123
McCabe, Timothy, 70–2
McCallum, Mary Jane, 16
McCrossan, Michael, 44, 50, 94
Melançon, Jérôme, 22
Memmi, Albert, 45, 80, 126
Métis Peoples, 19
   author ancestry in, 1–5
   fiduciary obligations to, 25, 64, 79
   Red River Settlement, *see* Red River Settlement
   resistance/resurgence movements by, 17, 121
   scholars, 15, 28, 39, 42, 120–1
   self-governance/legal orders, 104, 107, 120–1
Mi'kmaq Nation, 5, 116–17
Mills, Aaron, 51, 111, 121–2
mini-municipalities, 101, 103
Missing and Murdered Indigenous Women, Girls, and Two-Spirit People, 7, 42
Monture-Angus, Patricia, 25
Morris, Alexander, 109
Morse, Bradford, 70, 88, 91
multiculturalism, 15, 89, 116
multiplural sovereignty, 117, 121–2, 125
   concept of, 113–14
   examples of, 115–16
Murphy, Michael, 88, 97
Musqueam Nation, 52–3
myths,
   Canada as peacekeeper, 10, 16, 40
   national, 38–40, 42, 80
   settler colonial legitimizing, 37, 44, 49–50, 52, 124

Nagy, Rosemary, 18
narratives,
   imperial, 24, 33, 77, 126
   replacement, 43–4, 46, 50, 54
   settler colonial, *see* settler colonial narratives
nation building, 10, 74, 78–80
nationhood, Indigenous,
   alternative governance models and, 103–5, 108–13, 116, 120–1
   distinctiveness of, 24–5, 33, 125
   in Ecuador, 116
   provincial authority vis-à-vis, 72–3, 85, 97–100
   reconciliation and, 21, 100, 102, 122
   resurgences, 117–23
   settler state relationship with, 11–14, 46, 51–2, 61–3, 88–90, 119
   sovereignty/self-determination and, 27, 32–3, 58–9, 75–7, 94
nation-to-nation relations,
   alternative governance models and, 105–6, 110
   calls to restore/reaffirm, 10–11, 23, 58–60
   concept/principles of, 24
   historical, 23–4, 59
   provincial authority in, 35, 73, 88, 96, 104
   reconciliation and, 10–11, 38
   settler colonial government undermining of, 61–2, 73, 88, 96, 104
natural resources,
   colonial extraction of, 11–13, 30, 38
   jurisdictional tensions over, 71–2, 75, 83–4, 91, 98
   legal cases involving, 72, 81, 94
Nepinak, Derek, 62
New Brunswick, 72
new public management (NPM), 90–1
Nielsen Task Force report (*New Management Initiatives: Initial Results from the Ministerial Task Force on Program Review*), 85–6
Nohr, Liam, 110–12
Northwest Territories, 2, 18, 32, 72, 105
Nova Scotia, 18, 72
Nunavut, 72, 104

O'Brien, Jean, 43
off-reserve First Nations people,
   impacts of settler colonialism on, 26, 64, 104
   service delivery to, 69–70, 74, 84–6

on-reserve First Nations people,
    impacts of settler colonialism on, 26, 64, 104
    provincial relations with, 55–7, 67–8, 71, 87, 92, 97
    service delivery to, 69–70, 74–6, 84, 86, 95
original/prior occupancy, 47, 51, 61–2, 65–6
Orsini, Michael, 86, 103, 126
Others, Indigenous/Exogenous, 15–16
Otis, Ghislain, 89

Papillon, Martin, 24
    on alternatives to federalism, 77, 89–90, 112
    on devolution to provincial governments, 71, 95, 99
paradox of iterability, 14, 50
Parasam, Ajay, 114, 117
    on pluriversal sovereignties, 31, 33, 102, 113, 115
Patton, Paul, 48
Peeling, Albert C., 87
Penner Report (*Indian Self-Government in Canada: Report of the Special Committee*), 85–6, 97, 105
Perry, Adele, 16
pipe ceremony, 79
place-stories, 39, 43–4, 46, 48
pluriversal sovereignty, 31, 33, 102, 113–15, 117
politics of recognition, 29
    concept of, 20–1, 119
    federalism and, 101, 111
    reconciliation and, 21, 100
    subverting Indigenous agency via, 36, 75, 100
postcolonialism, 86
    concept of, 108
    Indigenous resistance/resurgence and, 124–6
    structural domination persisting in, 45, 80, 126
    treaty federalism and, 107–8, 110–11, 113
post–World War II era, 57, 78, 83, 85
poverty, disproportionate Indigenous, 3, 6, 8, 16

power (relations),
    colonial, 11, 21, 33, 38, 45–50, 126
    decentralized/provincial, 68, 71–2, 90, 99–100
    federalist decision making authority, 8–11, 35, 40–1, 57, 81, 127
    hegemonic settler state, 40–2, 115–16
    imbalances in, 20, 40–2, 54, 57, 106, 122
    Indigenous decision-making, 32, 113
    Indigenous erasure in, 6, 14, 80, 103–4, 114
    Indigenous resistance/resurgence in, 101, 117–22, 124–6
    institutional, 8, 40–1, 80, 105, 110–11
    poststructural understanding of, 41
    settler colonial narratives and, 12, 37–42, 45–7, 50–1, 54, 60–2
    shared jurisdiction models of, 13, 23, 35–7, 40–1, 56, 100–2, 119
    see also inequities
Pratt, Alan, 24, 92
Prince Edward Island, 72
Prince, Michael J., 106, 109–10
provinces, Canadian,
    colonial/historical jurisdiction, 68–72, 75, 79, 81, 86–8, 96–100
    court cases involving, 68–72, 81, 87, 93, 97–9
    decentralized power to, 9–10, 68, 71–2, 90, 99–100
    devolution of governance to, 35, 48–9, 54–7, 75–6, 84, 90–7
    fiduciary responsibilities, 70–2
    Indianness vis-à-vis, 67–8, 71–2, 74–6, 93
    land, authority over, 71, 91, 93–4, 98
    on-reserve First Nations and, 55, 57, 67–8, 87, 92, 97
    undermining Indigenous agency, 67–8, 73, 86

racism, anti-Indigenous,
    historical settler colonial/nation-building, 15, 19, 80
    ongoing experiences of systemic, 4, 7–8, 25, 114, 116–17
Rawson, Bruce, 85
Ray, Arthur J., 79

recognition,
    constitutional rights, 23, 27–9, 96
    days of Indigenous, 7, 116
    dialectic of settler state, 14–15, 52, 85–6, 110–11, 127
    politics of, *see* politics of recognition
    resistance/resurgence movements and, 17, 122
    sovereignty, 32, 53, 58, 61, 106, 114
reconciliation,
    addressing dispossession, 20–2, 27, 66, 110, 123–4, 127
    commemorative efforts toward, 6–7, 22
    concepts/components of, 6, 17–20, 36, 38, 41, 119–22
    as distinct from decolonization, 8, 22–3
    federalism limiting, 5, 9, 22–3, 34, 37–8, 100, 124–7
    federalist power-sharing models and, 101–2, 107–8, 110–13, 119–22
    economic structures/systems and, 6, 38, 126
    inequities amid, 6–8, 19, 29, 41, 121–2, 127
    nation-to-nation relations, 10–11, 21, 38, 100, 102, 122–5
    as performative, 20–2, 42–3
    politics of recognition, 21, 100
    power relations and, 40–2, 119–22, 124–6
    recognizing Indigenous autonomy/difference in, 6–7, 17, 29, 108, 118, 122–5
    settler colonial narratives about, 37–8, 40–2, 53, 66–7, 75–6
    Survivor advocacy for, 6, 17–19, 21, 36
    see also Truth and Reconciliation Commission of Canada
Red River Settlement, 1–2, 121
Reference Re. Eskimos, 25, 64, 82–3
Regan, Paulette, 40–2
relationality, Indigenous,
    non-human/land-based, 6, 9, 12–13, 32, 51, 120–3
    reconciliation and, 17, 19, 23
    sovereignty/resurgence and, 26, 32, 114–15, 117–18
relocation, forced, 15, 50–1, 104–5

reserve system,
    community knowledge sharing on, 54, 95
    enclave doctrine, 87, 93
    Indigenous marginalization via, 46–7, 54, 61, 104
    land used for, 57, 64–6, 71–2
    provincial jurisdiction amid, 55–7, 67–8, 71, 87, 92, 97, 104
    service delivery in, 69–70, 74–6, 84, 86, 95, 100
    violence of, 13, 46, 61, 104–5
resistance, Indigenous,
    decolonization and, 7, 120–1, 126
    histories/legacies of, 1–2, 16–17, 53–4, 79
    Indigenous knowledge systems/relationality in, 26, 64, 118–21
    Métis involvement in, 1–2, 17
    postcolonial, 107–8, 126
    reconciliation and, 6, 17–19, 120
    to White Paper, 86, 96
resource extraction, *see* natural resources
resurgence movements, Indigenous, 101–2
    concepts and theory of, 117–23
    decolonization and, 27, 119–22
    Indigenous knowledge systems/relationality in, 26–7, 36, 115–17, 119–23, 125
    sovereignty and, 34, 118–22
rights, Indigenous,
    Aboriginal rights versus, 8, 25, 28–9
    concepts of, 7–8, 33
    decolonization and, 7, 23
    Inherent, *see* Inherent rights
    settler colonial legal perspectives versus, 44, 52–4, 58, 61, 73, 96–100
    sovereignty/self-determination and, 28, 33, 44, 115, 117
Rocher, François, 83, 89
Royal Commission on Aboriginal Peoples (RCAP), 51, 105–6
Royal Proclamation of 1763: 23
    Aboriginal/Inherent rights tensions with, 61–2, 73, 106
    ambiguous wording of, 58–9
    land ownership/transfer policies in, 60, 65, 81
    nation-to-nation diplomacy in, 15, 58–9, 61, 73, 96, 110

property law vis-à-vis, 60–1
Russell, Peter, 80
R. v. Guerin, 52–3

Said, Edward, 45, 124, 126
Saskatchewan, 18, 47, 121
　land governance in, 7, 23, 72–3, 79, 83
Saskatchewan Indigenous Investment Finance Corporation, 98
Satzewich, Vic, 80
Saulteaux Nation, 73
Sayisi Dene, 104–5
Scott, Ian G., 92
section 35 (Constitution Act, 1982): 75, 117
　Aboriginal title vis-à-vis, 49, 52–3, 94
　Indigenous organizing for, 28, 96
　state-centric rights recognition via, 28–9, 62–3, 67, 88, 103, 106–7
self-determination,
　critiques of state-centred concepts of, 27–8, 33, 85, 103
　decolonization and, 27–8, 102, 113–15
　federalism undermining of, 8–10, 35, 77
　Inherent rights as basis for, 26–7
　multiplural sovereignty and, 77, 113–16
　treaty federalism and, 36, 112
self-government, Aboriginal, 104
　agreements, 17, 75, 98, 111
　alternative governance models and, 105–6, 110–11
　concepts of, 28–9, 32, 89
　Inherent rights as basis for, 26–8, 58, 65–6, 105–6
　international recognition of, 28–9, 115–16
　provincial authority versus, 66, 75, 89, 98
　settler colonial legislation/cases on, 28–9, 58, 66, 85–6, 106
Sen, Somdeep, 126
settler colonialism,
　concepts of, 8, 11–12
　impacts on First Nations, 12–15, 26, 64, 104, 118, 126
　imperial colonialism versus, 12, 45–6, 62
　narratives of, *see* settler colonial narratives
　violence of, 13, 16–17, 31, 116–17, 127
　see also colonization

settler colonial narratives,
　court reinforcement of, 44, 47–8, 50–3
　dispossession and settler benefit via, 10–12, 34–5, 37–43, 50–2, 61–6, 114
　doctrine of discovery, *see* doctrine of discovery
　federalism ordering and, 8–11, 35–8, 40–1, 57, 81, 127
　genocidal, 44, 80, 100, 104, 125, 127
　Indigenous erasure in, 12, 34, 38–40, 43–4, 50–1, 54
　institutionalized, 54–5, 108
　jurisdictional arrangements and, 8, 37–8, 80–3, 95–7, 123
　myths of, *see* myths
　obscuring/reinforcing of power relations via, 35, 37–8, 41–2
　of pioneers, 10, 40
　place-stories as, 39, 43–4, 46, 48
　power relations in, 12, 37–42, 45–7, 50–1, 54, 60–2
　on reconciliation, 37–8, 40–2, 53, 66–7, 75–6
　stereotypes in, 34, 37, 39–40
　terra nullius, *see* terra nullius
　violence in, 10–11, 42–3, 47
settler sovereignties, 12, 33, 50
Short, Damien, 21
Shrinkhal, Rashwet, 29, 33
Simpson, Audra, 31
Simpson, Leanne Betasamosake, 36, 102, 118–19, 123
Sinclair, Niigaan, 1
Sixties Scoop, 15
Slattery, Brian, 66, 106
Smith, Jennifer, 56
Smith, Miriam, 83, 89
Snelgrove, Corey, 21
Sossin, Lorne, 91
sovereignty,
　as collective, 32–4, 113, 117
　Crown, 14–15, 30, 44, 52–3, 94, 126
　cultural, 32–3
　debated concepts of, 10–11, 29–34, 99–102, 105–6, 122
　denial of Indigenous, 8–10, 37–8, 44, 50, 86, 103, 127
　harms of federalist Canadian, 9, 29–31, 41, 57–8, 80, 96, 114

Indigenous, *see* Indigenous sovereignty
Inherent rights as basis for, 26–8, 33, 44, 115, 117
multiplural, *see* multiplural sovereignty
pluriversal, 31, 33, 102, 113–15, 117
recognition of, 32, 53, 58, 61, 106, 114
settler, 12, 33, 50
state, 29–33, 44, 49, 114, 117
thesis, 121
as undefined/practised, 32–3
see also nation-to-nation relations
Stanley, Gerald, 47
Starblanket, Gina (*Storying Violence*), 47
Stark, Heidi Kiiwetinepinesiik, 32–3, 120
state(s), settler colonial,
assimilative policies of, 6, 13, 15, 24, 61
dialectic of recognition, 14–15, 52, 85–6, 110–11, 127
Eurocentrism in systems of, 104, 114, 117
fiduciary responsibilities, 25–6, 61–2, 65, 70–4, 80–2, 109
hegemonic power of, 40–2, 115–16
Indigenous nationhood versus, 11–14, 46, 51–2, 61–3, 88–90, 119
notions of Indigeneity, 24–5, 63, 66–7
rights recognition, 28–9, 62–3, 67, 88, 103, 106–7
sovereignty of, 29, 31–3, 54, 89, 107, 117
St. Catharines Milling and Lumber Co. v. R., 81–2
structure(s) of indifference, 16, 42
superior/inferior binary, 10, 30, 39–40
Supreme Court of Canada,
on Aboriginal rights and title, 49, 52–3, 72, 117
on "Indianness," 25, 63–4
jurisdictional cases, 72, 87
Survivors, 6, 17–19, 21; *see also* Intergenerational Survivors

terra nullius,
aim of dispossession, 11–12, 47–50, 53
calls to repudiate, 23, 51–2, 54
territories, Canadian, 18, 32, 105
governance authority of, 57, 72
Thobani, Sunera, 15
Thrush, Coll, 39, 43

title, Aboriginal, *see* Aboriginal title
Tobias, John L., 64, 68
Todd, Zoe, 120
Treaties, 7
Aboriginal title and, 66–8, 96
Canadian governance incorporating, 13–14, 106–7
conflicting concepts of, 111
Indigenous understandings of, 23, 59, 62, 79, 109–11, 120
Numbered, 12, 79
lands (un)ceded in, 23, 52, 71–3, 81, 92–3, 97
rights, *see* section 35 (Constitution Act, 1982)
settler actions while making, 15, 46–7, 59, 75, 79, 109
settler violations of, 17, 72–3, 98, 100, 116–17, 127
(sovereign) relations outlined in, 23–5, 59, 62–3, 79, 113, 120–2
treaty federalism, 36, 102, 107–13, 125
Treaty Land Entitlement (TLE), 73
Treaty Land Sharing Network (Saskatchewan), 23
Treaty of Niagara, 23
reflecting nation-to-nation relations, 59–60
Wampum Belt of, 59, 109–10
Tremblay, Arjun, 101
trilateral federalism, 101, 105–7, 112
Trudeau, Justin, 7, 20, 112
Truth and Reconciliation Commission of Canada (TRC), 4, 23
Calls to Action, *see* Calls to Action
concept of reconciliation, 6, 19–20, 41–2
Final Report of, 7, 19–20
formation and work of, 6, 17–19
importance of truth-telling in, 18–19
on settler colonial expansion, 40, 50
Tsilhqot'in Nation v. British Columbia,
on Aboriginal title, 52–3, 71, 93–5, 98
provincial jurisdiction vis-à-vis, 68, 71, 87, 93–5
on *terra nullius*, 51–2
Tsosie, Rebecca, 32–3
Tuck, Eve, 7, 22
Turner, Dale, 30

Two-Row Wampum Belt (Treaty of
    Niagara), 59, 109–10

ultra-constitutional practices, 84
ultra vires jurisdiction, 69, 71
United Nations Declaration on the Rights
    of Indigenous Peoples (UNDRIP), 27–8
United States, governance system of, 14, 78
    Indigenous influence on, 13, 108

Venne, Sharon, 48, 109
Veracini, Lorenzo, 10, 12
violence,
    Indigenous Peoples facing dispropor-
        tionate, 7–8, 116–17
    settler colonial, 13, 16–17, 31, 116–17,
        127
    state narratives masking/legitimating,
        10–11, 42, 47
Voth, Daniel, 121
Vowel, Chelsea, 42

Walker, Katherine, 114
water,
    Indigenous relationships with, 38, 108,
        120–1
    quality issues on reserves, 7
    settler delivery/control of, 64, 69
Weaver, Sally, 85–6
Westminster parliamentary system, 84
Westphalian state model, 29, 113–15
Wet'suwet'en Nation, 17, 49, 65
White Paper (*Statement of the Government
    of Canada on Indian Policy, 1969*),
    85–6, 96, 103
Wildcat, Matthew, 21
Williams, Meaghan Anne, 105, 110–11,
    113, 125
Winnipeg, 1, 3–4, 18
Wolfe, Patrick, 43–5, 49
World War II, *see* post–World War II era

Yang, K. Wayne, 7, 22
Younging, Gregory (*Elements of
    Indigenous Style*), 26
Yukon, 72